FORGIVENESS AND RECONCILIATION
And Other New Testament Themes

FORGIVENESS
AND
RECONCILIATION

And Other New Testament Themes

———

C. F. D. MOULE

First published in Great Britain in 1998 by
Society for Promoting Christian Knowledge
Marylebone Road, London NW1 4DU

British Library Cataloguing-in-Publication Data
A catalogue record for this book is available from the British Library

ISBN 0-281-05139-9

Typeset by Wilmaset Ltd, Birkenhead, Wirral
Printed in Great Britain by
The University Press, Cambridge

CONTENTS

PREFACE

In a long retirement, I have published little beyond what was already in writing if not in print, if only because I have lacked the energy and will-power to keep anything like abreast of the specialist monographs which proliferate like a rain forest, and with which one needs to be in dialogue. Some will deem this silence my finest achievement. However, since naturally I am unable to give up puzzling over questions of theology, especially those raised by New Testament studies, I have continued to read, though only selectively, in these areas; and I cannot help noticing that a good deal that is written goes over ground that I had already covered in the past, sometimes in considerable detail.

It is this, with encouragement from friends, which emboldens me to reprint selections from what has already appeared. Some of these are inevitably of their time, and I have not systematically updated bibliographies, though I have added references to relevant material that happens to have come my way; but I hope that they may still make a contribution to the continuing discussion of the questions which have exercised me most. Each section, or part, represents one of my major concerns, and I indicate their contents in the Introduction.

It is impossible to thank Professor Graham Stanton adequately for the support and encouragement he has given me throughout the project, and for the hours he has generously devoted, though himself under heavy pressure at the time, to the toil of organizing the material, checking innumerable references, and communicating with the publishers and others concerned. Without this help, the thing would never have got off the ground at all. It was he, too, who secured for me the benefit of the expert and accurate work of Mrs Lavinia Harvey in transcribing copy, much of it in very poor photocopy and some in my own hand. I am greatly indebted to her for uncomplaining patience and consistent efficiency. My thanks are due also to other friends – better for them if they stay anonymous – who have kept me going with their encouragement. To the publishers of course I owe very warm thanks: they have been consistently accommodating, patient and encouraging.

ACKNOWLEDGEMENTS

The author and publishers are grateful to the following sources for permission to reprint material:

To Cambridge University Press for 'The Scope of the Death of Christ', first published in *The Origin of Christology*, Cambridge, 1977, pp. 111–26.

To the Methodist Publishing House for 'Preaching the Atonement', first published in the *Epworth Review*, 10.2, London, 1983, pp. 70–78, and for 'The Holy Spirit and Scripture', first published in the *Epworth Review*, 8.2, London, 1981, pp. 66–74.

To Oxford University Press for 'Reflections on So-called Triumphalism', first published in *The Glory of Christ in the New Testament: Studies in Christology in Memory of George Bradford Caird*, edited by L. D. Hurdst and N. T. Wright, Clarendon Press, 1987, pp. 219–27.

To HM Prison Service for 'Retribution or Restoration?', first published in *New Life: the Prison Service Chaplaincy Review*, 9, Leyhill, HMP, 1992, p. 14–18.

To L. E. Keck and J. L. Martyn for 'The Christology of Acts', first published in *Studies in Luke-Acts: Essays Presented in Honor of Paul Schubert*, edited by L. E. Keck and J. L. Martyn, Abingdon Press, Nashville, Tennessee, 1966, pp. 159–85.

To Vandenhoeck & Ruprecht for 'Jesus of Nazareth and the Church's Lord', first published in *Die Mitte des Neuen Testaments: Festschrift für Eduard Schweizer zum siebsigsten Geburtstag*, edited by U. Luz and H. Weder, Vandenhoeck & Ruprecht, Göttingen, 1983, pp. 176–86.

To Mercer University Press for 'The Gravamen against Jesus', first published in *Jesus, the Gospels and the Church: Essays in Honor of William R. Farmer*, edited by E. P. Sanders, Mercer University Press, Macon, Georgia, 1987, pp. 177–95.

To SPCK and Epworth Press for 'The Holy Spirit in the Scriptures', first published in *Church Quarterly*, 3, SPCK and Epworth Press, London, 1971, pp. 279–87.

To Hodder and Stoughton Publishers for 'The Sacrifice of Christ', first published as a booklet with that title, Hodder and Stoughton, London, 1956. Reproduced by permission of Hodder and Stoughton Limited.

To Mohr Siebeck for 'The Function of the Synoptic Gospels', first published in *Glaube und Eschatologie: Festschrift für Werner Georg Kümmel*, edited by E. Grässer and O. Merk, J. C. B. Mohr, Tubingen, 1985, pp. 199–208.

To the *Reformed Theological Review* for 'An Unsolved Problem in the Temptation-Clause in the Lord's Prayer', first published in the *Reformed Theological Review*, 33.3, Victoria, Australia, 1974, pp. 65–75.

INTRODUCTION

'New Testament theology' is a notoriously ambiguous term (see Morgan 1973); but, without begging the question, it is still legitimate to ask what is the bearing on Christian doctrine of the convictions reflected in the New Testament; and it is soundings at various points in this area of inquiry that the essays in this collection represent.

The section on the theology of forgiveness, with which it opens, reflects one of my almost life-long concerns. Long ago I was asked what the prodigal son must have seen when he looked up at his father who was welcoming him home. Taking the story not in its original context (where the elder brother was probably the key figure and the point highly topical), but as a classic portrayal simply of the processes of reconciliation after estrangement, the answer might be that he saw grey hairs in the beard that was black when he left home, and lines of distress in a brow that was then more serene. The point of this observation (the son could see signs of stress) is that to offer forgiveness is possible only for one sensitive enough to feel pain at being wronged. Equally, if one is genuinely to repent, one must begin to suffer in sympathy with the person whom one has wronged. Forgiveness and the acceptance of forgiveness are both painful and costly and emotionally demanding. Whatever vicarious suffering may mean, it does not mean that the penitent is let off pain. This is a universal law of human relationship; and if Christians have reason to believe that the life, death, and resurrection of Christ (as 'one' both with God and with humankind) are decisive for reconciliation, and that 'he died for us' carries a special sense, it is not because this is not part of its age-long pattern, but precisely because Christ brings to its climax and absolutizes in a unique degree this very pattern. The death of Christ *is* 'the grey hairs' of the father as well as the response of the son. To put it paradoxically, God always has been a God of forgiveness because he has always been the God who, at a particular time and place, becomes incarnate. Further, a study of the processes of reconciliation and

ix

repair shows that retribution, in quantitative terms, is no component part of them: justice, on the deepest level of human relationship, is not mathematical. Forgiveness is, by definition, a waiving of *quid pro quo* justice; but that – contrary to popular opinion – does not make it a soft option. Costly in the extreme, the process is costly on a level far profounder than that of barter: it does justice to the repair of persons as no quantitative justice could ever do; and although such reflections may sound idealistic and absurdly far removed from down-to-earth legislation for the restraint of crime, these principles ought to motivate the legislators.

In the section on Christology, the first essay demonstrates (I believe this is not too strong a word) that, if Luke and Acts are by the same author, this Evangelist, at any rate, did deliberately represent post-resurrection estimates of Jesus as different from those obtaining before his death. Thus, although this essay is primarily a study of Lukan Christology, it incidentally supports the contention (highly unfashionable but, as I believe, worthy of serious attention) which is the subject of the essay in Part Five on the function of the Synoptic Gospels. It makes a difference whether one believes that they purport to present the full Christology of their respective writers and any communities to which they may have belonged, or whether they intended (however well or ill they succeeded) to describe, rather, some of the impressions made by Jesus on his contemporaries, before experiences and 'hindsight' after his death had led his followers to a new estimate. It has long seemed to me that this new estimate, reflected in the Fourth Gospel, the Epistles and the Apocalypse – new, but perfectly congruous with the traditions about the historical Jesus in the Synoptic Gospels – constitutes weighty evidence for the nature of Christ. The conventional rationalization which tries to account for the genesis of these convictions by the process of apotheosis or divinization is unconvincing: the alleged parallels do not actually match. It is positively more plausible to postulate an origin in the nature of Jesus himself. This proposal means that historians of Christian beginnings find themselves, paradoxically, driven by historical evidence to plant a bewildered footstep beyond the frontier of their own discipline and in the area of dogma. This may seem unprofessional and disturbing, but what can one do? The contemporaries of Jesus were confronted by exactly this dilemma: 'Who is this . . . ?' they exclaimed; and after the resurrection they found themselves answering their question in trans-historical as well as historical terms. This was the thesis of my 1977 book, *The Origin of Christology*, and it reappears in the remaining two essays of this section.

The essay on the Holy Spirit is simply a brief summary of biblical thought about the Spirit of God, with pointers to its doctrinal significance. It is this material that I tried to elucidate and relate to Christian doctrine in my 1978 book, *The Holy Spirit*.

The short book on the Eucharist which constitutes Part Four consists of lectures delivered at Cuddesdon College in 1955, and as such may serve as a small historical monument to a certain stage of ecumenical relations; but I hope that it may still be of some value also as reflections on eucharistic theology.

The first essay in Part Five has already been mentioned. The other two concern details within the Gospel traditions.

Finally, what kind of authority is carried by the documents comprising the New Testament and by the fact that they came to comprise it? The answer proposed by the final essay is not that their authors, or their assemblers into a canon, were somehow divinely inspired to avoid error and relay truth. Rather, the events and the interpretations of them, the aspirations and the convictions presented in Scripture may be seen to converge on and cohere in Jesus, in such a way as to justify mainstream Christian estimates of him. Scripture thus carries the authority of the proximate evidence for long sequences of events and experiences and reflections leading to a self-authenticating climax. If the word 'inspiration' is applicable, it is to interpretation rather than presentation.

Part One

The Theology of Forgiveness

1

THE SCOPE OF
THE DEATH OF CHRIST

C. F. D. Moule, *The Origin of Christology*. Cambridge,
Cambridge University Press, 1977, pp. 111–26.

We need to ask, first, what meanings attach to the statement
that somebody died 'for another'. And we ask it outside any
reference to Jesus, and, in the first instance, outside even any
specifically religious frame of reference. If this section is illustrated by biblical phrases, this is only a matter of convenience:
it does not, at this point, involve religious presuppositions. On
this 'secular' level, it is possible, first, to apply such a statement
to two individuals with purely external and physical connotations. To say that a good shepherd lays down his life for the
sheep need mean no more than that the good shepherd dies –
or is ready to die – in fighting the wolf to defend the sheep. He
dies quite literally *instead* of the other: the shepherd dies that
the sheep may live. The preposition in Greek could appropriately be ἀντί, 'in the place of', though in fact New Testament
Greek sometimes uses the vaguer and more general preposition
ὑπέρ, even when the sense is that the action is strictly
vicarious. In John 13.37 (cf. verse 38), Peter boasts to Jesus
that he will lay down his life for him (ὑπὲρ σοῦ). Perhaps it is
in no deeper a sense than this that, in John 15.13, the greatest
possible love is said to be exhibited when a man lays down his
life for his friends (ὑπὲρ τῶν φίλων αὐτοῦ). In Rom. 5.7, the
possibility is recognized that a man may die for a good person
(ὑπὲρ τοῦ ἀγαθοῦ), and in Rom. 16.4 Aquila and Priscilla are
said to have risked their necks for Paul's life (ὑπὲρ τῆς ψυχῆς
μου).

It is equally possible, of course, to speak in such terms when
the death is not successfully vicarious. The shepherd may be
said to die for the sheep even if he fails to save its life. When the
wolf has killed the shepherd, it may itself be unhurt and may
go on to demolish the sheep, or the entire flock. A parent may

3

fling herself in front of her child, but the gunman may still shoot them both. But one can still say, 'That shepherd gave his life for the sheep;' 'That woman died for her child.' But this is not strictly ἀντί, 'instead of': it is ὑπέρ, 'for the sake of', in an attempt to protect or help.

In either case, here are simple examples of lives surrendered with a view to the physical benefit – the preservation of the lives – of others. And it is evident that, in such cases, a single person is sometimes successful in rescuing many individuals. One shepherd might save the whole flock by killing the wolf at the risk of his own life. When, in 1 Macc. 6.44, Eleazar Avaran stabbed an elephant from beneath and suffered the inevitable fate, 'he gave himself', says the narrator, 'to save his people and to win himself an eternal name'.

In other ways, too, one person may, by a self-sacrificing act, contribute to the physical well-being of many, not only of his or her contemporaries, but of all generations to come. A friend of mine died young of a disease contracted in the course of pathological research. What he discovered by his dangerous experiments was, perhaps, not a spectacular breakthrough: but it must have contributed at least something to the conquest of disease for future generations. In that sense, this one man died on behalf of many. And if, as I suspect, he knew the risk, he gave his life consciously that others might live.

It is also possible, of course, for a life given unwillingly to save others. Millions of animals used in medical research die each year that men and women may live: but they die without willing it or knowing what it is for. Those who believe that the execution of a criminal has a deterrent effect, might claim that the criminal dies, in a sense, for others; but his life, like that of animals used in vivisection, is taken forcibly, not willingly given. It is in this sense that Caiaphas, in John 11.50 (cf. 18.14), is represented as saying that it is expedient for one man to die rather than that the whole nation should perish. It is the Evangelist who interprets the saying on a very different level.

But now, still not going beyond the secular ambit, there are other ways besides the purely material and physical, in which men and women may be benefited by the surrender of a life; for it is appropriate to say that one dies for others when the death in question exercises some spiritual or moral influence

4

for good. The death of Socrates set up in history a monument to integrity and courage which will never be forgotten as long as the story is told, and which will go on for an indefinite length of time having its effect on the hearts and minds and ideals of all who hear it. So, again, those who die in battle for what they genuinely believe to be a noble cause leave behind them an incentive to do likewise.

And here an important fact emerges. Whereas on the material and physical level one dies that others may live, when it comes to the spiritual or moral level, the level of ideals and of honour, the death of the one may carry the others with it through the same experience, rescuing them not from death but from cowardly escaping death. Socrates dies not instead of others, but in such a way that others, like him, may dare to die in the cause of truth. His life may be said to be given 'for' them (ὑπέρ), but not strictly 'instead of' them (ἀντί). The Vietnamese and Czechoslovak self-immolations of recent history, as extremist demonstrations against tyranny, constitute a special case of this sort of moral influence.

Thus far, nothing has been said which goes beyond the bounds of the secular and could not be accepted by a humanist. We have either kept within the limits of material and physical benefits, or, when these have been transcended, it has been in terms of moral uplift and influence, exercised by one on another by the direct, rational means of holding up an example. And it is noteworthy that, when such influence is analysed, it seems to work by an individualistic relationship: it is a matter of each person's being individually influenced. The story of Socrates has to be heard by each individual on whom his death is to exert its influence – unless, indeed, one is prepared to argue that, by an act of courageous devotion to truth and duty, a whole society is so lifted to new ideas, that any member of it, whether or not the story is heard, is placed in a more advantageous context. Even if one did allow this – and it would be difficult to establish – this change or reform in society would still only take place when each member of it was able to convince his neighbour that the new moral level was right and good: it would still be a rational process of mutual instruction and influence and interaction.

But, now, supposing a religious factor is introduced: supposing God is brought into the reckoning, or a mystical notion of the human being, what then? On the crudest level imaginable, when God is brought into the reckoning, the theory will be that it is possible to bribe God; and the most impressive bribe conceivable will be a human life offered up to God. When Mesha King of Moab sacrifices his own eldest son on a wall to his god (2 Kings 3.27), he believes that he is surrendering a very precious possession in order to propitiate the god and secure his favour for his army; and the Hebrew narrator seems to have thought that it worked. Similarly, Abraham's readiness to go to the same lengths, although he was excused from the actual deed, brought blessing, not only to Abraham but to his posterity (Gen. 22.18, as frequently, if wrongly, interpreted).

On an immensely higher but still essentially mercenary level, it is possible for a religious mind to interpret the heroic act of martyrdom as a deliberate self-immolation to persuade God to be propitious. In 2 Macc. 7.37f. the martyr hopes that he and his fellow-martyrs may have stayed the wrath of God: 'With me and my brothers may the Almighty's anger ... be ended.' So in 4 Macc. 17.21ff. the obedience of Eleazar and others in the extreme degree of maryrdom is treated as a propitiatory sacrifice for the nation's sin: ὥσπερ ἀντίψυχον γεγονότας τῆς τοῦ ἔθνους ἁμαρτίας. This curious phrase is taken by Dalman (*apud SB* ii. 279) to mean that Eleazar's obedience is offered in exchange for the sin-stained soul of the people. It seems to me more natural not to attach the -ψυχον part of the compound word to the nation, but rather to the martyrs, and to interpret ἀντίψυχον as meaning, perhaps, a 'life given in exchange', as a compensation to God for the despite done him by the nation's sin. But in any case, the generally compensatory (indeed, propitiatory) sense is clear; and the next verse reinforces it: 'and through the blood of those godly persons and the propitiation (ἱλαστήριον) of their death, the Divine Providence brought Israel through to well-being, whereas previously they had suffered ill' (my version).

The same sort of thing may be said of any single act of dedication and obedience to God's will, even when not expressed in actual death or in physical suffering at all. Thus, in the

Qumran Manual of Discipline, the inner group of twelve 'laymen' and three priests are, by their devotion, to atone for sin (לִרְצֹת עָוֹן 1QS 8.3). So, in Sirach 44.17, 'Noah was found perfect and righteous, and thus he made amends in the time of retribution...' (NEB), Νωε εὑρέθη τέλειος δίκαιος, ἐν καιρῷ ὀργῆς ἐγένετο ἀντάλλαγμα... And, much later perhaps, there is the well-known saying about the vicarious suffering of two rabbis, Judah and Eleazar ben Simon. It was said that for the duration of their sufferings (which included toothache!) no one died prematurely, there were no miscarriages, and there was no shortage of rain.[1] Going back to canonical Scripture, there is the noble passage in Exod. 32.32, where Moses asks to be expunged from God's book of life if that could save his people. And, most famous of all, there is the Suffering Servant of Isa. 53, whose suffering is described in terms of compensation, and through whose bruises healing comes to others. Whether the 'compensation' here is intended as a cultic metaphor or simply as a legal or quantitative one is a debatable point, though the NEB comes down on the cultic side, translating אָשָׁם by 'a sacrifice for sin'. But in any case it is to God, presumably, that the compensation, whether cultic or legal, is thought of as paid. (It is strange, incidentally, that the Maccabaean stories never apply Isa. 53 to the martyrs.)[2]

These allusions, from the lowest and most barbaric up to the most noble and sophisticated – from Mesha of Moab to the Servant of II-Isa. and the heroic martyrs under Antiochus Epiphanes – all illustrate an interpretation of the effect of the death or sufferings of the one on the many in terms of a corporate structure of relationship. It is not a matter of material gain – a person giving his or her life so that others may live – nor only even of spiritual or cultural uplift reaching other individuals directly from the sufferer's example. It is a matter, rather, of the sufferer's offering to God that which God will accept for the benefit of the rest. Essentially the same structure of corporate relationship is implied also by the rabbinic doctrine of the merits of the fathers. This religious (or at least mystical) interpretation of the ὑπέρ-idea, this interpretation of 'on behalf of', differs from interpretations which may be confined within a humanist (or rational) frame of reference, in its assumption that it is through God, or at least by way of some 'mystical' interconnectedness of persons with one another if not also with God, that the many may be affected by the one. Whereas those other interpretations of 'he died for us' – the interpretations which are not necessarily more than rational – operate in terms of essentially individual and horizontal relationship, the 'mystical' interpretations postulate a corporate interconnection, and the religious interpretations place this within the ambience of God's presence.

And this will hold good, even when ideas of propitiation and sacrifice are left behind. If one who believes in this mysterious relationship with God says 'such and such a person died for us', he or she means that the self-surrender of that person in obedience to the will of God constituted something that God could (as it were) use and 'relay' for the benefit of his whole family. And although to put it so, even if it obviates the crudity of propitiation, may still suggest a very crude 'model', as though heaven were a kind of clearing-house or telephone exchange, yet it need not be so. If one ponders on the structure of personal relationships, even in the limited degree to which any one of us understands it (say, within the organism of a family), vistas of immeasurable suggestiveness open up, in which the relation of one to another is part, ultimately, of the relation of all to God. It throws a new light on the sense in which one may be conceived of as giving his or her life for others. The analogy of the living body suggests itself – which means that we have arrived, by a different route, at the point where we left St Paul. He borrowed the analogy of the body. In its already established uses, in Stoic and other circles, it had served as an analogy for a corporation of persons in harmonious co-operation. The remarkable innovation in Paul was that he brought it into close relationship with the risen Christ, thereby reflecting an understanding of Christ as more than individual and describing experience of Christ in terms such as theists use of God. But even leaving Christ out of account, and even in pre-Christian contexts, conceptions of the transmission of the benefits accruing from some good life, or from the noble surrender of life in the cause of loyalty to God, seem to imply an organic understanding of human society within the providence of God. A religious use of ὑπέρ, unlike a secular use, goes beyond the rationalization of it in terms of the inspiring effect of a fine example or a noble ideal: it operates with an organic 'model' of society, and relates it to God. Thus, each limb or organ of the living organism of the community is conceived of as having its measure of influence on the entire 'body'; of acting 'on behalf of' all, not merely by the direct and rationally intelligible means of stirring the imagination or arousing idealism, but more subtly and mystically, inasmuch as the entire organism is seen as a living unity. It is in such a context of thought that the functioning of intercessory prayer may begin to become more readily conceivable.

So much, then, for conceptions of the sense of a phrase like 'he died for us' in a generally and broadly theistic context of thought.

Now, when Christians recite the death of Jesus as an article of their belief, they add (if they are using the Nicene Creed) that it was 'for us' that he was crucified: σταυρωθέντα τε ὑπὲρ ἡμῶν. This interpretation of that death goes back at least as far as the middle of the first century AD. Not all the New Testament writers express it. Acts, on the whole, associates the death with the vindication of Christ and of God's design, rather than with the redemption of others. But St Paul, reciting in 1 Cor. 15 information about Jesus which he had received by tradition, adds that it was 'for our sins' that he died (an example, incidentally, of the comparatively rare use of ὑπέρ with the sins expiated rather than the persons redeemed); and in other passages Paul says similar things, as do certain other New Testament writers, each in his own way. Here is a list of passages in which the death of Christ is related to others by a simple prepositional phrase, mostly with ὑπέρ, together with a few examples of other ways of expressing the same idea. Prefixed is a summary note on the use of prepositions in this connection.

A summary note on prepositions
'Υπέρ with genitive occurs only twice (according to Hatch and Redpath's concordance) in the LXX of the Pentateuch (Deut. 24.16 (עַל) and, in a purely literal sense, 28.23); but outside the Pentateuch Judges 6.31 (B, Hebrew לְ), 9.17 (A and B, Hebrew עַל) are good examples of its meaning 'on behalf of'.

Περί is usual in the LXX after ἐξιλάσκεσθαι (כפר), governing both 'sins', etc. and the persons atoned for. The Epistle to the Hebrews (with reference to the Levitical system) reproduces this double usage in 5.3 (περὶ τοῦ λαοῦ ... ἑαυτοῦ ... ἁμαρτιῶν), though it also uses ὑπέρ doubly (5.1, ὑπὲρ ἀνθρώπων ... ἁμαρτιῶν; so 9.7, cf. 10.12). The New Testament uses ὑπέρ mostly with persons. Departures from ὑπέρ with person and περί with sins, etc. are asterisked in the following list of significant New Testament passages according to the text of Nestle-Aland 27. (For variants, see Metzger 1971, *in locc.*)

Mark 10.45 (ἀντὶ* πολλῶν)
Mark 14.24 (ὑπὲρ πολλῶν); Matt. 26.28 (περὶ* πολλῶν); Luke 22.19f. (ὑπὲρ ὑμῶν); 1 Cor. 11.24 (ὑπὲρ ὑμῶν)
John 6.51 (ὑπὲρ τῆς τοῦ κόσμου ζωῆς – hardly to be asterisked)
John 11.51f. (ὑπὲρ τοῦ ἔθνους ... οὐχ ὑπὲρ τοῦ ἔθνους μόνον...)
Rom. 5.6, 8 (ὑπὲρ ἀσεβῶν ... ὑπὲρ ἡμῶν)
Rom. 8.32 (ὑπὲρ ἡμῶν πάντων)
1 Cor. 15.3 (ὑπὲρ* τῶν ἁμαρτιῶν ἡμῶν)
2 Cor. 5.14 (εἷς ὑπὲρ πάντων)
2 Cor. 5.21 (ὑπὲρ ἡμῶν)
Gal. 1.4 (ὑπὲρ* τῶν ἁμαρτιῶν ἥν)
Gal. 2.20 (ὑπὲρ ἐμοῦ)
Gal. 3.13 (ὑπὲρ ἡμῶν κατάρα)
Eph. 5.2 (ὑπὲρ ἡμῶν)
Eph. 5.25 (ὑπὲρ αὐτῆς, sc. τῆς ἐκκλησίας)
1 Thess. 5.10 (ὑπὲρ ἡμῶν)
1 Tim. 2.6 (ἀντίλυτρον ὑπὲρ πάντων)
Tit. 2.14 (ὑπὲρ ἡμῶν)
Heb. 2.9 (ὑπὲρ παντός). Note also 5.1, and cf. 5.3, 9.7, 10.12
1 Pet. 2.21 (ὑπὲρ ὑμῶν)
1 Pet. 3.18 (περὶ ἁμαρτιῶν ... δίκαιος ὑπὲρ ἀδίκων)
1 John 3.16 (ὑπὲρ ἡμῶν)
Cf. Heb. 5.9 (αἴτιος σωτηρίας αἰωνίου; 9.12 (αἰωνίαν λύτρωσιν εὑράμενος); 9.24 (νῦν ἐμφανισθῆναι τῷ προσώπῳ τοῦ θεοῦ ὑπὲρ ἡμῶν); 9.28 (εἰς τὸ πολλῶν ἀνενεγκεῖν ἁμαρτίας); 1 Pet. 2.24 (οὗ τῷ μώλωπι

ἰάθητε); 1 John 1.7 (τὸ αἷμα 'Ιησου ... καθαρίζει ἡμᾶς
ἀπὸ πάσης ἁμαρτίας)
1 Cor. 1.13 (μὴ Παῦλος ἐσταυρώθη ὑπὲρ ὑμῶν;) Yet, Col.
1.24; Eph. 3.1, 13; Rom. 9.3; 2 Cor. 12.10; Phil. 1.29.

If, now, with this list before us, we ask what, if anything,
marks these Christian uses of the 'on behalf of' formulae as distinctive, one feature, at least, is impressively persistent. This is
the universality – or, at least, potential universality – assumed
for the effects of the death of Christ. It could not be maintained
that this, in itself, is absolutely distinctive; but it is perhaps distinctive in its pervasiveness.

It is true, admittedly, that one particularly famous saying,
with echoes elsewhere, speaks of Christ's death as 'for many',
which might seem to suggest that it was not 'for all'. Mark
10.45 (Matt. 20.28) speaks of the Son of Man giving his life as
a ransom for many. So, too, the Marcan and Matthean words
of institution (Mark 14.24, Matt. 26.28), and the phrase in
Heb. 9.28. Many scholars insist that this represents a Semitic
idiom which uses 'many' for 'all'.[3] For my part, I am sceptical
of this claim. But I believe that, in all these sayings, the point is
in the contrast between the *one* and the many: it is the plurality
of results achieved by the one deed (exactly as in Rom.
5.12ff.). If so, it follows that the 'many' is not intended in the
least to suggest a limitation to only some rather than all, but to
emphasize the remarkable fruitfulness of the one act of self-
surrender.

In practically all the other phrases on the list, either the word
'all' occurs or some equivalent (such as 'the life of the world'),
or the reference includes persons who were not of Jesus' own
circle or even generation, but are alluded to simply because
they happen to be persons reached by the gospel, however
alienated from or oblivious of Jesus Christ they may have been
before. The same phenomenon could be illustrated also from
other statements in the Pauline epistles which happen not to
contain the ὑπὲρ-formula, such as Col. 1.21f., where Christ is
said by his death to have reconciled those who were formerly
estranged; and the same is true of some of the passages
collected at the foot of the list already given. Potentially, the
death of Jesus is 'for' all who will accept him.

The claim of a potentially universal applicability is very persistent in our documents, and this, as I have suggested, is one distinctive feature in the Christian application of the 'on behalf of' formula to Christ. However, it is impossible to deny that any such claim is ever made, outside Christianity, for the effects of one person's death on others. Others besides Jesus are conceived of as voluntarily suffering for the benefit of a plurality of persons; have we not already seen that there are certainly passages in Hebrew-Jewish literature before the New Testament, such as Isa. 53 and the Maccabaean stories, where such a conception is expressed? It is true that they are not numerous. In the Old Testament, Exod. 32.32 and Isa. 53 are practically alone. In Judaism, 2 Macc. is perhaps the earliest example. But still, they *are* to be found. Of an Eleazar (or, for that matter, of a Socrates) it may be intelligibly said that his death brought, and continues to bring, benefit to an unlimited number of others, whether because of the example he set, or because of the blow he struck for truth or, more 'mystically', because of the obedience he, as it were, injected into the total organism of humankind – and this (a theist would add) in its relation to God.

Interestingly enough, one can compile from Paul himself a catena of allusions to his own sufferings as in some way beneficial to others. He declares in Col. 1.24 that his own sufferings are on behalf of Christ's body, the Church; and there is something comparable in Eph. 3.1, 13. Again, he says in Rom. 9.3 that he would gladly become an accursed thing, cursed by Christ or banished from his presence (ἀνάθεμα ἀπὸ τοῦ Χριστοῦ)[4] if that could benefit his Jewish brothers (ὑπὲρ τῶν ἀδελφῶν μου) – an idea strongly reminiscent of Exod. 32.32 once more.

Incidentally and in parenthesis, there is even the passage in Phil. 1.29 where Paul speaks of Christians' suffering on behalf of Christ – but that evidently means suffering in loyalty to him, not (as it were) so as to benefit him(!). It is comparable to the phrase 'to suffer for the name' (Acts 5.41). It is a significant fact that nowhere in the New Testament are Christians really placed on a level with Christ in this respect. Contrast the following sentiment from an Indian lyric by Subba Rao: [addressing Christ] 'It is enough, if, like you, I don't die for myself, better still to become God like you by dying for others...'[5] It is significant that Paul, expostulating with his readers (or hearers) for attaching themselves to his own name in a partisan way, cries out in indignation (1 Cor. 1.13): 'Was Paul crucified for you?' (μὴ Παῦλος ἐσταυρώθη ὑπὲρ ὑμῶν;) – as much as to say, there is one, and one only, of whom it can properly be said that he died for you.

Why this indignation? Where lies the distinctiveness that is so intensely claimed by New Testament writers for the death of Christ? Whence is it derived, and what does it signify? To the remarkable and persistent, but not absolutely unexampled, claim to a wide and even, perhaps, universal scope for the death of Christ,[6] must be added a further factor. This is the claim that it is a *fait accompli* and one whose results are still actively present. It is its achievedness, its 'doneness'; and, in addition, the strange fact that it is constantly accessible, always and everywhere. The death of Christ is a past achievement, often spoken of in the aorist tense; and yet it is available and accessible now, in a special sense: it may be appropriated by all, anywhere and at any time.

In Mahayana Buddhism there is a noble universality and comprehensiveness of ideal: but it is as yet unfulfilled; it is a future aspiration. We hear of 'the man who truly knows the truth ... dedicated to the universalizing of enlightenment and willing to postpone his own final release from birth and death until the goal is achieved'.[7] Here, indeed, is a purpose with a universal scope: the redemptive intention of one on behalf of the many. But the Christian claim is distinctive, in that it is not only for the potential universality of the redemptive power of the death of Christ, but also for its being a fact already achieved. A past tense is attached to it: it is *there*, it is done. But also it is *here* and is now active, in a much fuller, more dynamic sense than the sense merely that a fine example is there for all time and is permanently effective. It is not a mere incentive, like the example set by a Bodhisattva or a great hero. It is not an ideal, realizable only in theory, but an achieved fact, extending into a present reality, which Christian faith may actually lay hold of. The Christian hope is an anchor as well as a goal (Heb. 6.19 as well as 12.1).

In a word, it is incarnation and resurrection that lends

distinctiveness to the Christian phrase 'Christ died for us'. It is the *fait accompli* of the cross, plus the constant accessibility of the risen Christ, and the universal scope of God's action in Christ. What Christ is, all others are potentially involved in becoming: 'one man died for all and therefore all mankind has died' (2 Cor. 5.15); but also, 'as in Adam all men die, so in Christ all will be brought to life' (1 Cor. 15.22). How natural it is for a Christian to find Christ's death all-inclusive is illustrated – though it might have been illustrated in countless other ways – by the following meditation. A young man lost his life in a road accident abroad. Somehow, in some unaccountable way, this led to illumination for his bereaved sister. Here is a friend's meditation on these events. (The jibe against the Pharisees is not essential to the meaning: the author is well aware of the criticisms levelled against Christian writers for their treatment of the Pharisees, and knows that any considered account of the circumstances of the death of Christ would need to reckon carefully with their actual status and outlook. What he intended to suggest was that physical and even mental reactions are a luxury, and that in moments of real significance there is neither time nor need for feeling. In this context, 'Pharisees' meant, at least partly, those who enjoy religious feeling, including the pleasure of acknowledging sin, more than the reality.)

> A sudden death, they say, has no Gethsemane;
> but perhaps in the moment of this other death
> our time lost meaning, and the swerving car
> was filled with a rhythm stronger than the world could
>   bear.
> For when He died, a sudden clarity
> gave death a content. Through the clouds of emptiness
> (for pain and feeling now had fled
> to titillate the well-fed Pharisees)
> a cry of 'Finished' saw life's end, and poured
> blood and water from his side
> upon the twisted metal and marks of scorching tyres.
>
> And as the mountain blossomed as a plain,
> Its dews baptised the awakened eyes of a girl
> which shone with love to undo that death

by which, although we gaze uncomprehending
at the silhouette of memory, she lives.

David Dunford, April 1968

If I have correctly located the distinctiveness of the Christian
claim, it still remains to ask how Christians were led to
recognize and express it. It seems to me that the only answer
that can be given is in the actual experience of the earliest
Christians: they found that Jesus was alive and (in this strange
sense) somehow inclusive. Paul may be the only writer in the
New Testament who formulates the idea of inclusion in Christ
and membership in his body. But – and this is the point of this
chapter and the next [in the book from which this section is
taken] – there are certain assumptions held by other writers in
common with Paul, which, when analysed, point to just this
same conclusion. One such assumption is precisely that the
results of Christ's death are (at least potentially) all-
embracing. Other Christians besides St Paul may not say 'We
are in Christ', or 'He is the body and we its limbs and organs';
but they freely say 'He died for us; in his death is our life'. And
that implies an 'Adam Christology', even when this is not formulated.

Dr Morna Hooker, in a notable article on 'Interchange in
Christ' (reprinted in Hooker 1990, pp. 13ff.),[8] stresses the representative and inclusive character of Christ, as against an
exclusive vicariousness, and (rightly, as I believe) traces the
basis of this not to his death alone but to his entire ministry
and person – in a word, to the incarnation: he was made under
law, that he might ransom those who are under the law (Gal.
4.4f); he became sin (?) for us that, in him, we might become
God's righteousness (2 Cor. 5.21). And Father Gerald
O'Collins (1973, Ch. 10) has warned us against tracing our
salvation exclusively to the incarnation and not also to the
death, or to either or both of these and not also the 'posterior
mysteries', as he calls them, of the exaltation, Pentecost, the
birth of the Church and the *parousia*. I take his point; and to
find salvation in the whole of this 'Christ-event' is the same
thing, I suspect, as finding the unique quality of the death of
Christ in the potentially total inclusiveness of the life thereby
made available.

And if humanity as a whole may be spoken of as having caused the death of Christ, all those who accept his Lordship will voluntarily admit this and identify themselves with his death, accepting his obedience as their own. Thus it comes about that, in the Pauline or near-Pauline epistles, words compounded with συν- ('together with') are used to describe this identification of any Christian and of all Christians with Christ's death: to share its form (Phil. 3.10), to become fused or united with it (Rom. 6.5), to die with him (2 Tim. 2.11), to be buried with him (Rom. 6.4; Col. 2.12), to suffer with him (Rom. 8.17), to be crucified with him (Rom. 6.6; Gal. 2.19). It is often pointed out that, whereas such verbs, denoting suffering and death, are found in a past tense in Romans and Galatians as well as elsewhere, verbs denoting sharing Christ's risen life are found in a past tense exclusively in the captivity epistles: to be raised with Christ, Eph. 2.6; Col. 2.12, 3.1, and to sit with him in the heavenlies, Eph. 2.6. However, Styler (1973) has pointed out that in Rom. 6.11, 13, Paul bids his readers reckon themselves, or present themselves as, alive to God, which shows that Paul does not relegate this aliveness exclusively to the future; and, from other phrases also, it is clear that Paul reckons that Christians enjoy here and now a new sort of life (Rom. 6.4; 2 Cor. 5.17).[9]

Thus, to gather up the features that seem to make Christ's death 'for us' distinctive, we may say that we have found that anyone who has the courage and devotion to go, or be willing to go, to death in his loyalty to God and to truth, brings benefit to others – in some cases, material benefit, but in all cases spiritual; and that such a one may therefore rightly be said to have endured 'for' others – for certain others, if not for all others. Isa. 53, for instance, may be read as denoting universal atonement.[10] But it is of Christ alone that Christians found themselves saying: This one 'died for us, that whether we "wake" or "sleep" [? survive to the *parousia* or die first] we might live together with him' (1 Thess. 5.10); or, again (with reference to any Christian whatever), 'You have been purchased at a price' – that is, at the price of his death (1 Cor. 6.20); or (with reference to any and every Christian 'brother'), he is one 'for whom Christ died' (Rom. 14.15); or, 'he laid down his life for us' (1 John 3.16); or, 'one died for all,

therefore all have died' (2 Cor. 5.14); or, perhaps most remarkable of all, 'for this purpose Christ died and lived again, that
he might be Lord of dead and living' (Rom. 14.9).

It is this universal scope, assumed by Christians as a matter
of course, that seems distinctive about their estimate of the
meaning of Christ's death; and it is dependent on his experienced aliveness and his universal inclusiveness.[11] And those in
every generation from then to now who know him alive are
able to turn A. E. Housman's bitterly ironical 'Easter Hymn'
into a genuine invocation:

> If in that Syrian garden, ages slain,
> You sleep, and know not you are dead in vain,
> Nor even in dreams behold how dark and bright
> Ascends in smoke and fire by day and night
> The hate you died to quench and could but fan,
> Sleep well and see no morning, son of man.
>
> But if, the grave rent and the stone rolled by,
> At the right hand of majesty on high
> You sit, and sitting so remember yet
> Your tears, your agony and bloody sweat,
> Your cross and passion and the life you gave,
> Bow hither out of heaven and see and save.[12]

If we ask what are the doctrinal implications of this understanding of Christ as making himself available, through his
death, to all men and women, the answer is that they constitute
one more factor in a Christology which finds in Christ not just
an example but the Mediator between God and humankind.
It means, if it is justified by the evidence, more than that Jesus
Christ indicates how we may become rightly related to each
other in an ideal society.[13] It means that Jesus Christ, crucified
and raised from among the dead, actually is, or constitutes
that ideal society: he is the ultimate Adam, to be incorporated
in whom is to belong in the renewed society.

Notes

1. b. Baba Mesi'a 85a: see SB ii. 281, and Lohse 1955, p. 32, n. 3.
2. See Lohse 1955, p. 72 n. 6; cf. 105, 110; and Hahn 1963, p. 55; it is
   possible that baptism for the dead, in 1 Cor. 15.29, means the

offering of total self-dedication by the living in baptism on behalf of the unbaptized dead.

3. See, e.g. Jeremias 1955, p. 171.
4. For a discussion of this, see van Unnik 1973, p. 119.
5. Quoted by Samartha 1974, p. 125.
6. See Young 1975[a] and 1975[b]. In 1975[a], she writes: 'The new dynamic is to be found ... in the startling way in which the death of Jesus Christ becomes the focus of all sacrificial thinking,' p. 308a.
7. Fox 1973, p. 197.
8. Cf., independently, Dunn 1974, p. 130.
9. See also Gundry 1976, p. 57.
10. Hahn 1969, p. 348 n. 12.
11. For remarks about the distinctiveness of Christian claims for Jesus, see Roloff 1972, suggesting that they go back to the *diakonein* of the eucharistic tradition. Cf. Traina 1966, p. 187: 'he accomplished something in his coming and in his life unto death on behalf of men which was necessary for atonement and which men could not have done for themselves, though their free response still remains indispensable to make complete at-one-ment.'
12. Housman 1936, p. 15.
13. See Peacocke 1971 and 1973.

2

PREACHING THE ATONEMENT

Epworth Review, 10.2 (May 1983). London, Methodist Publishing House, pp. 70–78. This article contains material from lectures and papers in many places and on many occasions, but, in particular, it is based on a lecture delivered in Wesley College, Bristol on 4 December 1981, at the invitation of the Principal, the late Dr W. D. Stacey. I am grateful to him for suggesting that it might be of interest to readers of the *Epworth Review*, and grateful to its editor for accepting it.

The doctrine of the atonement, which is at the heart of the Christian good news, is sometimes preached in terms which seem to set it apart from anything recognizable in ordinary experience. At best, it sounds like some transcendent drama played out over our heads. At worst, it is told as a positively immoral story – an angry God needing to be propitiated, and accepting by way of propitiation the sacrifice of an innocent victim in lieu of the guilty. This is, of course, a pernicious travesty of the gospel, and the first step towards putting it right is, no doubt, to see that God and Christ are one in being, so that the sacrifice of Christ is a sacrifice made by God, not made to him. But over and above this, is it not vital to recognize that what is happening on the cross is not something apart from human life but is only the climactic fulfilment and perfecting of what, in its measure – its incomplete measure – happens whenever there is a reconciliation between two estranged persons?

To explain the processes of reconciliation (so far as a great mystery may be explained at all), analogies are necessary, and a number of these are used in the New Testament. There is the analogy of conquest: just as, in creation-stories, God is pictured as triumphing over chaos, so, in the Christian good news, Christ the conqueror triumphs over sin and death: he is like a warrior riding to victory. There is the analogy of washing or purging: the blood of Christ cleanses from sin. There is the analogy from the law courts: through Christ,

God's forgiveness 'puts us in the right'; somehow, in some sense, we are made 'not guilty'. There is the analogy from the sacrificial system of ancient Judaism: Christ's sacrifice of himself is the means of annulling the estrangement caused by sin.

The limited purpose of this article is to suggest that this last analogy – that of 'cultic' sacrifice – may be dispensed with, not because it does not represent a vital part of the gospel, but because it may be translated without essential loss into the language of a different analogy, namely, that of expenditure, of giving in a costly way. To anybody familiar with the language of the Bible and of Christian liturgy, it may seem preposterous to propose to substitute something else for so time-honoured a part of preaching as the language of sacrifice; but there are serious grounds for the proposal.

'Sacrifice' has become an imprecise and blurred concept. Strictly, 'sacrifice' means the offering to a deity, by some ritual, of something that is one's own and, characteristically, this takes the form of the ritual slaughter of an animal as an offering. But, for several reasons, this has become an undesirable analogy for the work of God in Jesus Christ. First, in our day and in the West, it is alien: we do not slaughter animals in worship. Second, it is difficult (though perhaps not impossible) to use the word without its implying a propitiatory intention, whereas in good news which tells of God's giving himself for us in Christ, propitiation is altogether out of place. It is true that in ordinary English the word 'sacrifice' has already lost its cultic connotation, and means simply the surrender of something precious. 'The supreme sacrifice' often means laying down one's life for one's country. 'Sacrificial' simply means extremely generous. Conversely, the simple word 'gift' both in the Hebrew of the Old Testament and in the Greek of the New, can, in certain contexts, stand for a certain type of sacrifice. But all this only goes to confirm the thesis that words denoting cost and expenditure have come to do the same work as the metaphor of sacrifice, which may therefore more appropriately be replaced by them, free as they are of propitiatory associations. There is a further reason for 'translating' the language of sacrifice into the language of cost, namely that it is possible more easily to keep the language of cost on the level of fully personal action. Sacrifice in its strict, cultic sense may be external to the offerer; but cost is a metaphor that may more easily be kept close to the donor's own actions and intentions. Moreover, the main thrust of the Christian gospel itself is towards recognizing that Christ's self-giving, even if it crowns the sacrificial system as the ultimate sacrifice, also supersedes it as the sacrifice to end sacrifices, making obsolete the Levitical cult and rending the veil of the temple in twain.

Here, of course, there arise delicate and controversial questions about the propriety of calling the Eucharist a sacrifice and Christian ministers priests, and it would take this essay too far afield to go in adequate detail into these aspects of the question. That the Eucharist is not a sacrifice, but rather a means of uniting the worshippers with Christ's sacrifice, and that Christian ministers are not priests in a sacerdotal sense, seems to follow from the evidence: but this is not the moment to pursue that part of the argument. (See pp. 135ff. below.)

The thesis of this essay, then, is that all the strictly Christian meanings of the biblical sacrificial terms as used in preaching atonement can, instead, be conveyed in terms of expenditure, cost, or giving; and that these terms can play an important role in the preaching of atonement in Christ when they are used in the analysis of the processes of reconciliation.

It will be assumed here without further argument that personal values and the relations between persons are paramount. Analogies drawn from a sub-personal level are un-avoidable: conquest by force, cleansing, a judicial verdict, and the very one with which we are now concerned – 'sacrificial' cost or expenditure – are all sub-personal analogies; but it will be assumed that all such analogies need continually to be related, and kept subservient, to the fully personal realities of reconciliation between persons.

This being said it is obviously an advantage if 'preaching' (in the widest sense of communicating the meaning of the gospel) can start on a personal level – and best of all if it can start with experiences that are recognizably true and important whether for Christians or non-Christians. We have all experienced reconciliation, or know friends who have had the experience. If we ask what, precisely, takes place when reconciliation is achieved, anyone will recognize that it is a costly process on both sides.

This fact was first, and unforgettably, brought home to me in terms of the story of 'the prodigal son' (as we familiarly call it) in Luke 15. Not that the original purpose of this story was primarily to portray a reconciliation: the likelihood is that Jesus told it to justify his fraternizing with the social and religious outcasts, and to challenge his orthodox critics. It is really another story about the Pharisee and the publican. But it happens to be a literary gem depicting a reconciliation, and as such it can be used simply as a model or 'paradigm' for that.

When the son returns, then, and finds his father running to welcome him and embracing him, what will he see when at last he dares to look up into his parent's face? (Anyone who so wishes may substitute mother and daughter for father and son: the realities are the same.) The son, it was suggested to me, will see signs of wear and tear – physical signs of distress: his father will have been visibly aged by what the son has done; his hair and beard will perhaps be going white and his face will have aged. In other words, the process of reconciliation has 'taken it out of' the parent – it has been costly. It is not that the forgiveness and welcome are not glad and spontaneous: they are. They are not laboriously fetched up with conscious effort. But nobody can greatly forgive unless he or she is sensitive enough to suffer from the wrong that is forgiven. Thus, the offer of forgiveness is necessarily costly. It is not a matter of words – 'I forgive you'; or of a gesture – embracing. It is a creative act, costly and achieved only by the output of energy. It means thinking nothing about one's rights or about abstract justice, but surrendering one's self-concern altogether. It means absorbing the wrong, instead of retaliating; giving, and not demanding any *quid pro quo*. Most people, whether consciously religious or not, will recognize this as true to reality.

Of course, in this model or 'paradigm', absolutes are used for the sake of simplicity. In real life, there are sure to be both right and wrong on both sides: a measure of provocation before the offence was committed; a measure of decency on the side of the offender. It will not be black and white but two shades of grey. But for simplicity – and of course it becomes actual when it is between God and the sinner – we call one side innocent and the other guilty, without qualification.

On the side of the guilty party, the offender, then, what are the processes of repentance? It probably starts with mere remorse, which is self-regarding: 'I'm hungry; I've been a fool; I depise myself; I'm mortified.' This may be enough to start the prodigal homewards. But he will not really have repented, he will not have accepted his parent's forgiveness, he will not genuinely become part of the family again, until his concern has passed from himself to the one he has wronged, and – severest test of all – until he is able to treat those who wrong him with as much generosity as he has received from his forgiver.

St Luke's parable stops short with the father gently expostulating with the indignant elder brother (meaning, perhaps, in the original context, the Pharisees). The test will be when the younger son, the 'prodigal', is face to face with that brother of his. If he pays resentment with resentment, then he is not yet penitent. The forgiveness offered him has not yet been accepted. If he has accepted forgiveness from his father, he will himself be forgiving towards his brother: 'forgive us our debts, as we too forgive our debtors' (and the parable of the two debtors tells the same story – Matt. 18.21ff.).

This is dreadfully 'expensive'. It costs a lot to give oneself away like that. It feels like death to oneself. And this is where judgement comes in. A penitent person is one who recognizes his responsibility and the rightness of the judgement against him. So far from letting him off or condoning his fault, forgiveness is precisely that which calls him up to his full stature as a responsible person and makes him admit his sin and 'give himself up', as it were. Forgiveness is ruthless in the severity of its judgement, although judgement in its deepest sense is never a destructive condemnation but is essentially restorative: it is the rescue of the person from his less-than-self.

Thus, by the time the reconciliation is achieved – costly forgiveness responded to by costly repentance – two great expenditures of creative energy have taken place: the initial and initiating energy of forgiveness, without which the process could not begin – that 'grace' or generosity which ultimately comes from God alone – and the responsive energy of repentance, without which the reconciliation could not become a fact.

It is noteworthy that these funds of energy (an admittedly

sub-personal analogy, but used close to and under the para-mountcy of the personal) are not reciprocal – they are not exchanged; they do not represent a transaction. The forgiver does not say 'I'll sell you forgiveness, if you'll pay me repentance.' Of course not! It is noteworthy, too, that restitution, which is often prescribed in sacramental absolution after the hearing of a confession, is not that by which forgiveness is earned: away with the thought! Forgiveness, by definition, cannot be earned, and restitution (or some other 'penance') is not identical with penitence, though it may be an important sign, seal, or sacrament of penitence.

Thus, penitence is not 'paid' to the forgiver. No: the two 'energies' – the creative energy of forgiveness and the responding energy of penitence – are, so to speak, both poured out in the same direction. They do not, as it were, meet and cross; they both flow in the direction of repair, just as, in a lesion in living flesh, all the invisible armies of disease-fighters in the blood teem in the direction of repair. (Again, here are sub-personal, bio-mechanical analogies – but as part of the analysis of a personal process.)

So, forgiveness is costly, an expensive gift; but the forgiven is not 'let off', for repentance, though it cannot earn that gift, is a necessary 'cost', and a high cost: it is the surrender of self and of all *amour-propre*. Forgiveness, therefore, cannot be vicarious, if calling it vicarious means that it does not involve the offender in the cost, though it is vicarious in the sense that, by definition, the initiative of forgiveness cannot be taken by the offender: the process has to be started on his behalf.

The whole process is so obviously creative – bringing life into a dead situation or repairing a deadly wound in torn tissue – that it is impossible (for a religious person, at least) to imagine that human reconciliation can be achieved from human resources: they are always, even if unconsciously, derived from God, the Creator of life, whenever and wherever they have taken place, both before and after the incarnation of God in Jesus Christ. 'It is the pure victim alone who is capable of creative action,' says Williams (1982, p. 15). In other words, the Christian belief is that only in Christ is the source of the divine repair to be seen, and only in Christ does the process of reconciliation find complete implementation, since only by completely innocent suffering can forgiveness be completely proffered. Christ is one with God and one with us in a unique sense, and the death and resurrection of Christ are, in a supreme and decisive degree, God's expenditure of forgiveness and mankind's expenditure of responsive obedience.

This does not mean that God could not forgive until Christ's sacrifice had been offered. To say so would make nonsense of, for instance, the Old Testament's messages of forgiveness. Neither does it mean that the incarnation is an isolated 'invasion' from without, discontinuous from the long, perennial process of painful forgiveness and repentance and repair which God, immanent in the world, exercises throughout time within his suffering creation. On the contrary, the reason why God has always and in all ages and cultures been a redeeming God is that, as Creator, as the strength and stay upholding all creation, he is always immanent in all the processes of forgiveness, repentance, and repair, and has to reach in them, sooner or later, a climactic absolute. The distinctiveness of Christ is that, in him, God becomes wholly and completely incarnate at a particular time and place: in him the process reaches its absolute. The incarnation is the supreme and decisive expression and implementation in history of what God is always performing and will continue to perform in all creation.

That is as far as the story need be taken for the present purpose, namely, to show that the language simply of giving – the language of spending and of expending energy – can express all that, in certain parts of the New Testament, is expressed in terms specifically of sacrifice.

Of course it can be argued that the language of sacrifice is so important to 'the Israel of the Old Covenant', the Israel of the Jewish Scriptures, that if Christians jettisoned that language it would break one of the bonds of continuity between the ancient People of God and the Christian Church. In the face of this argument, one may concede at once that the recognition of this bond is essential to a Christian doctrine of the Church. In the New Testament there is no such thing as 'New Israel': the People of God is one and continuous. What is new is not Israel, but the covenant sealed by the blood of Christ. Hence the retention of the Jewish Scriptures by the Christian

Church, but, at the same time, their designation as the Scriptures of the Old Testament (or Covenant), in distinction from the Scriptures of the New. Nevertheless – one may go on to argue – community of language is not the only sort of continuity, nor necessarily the best; and continuity is secured no less by a sort of fulfilment that leads to supersession than by mere repetition and reaffirmation. The Epistle to the Hebrews is a great monument to the continuity of the People of God, yet also to the finality of Christ and the supersession of the Old Covenant by the New. Negatively, Heb. 8.13 is emphatic in its assertion that the Old Covenant is abolished by the New; but, positively, Chapter 10 is the heart of the argument. It declares that the whole system of sacrifices has culminated in and been replaced by Christ's self-sacrifice, which, no longer a 'cultic' sacrifice, sums up his total obedience to the designs of God, and in which Christians are consecrated to God: by that will – that is to say, by Christ's complete acceptance and affirmation of God's will – we are sanctified (10.10). Such total obedience to the will of God, in a life which turned out to be, in a unique sense, God's own life incarnate, cannot be a sacrifice offered to God to propitiate him. On the contrary, it is the expenditure, by God, of his creative, restorative energy. There is a sense, it is true, in which it is offered to God, for Christ is one not only with God but also with mankind; and his obedience is mankind's obedience offered up to God, as well as God's energy given for mankind. In the terms of our analogy, it is both the energy of the forgiver and also the energy of the penitent. But the human offering is still not a propitiatory sacrifice, but the offering of glad and affirmative obedience.

Of the other analogies which, as was observed at the beginning of this essay, the New Testament uses in its presentation of the good news of reconciliation, St Paul's law-court analogy, 'justification by faith' (or, more strictly, justification by God's grace responded to by mankind's faith), turns out to be part of the very analysis of reconciliation which has been made in this essay. Grace is, precisely, God's expenditure of generous forgivingness and faith is that costly response which is repentance. Paul is often accused of neglecting the theme of repentance; but faith, in its most characteristically Pauline sense, includes repentance.

As for the conquest of evil and cleansing from stains, these are both analogies that are still intelligible in our own day, and, within their limits, they are applicable to reconciliation. But these, too, take on a meaning fully in accord with the total Christian good news only when they are seen as analogies for certain aspects of the personal processes of reconciliation between persons. In all cases, it is the personal values that turn out to be paramount.

For the sake of any readers who wish to pursue further the question how far 'cultic' terms are used in the New Testament and whether they can be 'translated' without loss into terms of other analogies, an analysis of these follows.

Cultic Terms in the New Testament

to sanctify, ἁγιάζειν	It is difficult to be certain when this (and the related nouns and adjective) may be called ritual or cultic in their associations; but consider (out of the large number of occurrences) Matt. 23.17, 19; John 10.36, 17.17, 19; Rom. 15.16; 1 Cor. 6.11; Eph. 5.26; 1 Tim. 4.5; Heb. 9.13, 10.10, 13.12.
blood, αἷμα	Matt. 26.28 (and parallels); John 6.53, 56; Acts 15.20, 29, 20.28, Rom. 3.25, 5.9; 1 Cor. 10.16, 11.25, 27; Eph. 1.7, 2.13; Col. 1.20, Heb. 9.7–25, 10.4, 19, 29, 11.28, 12.24, 13.11, 12, 20; 1 Pet. 1.2, 19; 1 John 1.7, 5.6, 8; Rev. 1.5, 5.9, 7.14, 12.11.
shedding of blood, αἱματεκχυσία	Heb. 9.22.
lamb, ἀμνός	John 1.29, 36; 1 Pet. 1.19.
lamb (a second word), ἀρνίον	Rev. 5.6–13, 6.1, 16, 7.9–17, 12.11, 13.8, 14.1, 4, 10, 15.3, 17.14, 19.7, 9, 21.9, 14, 22, 23, 27, 22.1, 3.

without blemish,
ἄμωμος   Heb. 9.14; 1 Pet. 1.19. (As applied to Christians, more doubtful.)

gift
δῶρον   Matt. 5.23f., 8.4, 15.5 (and Marcan parallel), 23.18f.; Heb. 5.1, 8.3f., 9.9, 11.4. The word is also used, of course, outside ritual – a fact on which this essay turns.

to sacrifice,
θύειν   Mark 14.12 (and Lukan parallel); 1 Cor. 5.7, 10.20. (Other occurrences more general.)

a sacrifice,
θυσία   Rom. 12.1; 1 Cor. 10.18; Eph. 5.2; Phil. 2.17, 4.18; Heb. 5.1, 7.27, 8.3, 9.9, 23, 26, 10.1, 5, 8, 11, 12, 26, 11.4, 13.15, 16; 1 Pet. 2.5. (In Gospels and Acts, less relevant).

altar,
θυσιαστήριον   Heb. 13.10. (Other occurrences less relevant.)

expiate (propitiate),
ἱλάσκεσθαι   Luke 18.13; Heb. 2.17.

expiation (propitiation),
ἱλασμός   1 John 2.2, 4.10.

propitiatory (mercy-seat),
ἱλαστήριον   Rom. 3.25; Heb. 9.5.

propitious,
ἵλεως   Matt. 16.22; Heb. 8.12.

to cleanse,
καθαρίζειν   This can be a ritual word (compare ῥαντίζειν, below, and contrast, perhaps, the washing words), but the line is so difficult to draw that it would be unprofitable to give a list. Under αἷμα see Heb. 9.14–23.

cleansing,
καθαρισμός   This is mostly ritual, but, in the NT, almost wholly with reference to Jewish custom. See, however, Heb. 1.3; 2 Pet. 1.9.

a sweet-smelling savour,
ὀσμὴ εὐωδίας   Eph. 5.2; Phil. 4.18.

passover (victim),
πάσχα   1 Cor. 5.7. (Other occurrences less relevant.)

sin-offering (concerning sin),
περὶ ἁμαρτίας (-ιῶν) Rom. 8.3; Heb. 5.3, 10.6, 8, 18, 26, 13.11; 1 John 2.2, 4.10.

to bear,
φέρειν
to bear (offer) up,
ἀναφέρειν   Heb. 7.27, (9.28 = 'remove'), 13.15; Jas 2.21; 1 Pet. 2.5, (2.24 = 'remove' or 'sustain').

to bring as offering,
προσφέρειν   Matt. 5.23, 24, 8.4 (and parallels); John 16.2; Acts 7.42, 21.26, Heb. 5.1, 3, 7, 8.3, 4, 9.7, 9, 14, 25, 28, 10.1, 2, 8, 11, 12, 11.4, 17.

an offering,
προσφορά   Acts 21.26, 24.17; Rom. 15.16; Eph. 5.2; Heb. 10.5, 8, 10, 14, 18.

to sprinkle,
ῥαντίζειν   Mark 7.4; Heb. 9.13, 19, 21, 10.22.
sprinkling,
ῥαντισμός   Heb. 12.24; 1 Pet. 1.2.

In the original essay there followed a list of some relevant publications, in English only. This may be consulted in *Epworth Review* 10.2, May 1983, pp. 77ff. I now add these few which have come my way:

Marrow, S. B., 'Principles for Interpreting the New Testament Soteriological Terms', *NTS* 36 (1990) pp. 268ff.

Hamerton-Kelly, R. G., *Sacred Violence: Paul's Hermeneutic of the Cross*. Minneapolis, Augsburg-Fortress, 1992.

McLean, B. H., 'The Absence of an Atoning Sacrifice in Paul's Soteriology', *NTS* 1992, pp. 531ff.

Bailie, G., *Violence Unveiled: Humanity at the Crossroads*. New York, Crossroad, 1995.

Jones, L. G., *Embodying Forgiveness: a Theological Analysis*. Grand Rapids, Michigan, Eerdmans, 1995.

Sykes, S., *The Story of Atonement*. London, Darton, Longman and Todd, 1997.

3

REFLECTIONS ON SO-CALLED

TRIUMPHALISM

From L. D. Hurst and N. T. Wright (eds), *The Glory of Christ in the New Testament: Studies in Christology in Memory of George Bradford Caird*. Oxford, Clarendon Press, 1987, pp. 219–27.

When Haydn heard about the Battle of Aboukir Bay, he is said (probably apocryphally) to have added an entry of trumpets to the Benedictus of his D Minor Mass, the *Missa in angustiis*, now popularly known as the Nelson Mass. Subsequently the composer and the Admiral exchanged gifts: Haydn gave Nelson his pen, and Nelson gave Haydn his gold watch. Eucharist and paean seemed to be in the same key. By contrast, the note of triumph was studiously kept out of the service in St Paul's Cathedral at the end of the campaign to recover the Falkland Islands, to the disgust of some of the public who wanted to sing militant hymns and shout 'hurrah!' (It was then that the same public discovered for the first time the existence of a 'peace version' of the National Anthem, though churchmen had had it in their hymn books for decades.) The difference between the two occasions marks a revulsion in the Christian conscience from the idea that success in warfare is necessarily a gift from God. It registers a decisive repudiation of jingoism by Christians. Essentially, this is only the recovery of what has been at the heart of Christianity from the beginning; but at least it is a new awakening.

Awakening has come on a still deeper level also. It is not merely a matter of realizing that Yahweh of Hosts, the God of battles, is not the Father of our Lord Jesus Christ. More profoundly it is a recognition that 'triumph' and 'success' may themselves be disastrously misleading words to describe love's endeavour. If, by definition, love takes ultimate risks, passionately throwing itself away in the dark, with no guarantee of success; if the very essence of love is to love with no certainty of being loved in return; if it means dying without any certainty of life, then the language of victory and success is in danger of trivializing that which it is supposed to acclaim. This consideration is thrust home by W. H. Vanstone's two fine books, *Love's Endeavour, Love's Expense* (1977) and *The Stature of Waiting* (1982). Facile notions of the success of goodness, shallow presentations of Easter as a triumphant reversal of Good Friday, have come to be called by the regrettable but convenient name of 'triumphalism', and the thoughtful Christian is keenly on guard against it.

Rightly so; but when human language gropes for words to describe the indescribable, there is no expression that does not have its attendant drawbacks; and in resiling from 'triumphalism' there is a danger of losing the proper note of triumph for the Christian gospel. This essay, dedicated to the memory of a scholar whose precision and intellectual courage have set the highest standards, is intended to draw attention to two considerations which, though familiar, are perennially important in the face of this dilemma. The first consideration, to which George Caird's own book *The Language and Imagery of the Bible* (1980) is relevant, not least in its suggestive discussion of anthropomorphism, is this. The language of warfare, of conquest and victory, belongs among the many metaphors applied by Christians, from New Testament times onwards, to the work of God in Jesus Christ and, like the metaphor that it is, it must not be pressed beyond its proper function. The same applies to the biblical metaphor of washing and cleansing. The abolition of dirt ('Out, damned spot!') is a good analogy for what a guilty conscience longs for: 'though your sins are scarlet, they may become white as snow'. But the actual processes of forgiveness, repentence, and reconciliation – the mysterious work of God's love which engages the sinner's whole person with its relentless but gentle demands – are in the end not adequately matched by the action of an omnicompetent detergent. Impersonal metaphors can go only so far and no further towards illuminating personal realities. Therefore, we shall escape 'triumphalism' not by moderating the language of military success or royal dignity or radical cleansing. On the contrary, when used it should be used with abandon and zest. But what we must do is to recognize its function and so observe its limited scope, using the metaphor but not abusing it. Victory is a metaphor for success; but if it is allowed to imply success by main force, it hinders the presentation of a Christian gospel. If love 'wins', it is not by flattening the opposition, but by eliciting the good that is buried under self-concern, by redirecting the perverted, by liberating a person to be his or her true self.

The other consideration is this. While of course it is true that the deepest realities of life are incapable of proof – how could anyone prove that 'love never fails'? – nevertheless it is possible to point to very strong grounds for believing that the love of God in Jesus Christ did in fact create life out of death and love out of hatred. There is a sense in which 'success', that dangerous word, may with reason be applied to the outcome of the life and ministry of Jesus of Nazareth. He did see of the travail of his soul, and was satisfied.

When Christians began to look for words with which to express their faith, they naturally drew upon the Scriptures. These Scriptures – which Christians subsequently came to call the Scriptures of the Old Covenant – are full of battle language to describe the work of God, and they unashamedly ask for and proclaim success. Not only are there certain levels of Old Testament thought on which it is assumed that Yahweh will win literal and material victory for his people if they remain loyal to him, and that defeat in war must mean that their loyalty has failed. There are also the familiar passages where the language of conquest is applied metaphorically – for instance, to the work of creation. God the Creator, the God of light and order, is depicted in creation myth as subduing the monsters of chaos – Tehom, the great deep, Rahab the rager, Leviathan and Tannin, those primeval dragons. It is a theme of ancient religions generally, and Babylonian epic correspondingly has its battle between Marduk and Tiamat. When light and order overcome darkness and chaos, this is victory, this is success. So the New Testament represents Jesus as saying that he has witnessed the fall of Satan like lightning from heaven, and that he gives his disciples authority, like the psalmist in Psalm 91, to tread upon serpents (Luke 10.18f.). Paul looks forward to a time very soon when the God of peace will crush Satan under his people's feet (Rom. 16.20), and when all other government and authority shall be abolished (1 Cor. 15.24).

Revelation uses a spate of victory-language. It depicts war in heaven, when the dragon is thrown down (12.7); and a climactic battle in which the triumphant Word of God rides forth with his white-clad armies to conquer the forces of evil (19.11ff.). Of the martyrs it is said that they conquered by the blood of the Lamb (12.11). Disturbingly, the victory of Christ seems even to be depicted as a blood-bath (14.20), though G. B. Caird, and, after him, J. P. M. Sweet, in their commentaries (1966; 1979), argue powerfully that here the blood is not the blood of opponents but the blood of Christ and of the martyrs, which will ultimately be creative and constructive.

The same conquest-language, condensed from myth to metaphor, is exploited in the Johannine Gospel and First Epistle. Indeed, these, with Revelation, almost have the monopoly of words from the νικ-group. Outside this group of writings these words are sparse: Matt. 12.20, quoting from Isa. 42, has 'leads justice on to victory' (νῖκος); Luke 11.22 has 'when someone stronger comes upon him and overpowers him', in a parabolic saying; Rom. 3.4, quoting from the LXX of Ps. 51, has 'conquer', in the sense of win in a lawsuit (compare Hebrew 'come out clean'); Rom. 8.37 has 'overwhelming victory is ours' (ὑπερνικῶμεν) and Rom. 12.21 has 'do not let evil conquer you, but use good to defeat evil'. All the rest belong to John, 1 John, or Revelation, and all, in one way or another, refer to the triumph of good or faithfulness or right belief over evil and falsehood. It is a metaphor not uncommon in Philo (for instance *All.* 2.108 (metaphor from the Olympic Games), 3.190, *Abr.* 244).

To the actual use of words of the νικ-group must be added, of course, all the expressions for power or authority which are applied to God or Christ or their followers. Such − besides those already quoted − are the promise to Peter that the gates of Hades shall not prevail (Matt. 16.18), and the profusion of power-words in Ephesians, leading up to the Christian warrior's mastery and firm stand (Eph. 6.13). J. S. B. Monsell's hymn, 'Fight the good fight', so beloved by militants who have not altogether come to terms with its metaphorical nature, is a pastiche of phrases of this sort, mingled with the competitive language of the Olympic games. As it happens, the opening phrase itself is the Authorized Version's mistranslation of what is not a military but an athletic metaphor in 1 Tim. 6.12. Unambiguously military, however, is the campaign language of 1 Tim. 1.18 and 2 Cor. 10.3 f., as are 'soldier' and 'fellow-soldier', used metaphorically, in Phil. 2.25, 2 Tim. 2.3 and Philem. 2. Finally, the actual word θριαμβεύειν occurs twice in the New Testament – at 2 Cor. 2.14 and at Col. 2.15. In both instances there is controversy over the exact meaning of the verb (lead as captives in his triumphal procession, or as fellow-conquerors?); but certainly the image is that of a victor's triumphal procession, and it is paradoxically applied to the strange work of God through the cross and through those who accept it.

All in all, the New Testament is not shy of the language of coercion, and a study of the word ἐξουσία is instructive, for it points unequivocally to the conviction that God's authority is successfully exerted over authorities. In the temptation, Christ rejects the spurious ἐξουσία offered him by Satan (Luke 4.6, and the same sense in Matt. 4.8f., though without the word ἐξουσία). As a result, he can declare at the end of the story that all ἐξουσία has been given him in heaven and on earth (Matt. 28.18). So, too, the disciples are given authority over the unclean spirits (Matt. 10.1, Mark 3.15, 6.7, Luke 9.1). The Lucan saying (10.19) about authority to trample on serpents has already been mentioned. In Col. 1.13, the ἐξουσία of darkness from which Christians are rescued is contrasted with the kingdom of God's beloved Son into which they are transferred. The language is that of a commando raid to free hostages.

The 'warlike language' of the Johannine writings, says Brown (1982, p. 304),

is at home in a dualism where the forces of darkness seek to overcome or to kill the forces of light ... The Johannine community could have addressed to Christ the praise addressed to God in the Qumran *Scroll of the War between the Sons of Light and the Sons of Darkness* (1QM 11:4–5): 'The battle is yours and the power comes from you, not from us. Our strength and the power of our hands accomplish no mighty deeds except by your power and the might of your valor'

– a theme already familiar in the Old Testament. This warlike language, whether in a dualistic context or not, stands not only for man's dependence on divine help but also for the success of the divine forces: 'God does win in the end,' it affirms. And in the New Testament such assertions are sometimes cast in the form of a peripeteia, to emphasize the surprise and paradox of God's road to triumph: what seemed defeat turned out to be victory; what seemed humiliation ended in glory. 'God has made this Jesus, whom you crucified, both Lord and Messiah' (Acts 2.36); 'he died on the cross in weakness, but he lives by the power of God' (2 Cor. 13.4); 'he humbled himself … Therefore God raised him to the heights' (Phil. 2.8f.). Not seldom the New Testament adopts what might be called the victory-sign – a V-shaped pattern of descent to the depths followed by exaltation to the heights: a peripeteia from defeat to victory is woven into the texture of the gospel. But it is only a metaphor, with a strictly limited validity. If it stood alone, it would misrepresent the gospel, for the simple reason that the language of the reversal of fortunes from adversity to triumph suggests brute force whereas the Christian good news is constructive and is concerned with personal relations into which coercion may not enter. Indeed all the biblical metaphors relating to the processes of reconciliation suffer from some such limitation because they belong in sub-personal realms: conquest, cleansing, emancipation, acquittal, cancellation of debts, sacrifice, ransom – all are analogies borrowed from below the level of the fully personal. Applied metaphorically to the deeply personal reality of reconciliation between estranged persons, each of the metaphors performs some particular function in affirming God's ultimate success, in emphasizing the costliness of the process, in magnifying the sheer generosity of God, or in underlining the inability of men and women to save themselves. But to press the metaphors beyond their limited function is to court doctrinal disaster.

To safeguard against this, there are checks and balances built into the New Testament itself. What saves all expressions of victory from 'triumphalism' is not a sparing or muted use of them. It is the recognition that peripeteia – a story about the reversal of fortunes, and, as such, about chronologically successive circumstances – is only a device to illuminate one aspect of a reality in which there is no successiveness, for it is eternal and all its aspects coexist simultaneously. The 'descent' in the V-shaped story, and the apparent failure or humiliation, are not really preliminary to ascent and exaltation, for the eternal graciousness of God holds all together and simultaneously. The New Testament itself does not fail to make this point. Barrett (1973, p. 336), commenting on 2 Cor. 13.4 ('. . . died on the cross in weakness . . . lives by the power of God') writes:

> the weakness shown in his crucifixion, being a mark of his grace, is not an unfortunate lapse from strength but one aspect of the action God intended in his Son. Historically, he preferred crucifixion to the exercise of some kinds of power; he preferred crucifixion to the abandonment of the outcast groups of Palestinian society, with whose social and religious weakness he identified himself. Similarly, though it is true it is also inadequate to say that the resurrection was a signal manifestation of divine power . . . Christ is both weak and strong.

Similarly, the inadequacy of a one-sided statement is recognized in the well-known *double entendre* used by the fourth Evangelist when the word 'exalt' signifies both the uplifting of Jesus on the shameful cross and his uplifting in glory (John 3.14, 8.28, 12.32, 34). In other words, the New Testament itself as it were flattens out the V-pattern. If the V-pattern helps to bring home the marvel of Christ's humility, a straight line puts the humiliation on the same plane as the glory, as though to say, 'Marvel not, for the two are one.' It has even been proposed to interpret Phil. 2.6f. in a 'rectilinear' way so as to mean: 'Christ did not reckon equality with God to mean grasping: instead, he emptied himself.' See Moule (1970[a]), in which I revived a suggestion made by Ross (1909). Subsequent research seems to have established that ἁρπαγμὸν ἡγεῖσθαί τι means, rather, 'to regard as *something to be taken advantage of*' (see Hoover 1971). If so, the sense of the passage remains 'rectilinear', though this sense is reached by a different route: it means that Christ interpreted God-likeness in terms of self-emptying rather than of glorying (see the full and illuminating discussion in Wright 1986).[1] But supposing that this is what Phil. 2.6f. was intended to mean, then it is significant that one should find the 'straight line' pattern there 'bent', only a few verses later, into the V-pattern, in 'therefore God has more than exalted him'. So it is that, in human thinking, the two patterns need to alternate.

Again, it is noteworthy that, in St John's Gospel, the word ἐξουσία, which has already been mentioned as affirming the divine authority, is subtly handled so as to fall into the same pattern as is indicated by the *double entendre* of uplifting on the cross and in glory. For what is the authority given to those who accept Christ? It is the authority, the right, simply to be children of God (1.12, cf. 1 John 3.1). What is Christ's own authority? It is to lay down his life, as well as to take it again (10.18). Christ has authority to judge (5.27) and exercise authority over everybody (17.2), but it is clearly a moral authority, in contrast to Pilate's authority to sentence him, which is only a derived and secondary authority (19.10f.).

Again, one of the themes that runs through the teaching of Jesus as far as it is discernible through the Gospel traditions is that of 'the Son of man'. If it is correct to treat this phrase as a genuinely dominical reference to Dan. 7, then it is noteworthy that the human figure in that vision represents the martyr loyalists whose strength was in their obedience and their submission even to the length of death and that the 'success' of this way looks like failure, being vindicated only beyond death and in heaven. There it is that they are given favourable judgement and a kingdom. Thus, the adoption of this symbol by Jesus is one more way of declaring that for him the way of royal glory is the way of the cross. (Did the late Barnabas Lindars (1983), in regarding the Danielic reference as post-dominical, pay sufficient attention to the evidence provided by the definite article, and to the suitability of the phrase, not as messianic nor apocalyptic nor titular, but as a symbol of martyrdom vindicated beyond death? See p. 205ff.)

Thus, the New Testament itself reminds the reader that, in preaching the gospel, the metaphorical nature of the analogies and their limited function need to be observed. No analogy from a sub-personal level can ultimately do justice to the whole of a personal relation; but what it can do is to affirm some aspect of it. 'Glory follows humility' – that is a way of affirming faith in the glory; but 'the humility is the glory' represents a deeper insight, closer to the level of personal relations and very close to the cross. It is along the *via dolorosa* that the triumphal procession moves. If the preacher knows what he is doing he will not modify the triumph; yet neither will he fall victim to 'triumphalism'.

But if love never coerces, must not its triumph be at the mercy of the beloved? If love wins not by winning a victory over the other but by winning the other over, must not our gospel forever be an expression only of hope without certainty? Is it possible to point to any argument on which to rest such brave affirmations as the following, taken at random from contemporary theological writing? 'The Gospel is that Jesus's God is King, that the source of all things and the meaning of all things is what Jesus called *Abba* ...' (Williams 1983, p. 77). Describing the message implicit in the life and work of Jesus, the late Ben F. Meyer (1979, p. 250) wrote:

> Divine salvation would be nothing short of total victory over evil. Such was the *a priori* which evoked and linked the repulse of Hades, the ordeal and its resolution, the reversal of the lot of the depressed, the ransom for many, the destruction and raising of the temple, the banquet of the saved in God's reign. These themes incarnated the message that good would prevail, that the vicious circle of disorder and decline would be broken.

Once more, Newbigin (1969) speaks of 'the infinite power and resourcefulness of God to use men's rebellion as the means to his victory' (p. 86). On what is it legitimate to rest such confidence? Can we point – not of course, to proof, but – to considerations that at least constitute good grounds for such assertions? We can.

A starting-point is offered by the genesis of the Easter-belief. How came friends of Jesus to believe that, after his crucifixion, they saw him alive with life transcendent, the life of the age to come? 'Judaism', said the late J. Jeremias (1971, pp. 308f.), 'did not know of any anticipated resurrection ... to δόξα as an event of history. Rather, resurrection to δόξα always and

38

without exception means the dawn of God's new creation . . .'
In other words, it is not possible to account for the Easter faith
from any already existing Jewish expectations which might
have been entertained by the friends of Jesus. Then what did
generate their Easter faith? Notoriously attempts to rationalize
it as the result of psychological aberrations or subjective
visionary experience fail to reach plausibility. They do not
make sense of the sober, tenacious conviction which squeezed
this Jewish sect out of the synagogue and compelled them eventually to know themselves as a *tertium genus*. Then what did
generate this faith? It is not unreasonable, given the poverty of
alternative explanations, to conclude that what they seemed
to see did indeed correspond with reality: in Jeremias' words
in the same context, 'the disciples must have experienced the
appearances of the Risen Lord as an eschatological event, as a
dawning of the turning point of the worlds.'

But this turns out to be no isolated or rootless revelation.
Despite its overwhelming novelty, it became clear, on reflection, that the Jesus whom his friends had known was just such
a one as to fit this new dimension. As C. K. Barrett observed
(as already quoted), Jesus had in his lifetime identified himself
with the social and religious outcasts, insisting that what he
was doing in fraternizing with such persons was what God
does. Constantly, the Jesus who emerges from critical scrutiny
of the traditions is one whose work is God's work, in whose
presence God's sovereignty becomes a reality, who shows
God's mind directly without appeal to antecedent authority.
This immediacy, this directness, this embodying of the divine
presence is the sort of thing, it appears, that made Jesus intolerable to his own religious contemporaries; but now, in the resurrection appearances, his self-identification with God's way and
his being the vehicle of the immediate presence of God are
confirmed, and from such apprehension there springs, eventually, the articulation of a distinctive doctrine of the cross, a
Christology and a gospel. The belief that the strange and
gentle way of love is ultimately the only valid way is firmly
based on historical events.

If so, then the aliveness of Jesus is good news which may be confidently proclaimed. It is a well-authenticated triumph; it is a

victory for which no language of conquest can be too positive. Yet it is a victory on that mysterious level of personal relations, for which the language of victory is too small, and the language of coercion simply not appropriate. So far from being a reversal of the cross, this triumph is part and parcel of it and only endorses the absolute risk, the unqualified self-offering, of love's endeavour, love's expense. There is every reason why Christian triumph must on no account be 'triumphalist'; yet neither should a Christian, rightly rejecting 'triumphalism', be betrayed into singing the Easter hymns in a minor key: the evidence is strong enough for confidence. Love may be blind, but it will find out the way:

> Some think to lose him
> By having him confined;
> And some do suppose him,
> Poor thing, to be blind;
> But if ne'er so close ye wall him,
> Do the best that you may,
> Blind love, if so ye call him,
> Will find out his way.
>
> (Palgrave 1920)

Note

1. All this is now reviewed and discussed in Martin 1997.

4

RETRIBUTION OR RESTORATION?

New Life: The Prison Service Chaplaincy Review, 9 (1992),
pp. 14–18.

The thesis of this article, namely, that, *in the treatment of offenders,
not retributive but restorative justice is the only ultimately realistic
justice*, may already be familiar to many readers; but as far as I
can see, public opinion at any rate has hardly begun to be
reached by it. Yet, until this understanding of justice is
generally accepted, a vital factor will be lacking – or so it
seems to me – from the aims and motives behind any legislation
and procedures that may be designed to deal with wrongdoing.

When it is declared that terrorists must be brought to justice,
it is retributive, quantitative justice that is always meant, and
public opinion seems to regard this principle of retribution as
indispensable. It is often said that to abandon it would mean
condoning wrong and would rob the community of a voice
with which to repudiate evil.

Of course it is true that the principle of retribution is
prominent in the Hebrew Scriptures (known by Christians as
the Old Testament), and is by no means absent from the New
Testament. But the logic of Christian faith, borne out, even
without such a faith, by human experience, is, I believe,
against the principle, however zealously and often it has been
espoused by Christians as well as by many others. Moreover,
so far from condoning wrong or offering a soft option, it would
seem to be ultimately the only way to justice – yes, justice! –
on the deepest level, and the only ultimately effective reply to
wrong.

If this is true, it does not necessarily follow that legislation
and procedures designed to control wrongdoing may not still,
in the interim, have to measure sanctions by a roughly retributive scale, making the punishment more or less fit the crime, in
good Gilbertian style. What does seem to be clear is that the
deepest justice is never going to be achieved that way. Even if
quantitative, retributive justice dictates the fine or the

duration of imprisonment, retribution must not be among the ultimate motives behind legislation or the target aimed at by it, if offenders are to be successfully dealt with. Restraint, deterrence, and correction are all valid motives, but not retribution.

One does not need to be consciously religious to recognize this principle. It is evident when one reflects on the processes of the repair of human relations after damage. Retributive justice, measured by the estimated gravity of the offence, can be applied only externally and on a superficial level. This was pointed out by, for instance, the late Sir Walter Moberly (1968), and subsequently endorsed by Miss Elizabeth Moberly (1978). Retributive punition can be, they showed, no more than a symbol, or at best a kind of sacrament, of the real thing. The real thing is found only on the level of persons – the level of 'personality'. It cannot be externally applied or assessed on a scale of culpability. At its deepest and most realistic – that is, on the level of 'personality' – justice means a proper response to the demands of the situation. It is a response to what is needed for the restoration of the persons concerned to their full stature as persons in mutual relation.

It will mean, on the one hand, that the wounded and resentful feelings of the victim have to be amended. They must be respected, indeed, and not disregarded or made light of; but they do need to be changed. Did not Tom Sutherland, the hostage, say something to the effect that you diminish yourself if you go on harbouring resentment? We know, in our heart of hearts, that this is true. The first great step towards justice at the deepest level is, paradoxically, when the victim abandons quantitative justice, waives the demand for 'just' retribution, and begins to become ready to forgive – that is, to meet the damage by repair. This is the only attitude that can do justice to the diminished stature of the victim, though this is not for a moment to deny that it may well be proper for the victim to demand and receive compensation in some material form. It is the demand for penal retribution that is ruled out, if the victim is to return to the full stature of personhood.

The process of justice on the deepest level will also mean, on the other hand and similarly, that the offender, whose stature as a person has of course been diminished by his offence, must acknowledge the offence, accept responsibility, transfer his

42

concern to the victim, and so begin to rise again to his proper stature. On both sides, justice of a realistic sort will then begin to be done to the realities of the situation.

All this represents anything but a soft option or a lowering of moral standards. On both sides, the sheer pain, emotional and psychological, is likely to be acute. The process is emphatically 'penal' in a literal sense. Forgiving is costly, and so is repenting. Dr Howard Zehr (1990, p. 202), recognizes accountability in the shape of taking responsibility as a valid alternative to accountability in the shape of taking one's 'medicine'. There are no easy options in the process and no side-stepping of the moral law: justice is done, the offender is 'made to pay' far more dearly than he or she pays on the quantitative level; but there is nothing retributive about it – no 'tit for tat'. Instead, both sides are contributing, painfully and at great cost, to mutual repair and reconciliation. The process means an output of energy, directed to constructive repair, not destructive retribution.

All this – need it be said? – is highly idealistic. Everybody knows that, in practice, these lofty ideals of forgiveness and repentance and of the recovery of one's stature as a person are often simply not within sight at all. In some cases, there is no likelihood, humanly speaking, that they ever will be, though it is worthwhile to note, in parenthesis, that Dr Zehr, in the same book, writes: 'Victims are often open to non-incarcerative, reparative sentences – more frequently, in fact, than is the public' (p. 193). He quotes another writer, John Lampen, as saying that 'Restitution is at least as basic a human response as is retribution' (p. 192). All in all, however, it may well be, as has been said already, that legislation and procedures have to use a rough-and-ready framework of penalties and restrictions, to contain a situation; but the fact remains, I believe, that this cannot reach the heart of the matter on the level of damage to persons and personal relations. If this is so, then the motives behind legislation and procedures should spring from a recognition of what constitutes ultimate justice on the deepest and most realistic level. There seems to be little likelihood of advance, as long as the 'focus', to use Dr Zehr's metaphor, is on retribution. Dr Zehr's book bears witness to the difference that may be made in practice by a change of focus in one's presuppositions.

It may well be asked, however, whether this view does not mean playing fast and loose with important passages in the New Testament. The answer is that, if one believes that every word of the New Testament is equally authoritative, then obviously one must, indeed, somehow try to bring them all into a single coherent system. But what if, in fact, the Scriptures constitute a record of human response, with all its fallibility, to divine self-revelation? If that is so, then one will best perceive and receive that revelation by looking for criteria by which to differentiate between degrees of reality. The evidence from the New Testament and other relevant material for the origin, beginnings, and nature of Christian belief (evidence too elaborate to be reviewed here, but well established) seems to justify the estimate of Jesus as supremely the bearer of the divine self-revelation. Known as a historical person, yet known also transcendently after his death as the very presence of God, Jesus is the mediator – such is this estimate of an all-inclusive and decisive revelation of God. Hence the authoritative weight of the claim, in his life and person and through his death and resurrection, for the way of creative suffering and love (and the radical judgement that it constitutes) and not of retribution.

The life of Jesus and his death – the inevitable consequence of total dedication to the way of God – and his total aliveness through and beyond (not in spite of) death, all point in this direction, and exhibit the justice of God at its deepest level: 'God, in Christ, was reconciling the world to himself' (2 Cor. 5.19). No hangover of retributive systems still showing itself in the New Testament can negate this, though there are, in fact, fewer retributive sayings in it than is sometimes imagined. There are, it is true, some in the traditions of the parables of Jesus that come through the Gospels, and there is no compelling evidence that these are subsequent additions and do not belong to the original intentions of Jesus himself. But even if they do represent his mind, it is to be noted that they seldom, if ever, advocate the application of retribution. Rather they are a statement, in the black-and-white idiom of 'poster' communication, of the fact of retribution as the nemesis of wrongdoing. The nearest one comes, in the traditions of the words of Jesus, to a divine sanctioning of the application of retribution is, perhaps, in St Matthew 18.35 'So shall my heavenly Father do to you, unless you forgive...' – ironically a sanction, in terms of retribution, to instil a non-retributive attitude! The other phrase that springs to mind – 'vengeance is mine, says the Lord, I will repay' – is quoted from the Hebrew Scriptures by St Paul in Romans 12.19, precisely where he is enjoining non-retaliation. Outside the Gospels, there is a good deal in the Revelation that reflects retributive, not to say vindictive, motives. The Seer, fiercely defending Christian martyrs against their persecutors, seems sometimes to lose sight of 'Father, forgive them...', though never for a moment does he suggest that the victims should take retribution into their own hands. He writes in the same vein as the accounts of the Jewish martyrs in 2 and 4 Maccabees who threaten their torturers with divine retribution. Elsewhere in the New Testament there is retributive language in Romans 1 and 2 and in 2 Thessalonians 1, and in 2 Peter and Jude; but otherwise, extraordinarily little. Is it straining the evidence to say that what we see in the writings of the New Testament collectively is a gradual and as yet incomplete movement away from the pursuit of vindication by retaliation towards a response to the mystery of the release of repair and reconciliation and new life through Christ's creative, life-giving self-surrender? This is something that barely surfaces in the Hebrew Scriptures, though Isaiah 53 seems to reflect a wonderful insight into the mystery of martyr-suffering as a means of new life to others. With Jesus Christ this bursts into full view and gradually begins to oust retributive attitudes.

I find a great deal in Dr Zehr's book that confirms, from his practical experience in ministry to victims and offenders, what I have been led to by my study of Christian origins and theology. He draws up a series of statements in parallel columns, contrasting modern with biblical concepts of justice. One of these contrasts is between 'Rewards based on deserts, deserved' (in the modern column) and 'Justice based on need, undeserved' (in the biblical column) (p. 151). He elaborates this contrast in a later passage (p. 181), where he says that retributive justice holds that 'Crime is a violation of the state, defined by lawbreaking and guilt. Justice determines blame and administers pain in a contest between the offender and the state directed by systematic rules'; whereas, for restorative justice, 'Crime is a violation of people and relationships. It creates obligations to make things right. Justice involves the victim, the offender, and the community in a search for solutions which promote repair, reconciliation and reassurance.' 'Our system of justice', he writes (p. 152), 'is above all a system for making decisions about guilt. Consequently, it focuses on the past.' Biblical justice seeks first to solve problems, to find solutions, to make things right, looking towards the future. Again (p. 157),

> Whether the thrust of the Bible is on retribution or restoration is not a marginal issue. The question is at the heart of our understandings about the nature of God and about the nature of God's actions in history. It is not an issue which Christians can avoid.

For myself, as I have said, I believe that, although these principles are, indeed, biblical, they do, in fact, begin to take shape even if one does no more than analyse realistically the structure of any reconciliation between persons; and I believe that the process of reconciliation is not a violation of morality but is, on the deepest level, justice.

As I have repeatedly acknowledged, it may be necessary, for all I know, for legislation and procedures to deal with the past and to fix quantitative penalties, so as to contain the situation. But what I find myself affirming is that it is attention to the future and to the solving of problems that is creative and that holds out hope of building a better society; and that, therefore, it is vitally important that this should be in the forefront of the minds of legislators and planners, determining their approach to the task and their long-term aims and motives.

Here, then, is an ideal which, as a student of New Testament thought, I have long seen to be central to Christian faith, and which seems to receive impressive support from the level of practical efforts to sort out the tangled skein of human relations. Many who are associated with the planning and administration of justice have, no doubt, been actively pursuing these principles; but since they need to reach the consciousness of the public, perhaps it is not a waste of time to reiterate them.[1]

Note

1. In addition to the books mentioned in this article and relevant articles of my own, in this collection and elsewhere, mention may be made of Travis 1986.

Part Two

Christology

5

THE CHRISTOLOGY

OF ACTS

L. E. Keck and J. L. Martyn (eds), *Studies in Luke-Acts: Essays Presented in Honor of Paul Schubert.* Nashville, Abingdon, 1966, pp. 159–85.

Professor Schubert knows, far better than I, the formidable output of literature, even over the last two or three decades, relevant to the Christology of Acts and providing evidence of an increasing awareness of the complexity of the subject. In gratefully dedicating this small offering to him I am glad, therefore, that it is not the only essay in this volume [i.e. the Schubert *Festschrift*] which is responsible for Christology. The essay by Professor Schweizer (on the Davidic 'Son of God') is also relevant, not to mention the less direct light shed on the subject by others; and I am sure that errors and deficiencies both of fact and of judgement will not go wholly uncorrected and uncompensated, even within these two covers. What matters most, however, is that any true insights into the meaning of Luke or of his sources should not be left on a merely academic level, but should be made available and applied to the Church's witness at the present time. It is not my responsibility to attempt this in this essay; but it is good that this aspect, too, of the study of Luke-Acts does not go unmentioned.

Within the limits of a single essay, I have decided to confine my investigation to a series of comparative studies: first, between Acts and Luke's Gospel; second, between different parts of Acts itself; and third, between Acts and certain other New Testament documents. A great body of scholars have done this before me: the names of some of them appear in the notes. If there is anything at all that I can add, it will only be in the arrangement and presentation and, possibly, fresh assessment of some of the facts. In writing this essay without access to the others, I am well aware that any such assessment, insofar as it bears not only on Christology but also upon the methods and motives of the author of Acts, will need to be counterbalanced – perhaps to the degree of flat contradiction – by other contributors.

The Christologies of Luke's Two Volumes Compared

It is a commonplace of New Testament criticism [see, however, pp. 179ff.] that the Gospels are theological documents and, at the very least, reflect the faith of the writers and of their communities. Some would go further and say that the Gospels do not merely reflect such faith, but have been largely created by it. In its extreme form, this view would mean that the evangelist was making little or no attempt to reconstruct what Jesus may have seemed to his contemporaries: his only aim was to present Jesus as the Lord of the Christian confession – the Lord he was now acknowledged to be.

The Christology of Acts is exceptionally interesting, because it offers the only fully authentic test of this theory. Few critics doubt that the same person wrote both Luke's Gospel and the Acts of the Apostles. If the Christology of the two is one and the same, then the view just indicated is, to that extent, supported; but if there is a difference, it is practically conclusive proof that the view needs to be modified.

The fact is that there is a difference.[1] And the first step in defining the difference may as well be to clear away once and for all a misapprehension which sometimes appears in accounts of Luke's Christology. It is well-known that Luke, unlike the other Synoptists, sometimes refers to Jesus in his Gospel as ὁ κύριος. It is not always stated that until the resurrection this is, with very rare exceptions, confined (on the lips of men) to passages in which the Evangelist is himself as the narrator alluding to Jesus.[2] Except in the vocative – and κύριε as a common form of respectful address hardly holds the same possibilities as κύριος – κύριος is not, until the resurrection, applied to Jesus in Luke's Gospel by the human performers in the drama itself, except in Elizabeth's phrase, Luke 1.43, ἡ μήτηρ τοῦ κυρίου μου (see further below), possibly Zechariah's phrase, Luke 1.76, ἐνώπιον κυρίου (but only as Christianly interpreted), and Christ's own phrase, Luke 19.31 (cf. 34), ὁ κύριος αὐτοῦ χρείαν ἔχει. Angels are allowed it (Luke 2.11) but not men, with those two or, at most, three exceptions. Thus Luke is, as a rule, not anachronously (if it is anachronous) reading back into the historical situation of Jesus' ministry what seems to have been a post-resurrection title. To use it in his own capacity as a narrator is different: a Christian narrator at any period might, without incurring blame for anachronism, say, 'The Lord was not styled "Lord" while still on earth'; and that is how Luke uses the title almost exclusively up to the resurrection.[3]

But as soon as his narrative reaches the post-resurrection period, both in the Gospel and in Acts, it is immediately different. In Luke 24.34 and from the beginning of Acts onwards, the disciples themselves are represented as doing precisely what they do not do in the Gospel before the resurrection: they freely apply the term κύριος to Jesus. Among its many occurrences there are perhaps three particularly striking phenomena. The first is the strangely absolute phrase in the preaching of Peter to Cornelius (Acts 10.36): οὗτός ἐστιν πάντων κύριος. This – the more striking when it precedes the 'adoptionist' type of language in verse 38 – is capable of being equated with παντοκράτωρ; but it is more likely that πάντων is here intended to be masculine rather than neuter, and to mean that Jesus is Lord of Jews and Gentiles alike[4] (so Haenchen and Conzelmann). Comparable phrases applied to God in Jewish literature are adduced by H. J. Cadbury (1933). It is not demonstrable that such a phrase – if it has a plausible Aramaic equivalent – could not have been used by Peter himself. (See further discussion.)[5] The second phenomenon is the free interchange between κύριος meaning God, and κύριος meaning Jesus, especially in the application of Old Testament *testimonia*. It is sometimes impossible to be certain which is intended. And the third phenomenon, cohering closely with this latter, is the use of the phrase ἐπικαλεῖσθαι τὸ ὄνομα which, undoubtedly used in certain instances with reference to the name of Jesus, is irresistibly reminiscent of the Old Testament idea of invoking the name of Yahweh (cf. Acts 2.21 with 7.59, 9.14, 21, 22.16) and implies the invocation of the divine.[6]

The mainly consistent restriction of κύριος, on the lips of human observers, to the post-resurrection context is at least a hint that Luke may not have used his terms as indiscriminately as is sometimes suppposed. It certainly does not prove that he avoided anachronisms or that his reconstruction was accurate: it is open to anyone even if he or she concedes the use of sources, to assume that a phrase like οὗτός ἐστιν πάντων κύριος is Luke's own insertion; equally it could be argued that, since κύριος *need* mean no more than מרי, etc., there is nothing necessarily transcendental about it, and that it is perhaps mere chance that it practically never renders a pre-resurrection designation of Jesus.[7] However, as far as it goes, the use of κύριος in the Gospel and Acts suggests that Luke at least was deliberately making a distinction (see further, below); and that its associations in Acts are decidedly transcendental.

Are there any other features emerging from a comparative study of the Gospel and Acts which point in the same direction? The answer is 'Yes.' First, take the use of the term 'prophet' for Jesus. This indicates a subtle but consistent contrast, as between the Gospel and Acts. With O. Cullmann (1959, pp. 30ff.), and others it seems correct to draw a distinction between the identification of Jesus as merely a prophet, and his designation as *the* prophet expected in the last days – an expectation often associated with the famous words in Deut, 18.15: 'The Lord your God will raise up for you a prophet like me from among your brethren.' In the original context this meant clearly that God wished to speak to his people through the living voice of a man of God like Moses and not through the pagan techniques of divination, necromancy, and so forth. But it had come to be regarded as an eschatological promise of a second Moses or even of Moses *redivivus*; and to identify Jesus with this figure ('the coming one' of Samaritan expectation[8]) was not the same as to find in him merely a prophet – one of the prophets. If so, it is significant that it is not until Acts that Deut. 18.15 is explicitly used as a *testimonium* about Jesus. In Acts 3.22f. in a Petrine address, and in Acts 7.37 (by clear implication) in Stephen's speech, it is so applied. In the Gospel, by contrast, Jesus is spoken of as simply a prophet – and with only one exception, by those who are not yet full believers (Luke 7.16, 39 (but *v.l.* ὁ π.); 9.8, 19, 24.19, this last being no exception since it is on the lips of the two on the way to Emmaus before their disillusionment had been dispelled by the epiphany of Jesus). The only exception is in the sayings of Jesus himself in Luke 4.24, 'no prophet is recognized in his own country,' and 13.33, 'it is unthinkable for a prophet to meet his death anywhere but in Jerusalem'. These passages imply that he is styling himself a prophet; but the fact that they are in proverbial form and, in any case, on Jesus' own lips, not those of a follower, makes them scarcely exceptions.

There is, however, one further passage in Luke's Gospel to be considered in this connection. Without an express citation of Deut. 18.15, a subtle hint appears to be intended in the story of the transfiguration (in all three Synoptics). The two figures of Moses and Elijah are, no doubt, themselves significant as pointing to him who is to succeed and supersede them. But there is the further phrase (Luke 9.35 and parallels) 'listen to him,' which is exactly like the αὐτοῦ ἀκούσεσθε of Deut. 18.15 as quoted in Acts 3.22. If this is an intended hint in the transfiguration narrative, then it will mean: 'This is the Moses-prophet, and more than a prophet – one who is a Son.' But even so, it is uttered not by a man but by the divine voice.

In sum, then, Luke does maintain a subtle but precise distinction between the recognition of Jesus during his ministry as one of the prophets, and the express claim of the post-resurrection Church, together with the anticipatory hint in the divine voice at the transfiguration, that he is the fulfilment of the Deuteronomic expectation – the Moses-prophet. Whether this is historically correct or not, Luke seems to be doing it with his eyes open.

It must be added that Luke 9.8, 19 (in company with Mark 6.15, 8.28; Matt. 16.14) represents the public as speculating whether Jesus might not be Elijah. Elijah was in some traditions[9] as great an eschatological figure as the Moses-prophet, and it could be argued that, when Luke allows this speculation to have been current before the resurrection, he is giving away with the other hand what he had withheld with the hand containing the Moses-prophet. Yet, once again, there appears to be method in what he does. Like the other Evangelists, Luke seems to suggest that popular speculation was mistaken in using Elijah as a term for Jesus, and there is never a hint anywhere of Elijah as a post-resurrection title for Jesus. Thus the Moses-prophet, excluded from pre-resurrection language, is brought in explicitly in the Church's preaching; and, conversely, Elijah, speculatively offered by public rumour during the ministry, is not heard of afterwards.

Another impressive example of apparently deliberate contrast between the Gospel and Acts is furnished by the use of the term 'the Son of man' in Acts 7.56. It is a familiar fact that, while in all four Gospels the Son of Man is a phrase occurring frequently and on the lips of Jesus alone (John 12.34 is hardly an exception to this latter rule), Acts 7.56 is the solitary occurrence in the New Testament outside the Gospels and on the lips of another (unless one reckons Rev. 1.13, 14.14, which are virtually direct quotations from Dan. 7,[10] and are used in a visionary context). When compared with the Gospel uses, this occurrence differs not only in being on the lips of another, but also in two further respects: first, such Gospel references as associate the Son of Man with glory are all in the future; here, by contrast, the glory is an already realized fact: he is already at God's right hand. And secondly, in Stephen's vision, the Son of Man is not seated but standing. It is natural to see the Gospel use as referring to a future vindication of the martyr-community in its central, representative figure, Jesus; at present, the Son of Man is still on earth, destined to suffer, and destined for glory only after the suffering. This solitary post-resurrection occurrence, by contrast, shows the Son of Man already in glory and standing – perhaps as in a Jewish court of law to champion the cause of the 'defendant', Stephen, on earth.[11] The term is used to denote Christ's already achieved glory and his championship of the first martyr. It has been subtly and convincingly adapted to a distinctively post-resurrection martyr-situation.[12]

Conzelmann (1961) has familiarized us with the idea that Luke saw the era of the Church as a new phase, distinct from that of the ministry. It is entirely in keeping with this that Luke should be thus conscious of an explicit Christology characterizing this new phase in contrast to the veiledness of the ministry. And the same is borne out by the way in which the theme of the Spirit is handled. In the Gospel and in Acts 10.33, which is part of the deliberately retrospective and Gospel-like preaching by Peter to Cornelius, Jesus, while himself uniquely endowed with Spirit, does not yet bestow the Spirit on others, although in the Gospel he promises the Spirit's help and presence. In the Acts, however, he is explicitly spoken of as bestowing the Spirit (Acts 2.33) and working through the Spirit (Acts 16.7). [See now Turner 1982 and 1996[a], Ch. 11.]

Once again, the designation of Jesus as 'Saviour', although common to the Gospel and Acts, is used in a significantly different way in the two. In the Gospel it is only on superhuman lips – in the angel's announcement to the shepherds (Luke 2.11). Only two other approaches to the same sense are found within the Gospel. When Simeon, holding the child Jesus in his arms, says (Luke 2.30): 'I have seen with my own eyes the deliverance (τὸ σωτήριον) which thou hast made ready' (cf. Luke 3.6), this is God's act of deliverance, but Simeon is certainly associating it with the child he is holding. The second place is at 24.21, where the disillusioned two on their way to Emmaus say that they had hoped that Jesus was going to be the one who would rescue Israel (ὁ μέλλων λυτροῦσθαι τὸν Ἰσραήλ). An angelic anticipation, a prophetic vision, and a frustrated hope – that is all in the Gospel. But after the resurrection a far more explicit phrase occurs, in Acts 4.12: 'There is no salvation (σωτηρία) in anyone else at all, for there is no other name under heaven granted to men, by which we may receive salvation' (σωθῆναι); and again in Acts 5.31, where Peter before the Sanhedrin speaks of Jesus as exalted by God to be ἀρχηγὸς καὶ σωτήρ, so as to give remission of sins to Israel; and in Acts 13.23 where Paul at Pisidian Antioch again relates Jesus to Israel as Saviour. In Luke 2.11, Acts 5.31, and Acts 13.23, it looks like an allusion to the etymology of 'Jesus'; and the salvation is, expressly or by implication, a moral one from sin. The term is appropriate to the Jewish contexts, but especially to the insights brought by the resurrection: Jesus now assumes the function of God as *go'el* or Champion of Israel.

Yet once more it is noteworthy that the title υἱός is given to Jesus in the Gospel only by other than human voices – divine, angelic, or satanic (Luke 1.32, 35, 3.22, 4.3, 9, 41, 8.28), or in his own monologue (Luke 10.22), until the climax of the story when, at the trial before the Sanhedrin, Jesus is asked whether he is the Son of God and gives, perhaps, a noncommittal reply

(Luke 22.70). But in Acts after the resurrection Paul – though only Paul, unless the δ-text of Acts 8.37 be accepted; cf. further discussion below – explicitly affirms the title (Acts 9.20, 13.33).

One further specific piece of evidence pointing in the same direction is in Acts 18.9f., where 'the Lord' (evidently Jesus) says in a vision by night to Paul: 'Have no fear: go on with your preaching and do not be silenced, for I am with you and no one shall attempt to do you harm; and there are many in this city who are my people (λαός ἐστί μοι πολὺς ἐν τῇ πόλει ταύτῃ): Luke's Gospel shows nothing parallel to the astonishing Matt. 16.18 οἰκοδομήσω μου τὴν ἐκκλησίαν; but in Acts in contrast to Luke's Gospel, the risen Lord is represented as speaking about a λαός belonging to him.

The common factor behind the contrasts that have been described is, of course, the consciousness of the resurrection as marking a decisive vindication of Jesus. Consistently in Acts, Jesus is recognized as the one who, though crucified, has been raised,[13] – absolutely, for like the other New Testament writers Luke clearly means that the raising is abolute.[14] There is no question of temporary resuscitation to a continued mortal life: in its own peculiar idiom, the ascension[15] narrative makes that clear. Jesus is shown in Acts as raised from death, exalted to heaven, destined ultimately to return, and meanwhile represented in the Church's activities and expansion by the Holy Spirit, whose advent is the result of Christ's 'withdrawal'. More will be said about this conception of Jesus' withdrawal when the Christology of Acts is compared with that of Paul but it is enough meanwhile to recognize the resurrection as the Christological watershed dividing the Gospel from the Acts.[16]

If the contrasts just reviewed are undeniable, it is the more significant that Acts evinces an unshaken awareness that the exalted Lord is identical with Jesus, the man of Nazareth. There is no trace of discontinuity: indeed, the opening words of the prologue expressly forbid it; and the emphasis upon the Galilean and Nazarene origin of the Church is in keeping with this. The 'two men in white' at the ascension (Acts 1.11) expressly address the disciples as 'men of Galilee'; they are described at Pentecost (Acts 2.7) as 'all Galileans'; and the term Ναζωραῖος is freely used of Jesus (Acts 2.22, 3.6, 4.10, 6.14, 22.8, 26.9) and once of his followers (Acts 24.5, ἡ τῶν

Ναζωραίων αἵρεσις). Much discussion has been devoted to this obscure title.[17] Gärtner (1957) suggests its association with נצר (i.e., the holy remnant, 'preserved' by God); Schweizer (1960) offers the guess that it originally meant 'the Nazirite' – not in the strict sense, but as 'a holy man of God' – and that the topographical association was an afterthought; Cullmann[18] alludes to the possibility, suggested by Lidzbarski, that it may have attached to a pre-Christian Jewish sect of 'observants' (נצר) and then been transferred to the Christian sect. But Schaeder[19] seems to have shown that the simple, topographical meaning ('of Nazareth') is, in fact, unexceptionable; and it is easy to imagine that the common name 'Jesus' came to be distinguished by the name of his home, and that so, in turn, the epithet passed to his followers. If this is really its origin, then its frequent use for Jesus in post-resurrection settings seems to reflect an awareness of his continuity with the Jesus of history.

If a cumulative case is thus made for Luke's recognizing continuity of person but novelty of interpretation in the post-resurrection period, this is not to say that his post-resurrection Christology is the same as that of other New Testament writers, or is even consistent with itself. These are precisely the matters which will occupy the other sections of this essay. But it can be said at once that the Acts' Christology is consistently 'exalted'[20] in type. Although there are phrases which in a later context could be classed as adoptionist – Jesus is twice called ἀνήρ (2.22, 17.31; cf. Luke 24.19) – there is never any doubt that he is more than a mere prophet or rabbi of the past. Christians are commonly called 'disciples'; but their Master is always an exalted, heavenly figure. This would follow from the resurrection, even if κύριος meant no more than 'Master', and if its non-application before the resurrection were due to mere chance.

Various Christologies within Acts

The question whether there are different levels of Christology within the Acts now requires investigation. It is difficult – perhaps impossible – to come to the inquiry without presuppositions about Luke's method. Did he freely invent words for the actors in his play, handling them, indeed, with the creative insight of a dramatist? O'Neill (1961, p. 145 [but see [2]1970, p. xi]), was typical of many when he saw the exuberance of uncommon titles of Christ in Acts 3–5 as due simply to Luke's attempt to give this part of his story an archaic, scriptural ring. There are others who imagine that he made considerable use of sources, oral or written, and that, although he exercised his editorial prerogative of selecting and placing, the language is in large measure the authentic language of the period in question. On this showing, if there is a marked difference[21] between certain passages in the earlier chapters and others later in the book, it will be due not to Luke's creative imagination but to an actual difference of environment and outlook for the leading figures in the respective sections.

Nothing approaching an objective judgement will be reached without a comparative study of the phrases – though even this, of course, is at the mercy of a good deal of subjectivism.

We may start with Acts 3.19–21, for it has been claimed by Robinson[22] that in these verses a very primitive type of Christology seems to show through, like an outcrop of primeval rock in a contrasting landscape. The crucial words are (vss 19b, 20, 21a in RSV, NEB, or in the Greek, 20, 21a): 'Then the Lord may grant you a time of recovery and send you the Messiah he has already appointed (τὸν προκεχειρισμένον χριστόν), that is, Jesus. He must be received into heaven . . .' Robinson interprets this to mean that Jesus, though indeed designated Christ (*de jure*, as it were), has yet to be actually sent as Christ (*de facto*) to the world. The disciples had seen him suffer and had seen his 'private' vindication: they believe that he is God's chosen Suffering Servant. But they cannot bring themselves actually to style him Messiah until some more public vindication, which they still look for in the future. This, Robinson thinks, is an extremely primitive way of thinking about Jesus, which did not long survive, and which was soon superseded by the kind of outlook which is reflected in Acts 2, although Luke has represented that as chronologically prior to this phrase in Acts 3. Indeed in this very context, in Acts 3.18, Luke has fused with the alleged antique fragment from the earliest traditions his own summary of a much more advanced stage of thought, namely that it is the Messiah himself, startling and paradoxical though this may be, to whom suffering belongs (παθεῖν τὸν χριστόν): it is not only as the Servant, it is actually as already the Christ that he suffers.

It is probably true that παθεῖν τὸν χριστόν is Luke's own summary.[23] It (or παθητὸς ὁ χριστός) is a distinctively Lucan refrain (cf. Luke 24.46; Acts 17.3, 26.23), and the idea is rarely found explicitly stated elsewhere in the New Testament, although there are a few instances (1 Peter 2.21, 4.1, though here Χριστός is anarthrous and perhaps only a proper name; and 1 Cor. 1.23, if Χριστός is, though anarthrous, a title there). But the mere fact that παθεῖν τὸν χριστόν (or παθητὸς ὁ χριστός) is characteristically Lucan does not necessitate the conclusion that a possibly pre-Lucan phrase now fused with it must be interpreted as alien and opposite in meaning merely because pre-Lucan. And we are not compelled so to interpret this phrase as to make it mean that the suffering one is not (yet) the Christ 'in fact', but only the Christ potentially and as 'designate'. If that had been the meaning, it is difficult to see why Luke placed the phrase side by side with παθεῖν τὸν χριστόν which, on this showing, is contradictory to it. Why did he not rather alter it or even reject it outright,[24] or, alternatively, retain it in its isolation as a specimen of primitive thought, without confusing the issue by juxtaposing his own summary of a later viewpoint? The 'outcrop' theory, in other words, suggests an unlikely coupling of a reverence for ancient tradition with an arbitrary reversal of its meaning. It is simpler, surely, to interpret the crucial words to mean that Jesus is already recognized as the previously predestined Christ (the term προκεχειρισμένος, so interpreted, is in line with Luke's penchant for predestination), who at the end is to be sent back again into the world.

Admittedly, the 'back again' has to be supplied from the context, and the phrase is a slightly peculiar one, as is the notoriously ambiguous ending of the sentence in verse 21 ('the time of universal restoration ... of which God spoke by his holy prophets'). But the whole might not unreasonably be paraphrased as follows:

Therefore repent and turn back (to God), so that your sins may be obliterated, and so that a period of recovery (i.e., a new age of godliness) may come from the presence of the Lord (God), and so that he may send (back) the one who was long ago designated to be your Messiah, namely, Jesus. He must be received in heaven (i.e., must remain removed from mortal sight) until the time, spoken of by God through his holy prophets ever since the earliest days, when everything is to be restored to its proper position (i.e. when there is going to be a general reduction of the world's dislocation and chaos).

This makes the passage similar, in its eschatology, to Acts 1.11, although that is devoid of the problematic titles for Jesus.

In this same context verse 26 is difficult, on any showing, to harmonize with verse 20; for verse 20 speaks of God's sending of Christ Jesus as a future boon, whereas in verse 26 God's Servant (παῖς) has already been 'sent with a blessing'. If this latter referred to the ministry of Jesus (and the aorist, ἀπέστειλεν, is easier to translate by 'sent' than by 'has sent'), it would fit Robinson's theory well. But in spite of everything (aorist included), it is difficult to take ἀναστήσας ... τὸν παῖδα αὐτοῦ ('having raised up his Servant') as an allusion, not to the resurrection but the 'raising up' (or 'letting appear') of a figure upon the stage of history. The verb is so used, of course, in the original context of Deut. 18.15; but as quoted in a Christian context in Acts 3.22 and 7.37, this becomes almost inevitably an allusion to resurrection.[25]

On the whole, then, it seems that the case for finding two decidedly different Christologies side by side in chapters 2 and 3 (not to mention in 3.18 and 20) is far from established. The matter is different with the twofold use of παῖς in Acts 3 and 4. Here, I believe, there are two recognizably distinct conceptions of Jesus. But even so they are not mutually incompatible nor incompatible with Christologies in other parts of the book. Cullmann (1953, pp. 67–88, 1959, p. 73) among others has stressed the remarkable fact that παῖς is confined, in Acts, to these two chapters; what is less often discussed is whether its significance is the same in both chapters. I have elsewhere[26] suggested that, whereas in 3.13 (and perhaps verse 26) παῖς is an allusion (as most commentators agree) to the Suffering Servant of Isa. 53, in 4.27 and 30, by contrast, it is rather a parallel to the royal Davidic Servant in Jewish liturgy. In Acts 3.13, ἐδόξασεν looks like an echo of Isa. 52.13, and the context, which is essentially that of Christian apologetic and explanation, suits such a reference; but in 4.25, παῖς is expressly used of David, so that it is a natural conclusion that, when it is used of Jesus in verse 27, it is intended in the same way. This would present a phenomenon very much like that of *Didache* 9, where the Jewish liturgical reference to David as the Servant of God is parallel in just the same way to its distinctively Christian adaptation in terms of Jesus as the Servant of God. This would mean that there is a clear distinction between the uses of παῖς in chapters 3 and 4, respectively. In Acts 3, the intention is to explain how it is that glorious and daring claims are now being made for a recently crucified criminal; and the method is to identify him with the Suffering Servant who was indeed, according to Isa. 53, treated like a criminal, and whose vindication also has the authority of Scripture. In Acts 4, by contrast, the context is not explanatory and 'apologetic' but exultantly adorative and liturgical; and ὁ ἅγιος παῖς σου 'Ιησοῦς (verse 27) is placed in a position parallel to that of Δαυὶδ παῖς σου (verse 25) in Jewish liturgy.[27]

Guesses about what a writer might or might not have done are always precarious; but one cannot help thinking that, if Luke had been composing freely as a dramatist, he might have used this παῖς-language again quite suitably in Pauline speeches. If he only used it as dramatically appropriate to a primitive stage of the Church's development (although evidence for its 'primitiveness' seems, actually, not to be forthcoming), would not 'early Paul' have been as plausible a setting as 'early Peter'? But in fact this use of παῖς does not recur in Acts; and the only other use of Isa. 53 in Acts – though here without παῖς – is in the story of Philip and the Ethiopian (8.32ff.).[28] In Luke's Gospel there is the one quotation (Luke 22.37) from Isa. 53.12. It is a standing problem why Paul in his epistles does not make more of the Servant-theme. But the fact is that he makes only slight and allusive use, and that in the whole New Testament the theme is remarkably scarce.[29] If it is right to question whether even the λύτρον-saying (Mark 10.45, Matt. 20.28) is Isaianic,[30] the Gospels contain strikingly little evidence for it; and the most notable exception, beyond the Acts passages, is 1 Peter 2.22ff.

Thus in sum there is no clear evidence either that the Servant-terminology was exclusively primitive, or that Luke was inventing its application: it would appear, more likely, to belong by idiosyncratic use (perhaps Petrine) or by liturgical appropriateness on the lips on which it is, in fact, placed. The likelihood is that in Christian liturgical contexts, especially when under the influence of Jewish *berakoth*, 'thy Servant Jesus' was a common usage, perhaps for a considerable period.

The examination, first of the passage Acts 3.19–21, and then of the use of παῖς in Acts 3 and 4, has led to the conclusion that in the former case we are not compelled to detect a discrepancy in sense between traditional and Lucan Christologies, and that in the latter it is not impossible that we may be witnessing the faithful representation of two different usages in two different settings – usages which, again, are Christologically not incompatible with one another or with other usages.

A third example of the same phenomenon – variation, though not discrepancy – may be found in the doctrines of salvation attached in Acts to the work of God in Jesus Christ. There is in Acts almost as complete an absence of any explicitly redemptive interpretation of the death of Christ as in Luke's Gospel. The Gospel does not even include the λύτρον-saying of Mark and Matthew; the words of institution (and then only if the longer text, 22.19–20, be accepted) are the only exception. The same is maintained in the Acts with the one exception of Acts 20.28: 'the church of God (*v.l.* of the Lord), which he purchased διὰ τοῦ αἵματος τοῦ ἰδίου'. Whether one reads 'God' or 'the Lord', and whether one renders the ambiguous words as 'his own blood' or 'the blood of his Own', in any case the phrase contains an allusion to the death of Christ as redemptive blood by which a 'purchase' is achieved. But in Acts this is the solitary exception. Otherwise the death of Christ is represented simply as turned into triumph or vindication by the resurrection. 'Salvation' is associated with Christ clearly enough; but not explicitly salvation by his redemptive death. Is it significant, then, that the one exception should be on the lips of Paul and in an address to an already Christian community? This is Paul, not some other speaker; and he is not evangelizing but recalling an already evangelized community to its deepest insights. In other words, the situation, like the theology, is precisely that of a Pauline epistle, not of preliminary evangelism.

It is tempting to add at this point the familiar observation that the distinctive features of Stephen's speech in Acts 7 show affinities with the Epistle to the Hebrews and can be regarded as a distinguishable strain within the Acts, in character with the Hellenistic Judaism which is associated with Stephen. But, although this is probably true, it is not the Christology of Stephen's speech, strictly speaking, that is part of its distinctiveness. The allusion to the Moses-prophet (Acts 7.37) and the title 'the just one' (Acts 7.52) are not peculiar to this chapter. The former has already been discussed; the latter will be considered shortly.

But the two themes that have been isolated as distinctive – the Servant, and the redemptive death – do mark their respective contexts; they appear to be in character and, though distinctive, are not mutually discrepant.

Before leaving this section of the inquiry, it will be well to add a further comment (see p. 53 above) on the striking phrase in 10.36, οὗτός ἐστιν πάντων κύριος. Striking in itself for its absoluteness and universality[31] the phrase is the more arresting by reason of its juxtaposition with the 'adoptionist' language of verse 38 (ἔχρισεν αὐτὸν ὁ θεὸς πνεύματι ἁγίῳ καὶ δυνάμει ... ὁ θεὸς ἦν μετ' αὐτοῦ). Is it necessary to argue that here, too, as in the view of 3.18ff. discussed above, two discrepant Christologies are incongruously united – a comparatively late and well-developed, perhaps Hellenistic, affirmation of Christ as world-ruler, and a primitive, perhaps Palestinian, conception of him as a man whom God had exalted to messianic status? I think it is not necessary. Given the resurrection, the two are logically compatible at one and the same time. Indeed, in effect they are together similar to the climax of Peter's Pentecost address in Acts 2.36: καὶ κύριον αὐτὸν καὶ χριστὸν ἐποίησεν ὁ θεός, τοῦτον τὸν Ἰησοῦν ὃν ὑμεῖς ἐσταυρώσατε. The real question is whether this kind of collocation is linguistically and psychologically conceivable in the situation depicted by Luke. What language would Peter have been speaking – Aramaic, Hebrew, Greek, or Latin? Would his language and his world of thought have compassed such terms? If Peter was speaking Aramaic (and using an interpreter) would some such phrase as is used here by the Peshitta *hanā māryā d^ekāl*) be conceivable? If he could speak Greek or Latin, would he be likely to use the words in the text or their Latin equivalent? Epictetus (4.1.12) uses the phrase ὁ πάντων κύριος Καῖσαρ. Is it impossible that a phrase used of the emperor by a Hellenistic writer in about AD 110 should be applied (*mutatis mutandis*) by a Jew in about AD 30? It is extremely difficult to find any decisive evidence. One can only reiterate that the logic of the phrase is no more difficult than that of Acts 2.36, which in itself does not sound implausible for its ostensible setting.

To revert for a moment to Luke 1.43, where Elizabeth uses the phrase ἡ μήτηρ τοῦ κυρίου μου, it would be useful to know whether, in the type of Aramaic used by Elizabeth, '*my* Lord' would have had a distinctly different significance from '*the* Lord'. One can imagine that the former might have been a more natural, and therefore less significant, honorific than the latter, which might have been more like a title of divine exaltation (מרא?).

Any decision whether Luke's words represent primitive historical sources or spring simply from his own, perhaps Hellenistic, background must take such questions into account; but the answers to them are hard to come by.

In sum, although it cannot be proved, so far as the evidence does go Luke may be following reliable sources in the passages here examined.

The Christology of Acts Compared with That of Other New Testament Writings

It is sometimes remarked (e.g. Dibelius 1956, p. 165) that what purport to be Pauline speeches or sermons in the Acts bear little resemblance to the Pauline epistles and a great deal more resemblance to the ostensibly Petrine speeches in Acts; or, in other words, that both Pauline and Petrine speeches are equally Luke's own invention. Such a statement exaggerates the uniformity within Acts, as the previous section of this essay may help to show. It also neglects certain factors essential to any significant comparison with the Pauline epistles. Not that this in itself shows that Luke did not extemporize but adhered to sources;[32] it only means that the facts are more complicated and require more sensitive formulation.[33] In particular, it needs to be remembered that it is *a priori* likely that there should be differences between a speaker's initial presentation of the gospel to a non-Christian audience and the same speaker's address to those who have already become Christians; and that, with rare exceptions, the Acts speeches belong to the former while the Pauline epistles belong to the latter class. The moment one examines the rare exceptions on either side, a striking *rapprochement* occurs. Acts 20.18ff. represents Paul speaking to Christians; and it is precisely here, as we have already seen, that the solitary 'Pauline' redemptive phrase occurs (Acts 20.28). Conversely, there are a few passages in the epistles where the writer explicitly recalls, retrospectively, the terms of his initial evangelism: 1 Thess. 1.10; Rom. 1.3–4 (by implication), and – most famous of all – 1 Cor. 15.1ff.; and it is precisely here that we approximate to the bare κήρυγμα of the Acts – save only that in 1 Cor. 15.3 there is admittedly the redemptive phrase Χριστὸς ἀπέθανεν ὑπὲρ τῶν ἁμαρτιῶν ἡμῶν which we have seen to be lacking from the initial κήρυγμα in Acts. As for the alleged uniformity of the speeches in Acts, we are not to forget that it is in Petrine contexts only that παῖς (Acts 3, 4) and the scripture of the rejected stone (Acts 4.11) are applied to Jesus (cf. 1 Peter 2.7 and for the Servant theme 1 Peter 2.22ff.);[34] that it is only by Philip the Evangelist that Isa. 53 is again applied to Jesus (Acts 8.32ff.); and that, in the Pauline speeches alone occur not only the redemptive language just referred to, but one or two other 'Paulinisms'.

At the end of Paul's address at Pisidian Antioch in Acts 13.38f. there is the celebrated passage:

> You must understand, my brothers, that it is through him that forgiveness of sins is now being proclaimed to you. It is through him that everyone who has faith is acquitted of everything for which there was no acquittal under the Law of Moses.

This, though not the only possible interpretation of the words,[35] seems the most natural and, if it is correct, represents a rough summary of the Pauline doctrine of faith.[36] So, too, do the words from the dialogue on the Damascus Road in the form which it takes in the hearing before Agrippa, Acts 26.18:

> I send you to open their eyes and turn them from darkness to light, from the dominion of Satan to God, so that, by trust in me, they may obtain forgiveness of sins, and a place with those whom God has made his own.

This is reminiscent, in particular, of Col. 1.12f.

Once again, the use of υἱός as a title for Jesus (cf. discussion above) presents certain affinities with the usage of the Pauline epistles. Excluding the Ethiopian's baptismal confession, which occurs only in the δ-text of Acts 8.37, the title υἱός is applied in Acts twice, and both in Pauline contexts: Acts 9.20, 'Soon he was proclaiming Jesus publicly in the synogogues: "This", he said, "is the Son of God" '; and 13.33, where at Pisidian Antioch Paul quotes from Psalm 2.7, 'You are my son; this day have I begotten you.'[37] Now it is clear enough that in Christian – if not in pre-Christian – circles the use of Psalm 2 is essentially messianic; indeed, a good case may be made for recognizing that it was associated even in certain pre-Christian circles with the specifically messianic passage in 2 Sam. 7.12–14 (especially through the key-words σπέρμα, υἱός, ἀνάστασις).[38] Acts seems, thus, to represent Paul as using a recognized argument for the messiahship of Jesus. By contrast, there is no doubt that the most interesting and most distinctively Pauline use of υἱός, in Rom. 8 and Gal. 4, goes much deeper than mere messianism. Nevertheless, the messianic use is not in the least incompatible with the profounder use, and Psalm 2.7 may well have been in Paul's mind in Rom. 1.4, if not elsewhere.[39] It looks, then, as though Luke may have represented Paul quite correctly, although on one of the shallower of Paul's own levels of thinking. There is another New Testament writing which makes use of the *testimonium* from Psalm 2.7, namely, Hebrews (1.5, 5.5); and Hebrews also shares with Paul and John something, at least, of the deeper connotations of υἱός, while it shares with Acts the less profound, more 'external' title ἀρχηγός (Acts 3.15, 5.31; Heb. 2.10, 12.2), which seems to mean something like 'pioneer'. The two levels are perfectly compatible within a single writer's thought.

The use of the term χριστός in the allegedly Pauline scenes in Acts seems at first sight, in contrast to the phenomena just examined, to strike a recognizably un-Pauline note. It is a familiar fact that Χριστός in the Pauline epistles is, broadly speaking, nearer to a proper name than to a title, however much qualification and subtle nuances might be demanded for a more precise definition.[40] If one did attempt to qualify, perhaps one might say that in the Pauline epistles Jesus is characterized as one who was anointed, rather than identified as the long-expected Anointed One: that is, it is not so much that the datum is 'the Christ' (unidentified) and that Jesus is then identified as that Christ; rather, the theme is simply 'Jesus, called Christ'. In the Acts, however, there are two verses, both associated with Paul, where the whole point is that Jesus is identified as the Christ: Acts 17.3; (cf. 18.28, of Apollos' preaching); and 26.23 (this presents the form which we have already recognized as a peculiarly Lucan formula – εἰ παθητὸς ὁ χριστός). But the facts are not altogether simple; for there are three, possibly four, other ostensibly Pauline contexts where Χριστός, as in the Pauline epistles, is used more as a proper name: 16.18, 20.21, v.l.; 24.24, 28.31. On examination, however, the last two of these could be called editorial, for Luke is describing Paul's ministry rather than purporting to report his very words: and if 20.21 is a false or, at best, a doubtful reading, this leaves only 16.18, where Paul is using the name of Jesus in exorcism. The other instances of the same sort of use (nearly as a proper name) are all Petrine (Acts 2.38, 3.6, 4.10, 9.34, 10.48, 11.17) except for 15.26, which is in the letter from the Jerusalem council.

This looks at first as though Luke himself used Χριστός as (roughly speaking) a proper name and attributed a similar use also to Peter and the apostolic council, but, with only one exception, he gave Paul the strictly messianic use, exactly reversing the evidence of the epistles. In fact, however, the distinction attaches not to the person speaking but to the occasion. The messianic use is invariably in apologetic contexts (which happen to be Pauline), while the other use is liturgical or quasi-liturgical: it is, as one might put it, a 'formula' use.[41] When once this is recognized, one may go on to recognize that, equally in the Pauline epistles, there is

ample evidence that Paul did presuppose a messianic identification for Jesus, e.g. in Rom. 1.3 and 9.5. In other words, once
again an apparent discrepancy between Acts and the epistles
seems rather to represent the difference between two different
situations which, however, could both be genuinely apostolic.
In the one situation the apostle is arguing to establish his
primary case for the Christian position. In the other he is
building on these foundations for the benefit of those who had
already accepted them.

Closely related to the theme of messianism is the question of
rivalry with the emperor. This is of particular interest in any
study of the Christology of Acts in comparison with that of
other parts of the New Testament. It is plausible to suggest
that those parts of the New Testament where a comparatively
developed imperial vocabulary is applied to Christ, namely,
the Pastoral epistles and the Revelation, reflect actual conflict
between the imperial cult and Christianity; and that, whereas
before the actual clash there was a hesitancy on the part of
Christians to borrow the pagan terms of adulation, once
war had been declared it was better policy boldly to raid the
enemy armouries and use their ammunition.[42] But if so, it
needs to be recognized that at least one passage in Luke and
one in Acts explicitly allude to the rivalry.[43] In Luke 23.2 the
charge laid by the Jews against Jesus before Pilate is the
charge of treason – that Jesus had been perverting the people
from loyalty to Caesar and declaring himself 'an anointed
king'; and in Acts 17.6f. the Jews who are inciting the Thessalo-
nian population against Paul and his friends describe them as
those who have upset the whole world and who violate
Caesar's decrees, declaring that there is another emperor
(βασιλεύς), namely, Jesus. Yet on further reflection one cannot
help noticing that in both cases these are represented as
charges levelled against the Christians by Jewish opponents
and obviously understood by the narrator himself to be false.
Nowhere in the Acts are Christian evangelists themselves
represented as using of Jesus such markedly imperial language
as occurs in the Pastoral letters where 'epiphany' and 'Saviour'
are used together, and where Christ is even styled (if this is the
correct exegesis) 'our great God and Saviour' (Titus 2.13).
Thus once again Luke seems to know what he is doing.

Whether he is doing it as a good dramatist realistically recon-
structing his imagined situation, or as a cool historian using
traditions faithfully, is another matter. He does, it is true, once
represent an official as using κύριος of the emperor (Acts
25.26). Whether this is an anachronism or not[44] is not relevant
for the present purpose; but the use of κύριος as applied to
Jesus (see discussion above) is not such as necessarily to imply
any intended parallelism or rivalry any more than the use of
χριστός is; indeed, it is a commonplace of criticism that Luke
is deliberately trying to present Christianity as a religion
which the empire has no need to regard as subversive or
dangerous to its peace. Is this why Acts never uses βασιλεύς for
Jesus in the apostolic preaching? (In Acts 17.7 it is, as we have
just seen, part of a charge brought by opponents of Christianity.) Χριστός is just as royal but possibly not so readily intelligible. 'Saviour' is applied to Jesus in two passages in Acts, 5.31
and 13.23, but, as has already been remarked, the contexts, as
in Luke 2.11 also, are appropriate to an essentially Jewish,
messianic connotation and are perhaps in this respect different
from those of the Pastoral epistles and, for that matter from
2 Peter 1.1, 11, 2.20, 3.18 where an emperor cult context seems
more fitting. It is a familiar fact that the word is very seldom
applied to Jesus in the recognized Pauline letters, Phil. 3.20
being the chief exception. That πολίτευμα also occurs in the
same context may be significant.[45]

However, the use of λαός must still be mentioned. Although
not directly Christological, Acts 18.10 has already been
pointed out as indirect evidence of a distinctively post-
resurrection Christology. We must now note that this use of
λαός for a Christian Community is not exactly paralleled in
the epistles of Paul, where it occurs only in Old Testament
quotations and then more often of Israel than of the Church
(see Rom. 9.25, 26, 11.1–2, 15.10, 2 Cor. 6.16). The other occurrence in Acts, apart from the direct Old Testament quotations
in Stephen's speech (7.34), is on the lips of James (15.14 with
which cf. 1 Peter 2.9–10; Titus 2.14). Does this indicate that
Luke, though faithful to an early line of Christian apologetic,
has this time made a mistake in attributing it to a specifically
Pauline vision?

So much for possible test cases for Luke's historical precision.

When we turn to the use of ὁ δίκαιος in Acts and compare it with the use elsewhere in the New Testament, the results are inconclusive. It is an extremely elusive term. Just as it has been suggested that παῖς is used in Acts 3 with reference to the Suffering Servant but in Acts 4 as a parallel to God's Servant David, so it may be that ὁ δίκαιος is capable of containing an allusion both to the Suffering Servant and to royalty (see Descamps 1950, pp. 57ff.). Isa. 53.11 describes the innocent sufferer as 'my righteous Servant'; and the innocent one who suffers undeservedly is the idea uppermost in the Petrine passage, Acts 3.14, '(you) repudiated the one who was holy and righteous when Pilate had decided to release him.' (Cf. the Lucan version of the centurion's words at the cross, Luke 23.47, 'Beyond all doubt ... this man was innocent.') But to the other two occurrences something, at least, of messianic royalty may be intended to attach. The first is Acts 7.52 (Stephen's speech): 'They killed those who foretold the coming of the Righteous One.' Here, no doubt, the murderous attack suggests innocent suffering; but ὁ δίκαιος is explicitly connected with ἔλευσις, 'coming', which lends a strong colour of messianism to the term.[46] In the second passage, Acts 22.14, Ananias, the devout Jewish Christian (verse 12) of Damascus, is represented as saying that God had predestined Paul to know his will and 'to see the Righteous One and to hear his very voice'. This most readily suggests a messianic vision, and it has been pointed out further that the royal associations of ὁ δίκαιος are illustrated by such passages as Zech. 9.9; 1 Enoch 38.2; Ps. Sol. 17.32.[47]

If one asks how far the application of the term to Jesus elsewhere in the New Testament helps to determine the meaning, the answer is obscure. In 1 Peter 3.18 the stress is clearly on the innocence of the sufferer, and the allusion is probably to Isa. 53. But in 1 John the question is harder to decide. In 1 John 1.9, 'he is just, and may be trusted to forgive our sins', the allusion to Isa. 53 is perhaps uppermost, but this is certainly not beyond question; the same is true of 1 John 2.1, 'one to plead our cause with the Father, Jesus Christ, and he is just'. But the only other instance in 1 John, namely 3.7, is evidently an allusion to Jesus as being just in the sense of 'moral', 'upright', and therefore as making moral demands on

Christians.[48] Perhaps we may tentatively conclude for the Acts uses that in the speech of Peter, as in 1 Peter 3.18, the allusion is to innocent suffering, while Ananias' phrase may be primarily messianic and Stephen's may combine the messianic with the suffering in a manner very suitable in a martyr's defence.

Finally we come to certain aspects of the Acts' Christology which seem definitely to mark it off from that of the more theological of the epistles. There appears to be no doctrine of the pre-existence of Christ in Acts, either in the speeches or in the narrator's comments, unless conceivably in 2.25. It is at this point in Peter's Pentecost speech that Ps. 16.8ff. is introduced. In the Hebrew this begins: שִׁוִּיתִי יְהוָה לְנֶגְדִּי תָמִיד but Acts, following the LXX, reads: προορώμην τὸν κύριον ἐνώπιόν μου διὰ παντός. The προορώμην, which one would expect to mean 'I foresaw' or 'I had or was having a preview of', causes commentators difficulty. Either this phrase must be taken as part of the verses which follow and which in the context of Acts are clearly intended to be spoken, though *by* David, yet *in the person of* David's successor, the Messiah. In that case the προ- can hardly be pressed, and one must imagine the Messiah, speaking by anticipation through the prophetic lips of David, to be saying that he was simply *seeing* God continually before him – an expression of trust and confidence. But this surely does less than justice to the προ-[49] and, still more, ignores the patent reference to *pre*vision in the προϊδών of the interpretation in verse 31. Or else, verse 8 might be given to David himself and προορώμην correctly translated 'I foresaw' or 'I had, or was having, a preview of', in which case the difficulty is that the speaker will have to be deemed to change suddenly in the subsequent verses, because the 'not being left in, or to, Hades' and the 'not seeing corruption' are explicitly applied in the interpretation to Christ (verse 31). Further, the προϊδών of verse 31 is related to the 'seeing' of the resurrection of Jesus, not of his person. This is not the place for a full-length investigation into the passage.[50] The only point relevant to the present discussion is that, if one chooses to accept the second method despite the difficulty attending it, one might have a hint of a doctrine of pre-existence for Christ. For it would then be possible to translate προορώμην not 'I foresaw *that* the

Lord', but, a more natural translation grammatically, 'I had a preview of the Lord', and 'the Lord', in that case, would mean the Lord Christ.

Unless one accepts such an interpretation – and it is precarious, to say the least – there is no doctrine of Christ's pre-existence in Acts, though there is ample stress on foreknowledge and God's predetermined plan (see, e.g., 4.28, 9.15, 10.42, 13.27, 48, 16.14, 17.31). Neither is such a doctrine entertained in the Gospel: the Lucan allusions to the virgin birth certainly do not imply it. Thus a decided contrast is presented at this point between Luke-Acts and the Pauline and Johannine writings.

Even more clearly Acts is marked off from the Pauline writings, at any rate, by its conception of Jesus as now no longer 'on earth' but 'in heaven'. The narrative of the ascension in Acts 1.9–11 is consistently presupposed throughout the story. In Acts 2.33 the exalted Jesus is described as having poured out the Spirit. In Acts 3.21 heaven must receive him until the proper time comes. When he appears to Paul on the Damascus Road, it is a special visitation from heaven (9.3, 22.6, 26.13). On the only other occasions when he 'appears' at all it is only in a vision (9.10, 22.17–18, 23.11 – by implication); otherwise it is by the Spirit (or by his Spirit) or by an angel that action is taken on earth (8.26, 29, 39, 11.28, 12.7, 13.4, 15.28, 16.6, 7, 20.23, 21.11, 27.23). More consistently than in any other New Testament writing, Acts presents Jesus as exalted and, as it were, temporarily 'absent', but 'represented' on earth in the meantime by the Spirit (except that, undeniably, in the vision of Acts 18.10 Jesus says ἐγώ εἰμι μετὰ σοῦ). That this is Luke's own attitude seems to follow from the fact that his narrative and his handling of whatever sources he may be using convey it, as well as explicit 'preaching' on the lips of the apostles.

A similar 'absentee Christology' does occur, indeed, in 1 Thess. 1.10, where the Christians are to await God's Son from heaven. But for the most part the Pauline epistles reverse this impression of temporary absence by the sense of intimate relation between Christians and Christ which pervades them. For Paul, Christ is indeed 'in heaven' in the sense that he is no longer a limited individual 'on earth'; but Christians are limbs of his body and are incorporated in him in such a way that all sense of remoteness is completely obliterated.[51]

Here, then, it would seem is a theological standpoint which for the reasons stated must be ascribed to Luke himself and marks a difference between his outlook and Paul's. And when one begins to ponder on its implications, it becomes clear that the conception of Jesus in the Acts is mainly an individualistic one. Despite his royal exaltation and his undoubtedly divine status, it is still as an exalted and divine individual that Jesus is viewed. But in Paul's robustly 'inclusive' Christology the gap between the risen Lord and the believer is transcended and no 'substitute' or *locum tenens* is needed. The Spirit is for Paul certainly the 'mode' in which Christ is among his people: the Spirit is as vital in Paul's conception of daily living on earth as in the conception of Acts; but for Paul the Spirit is not the representative and substitute of an absent Christ but the mode of his very presence. And in the Gospel and Epistles of John the connection between Jesus and the Spirit, though differently expressed, is equally close.[52]

The 'individualistic' Christology which is here contrasted with Paul's corporate conception has been, for the reasons stated, attributed to Luke himself. But this is not to say that he shares it with no other writer in the New Testament. Insofar as it is expressed not by Luke's narrative and handling of his material but by actual words attributed to early Christian preachers, it is represented by the phrase (Acts 3.15) ὁ ἀρχηγὸς τῆς ζωῆς, which seems to imply the kind of hero-Christology or leader-Christology which is to be found in parts of Hebrews (e.g., the ἀρχηγός passages in that epistle, Heb. 2.10, 12.2); and by the other Petrine statements, especially in Acts 2.33 and 3.21, which are not unlike another Petrine document, 1 Peter 1.8. It is therefore conceivably significant, that, whereas such expressions are not unrepresented in the non-Pauline epistles, the relevant Pauline statements in Acts represent, as a matter of fact, the nearest approach within Acts to the contrasting, corporate conception of Christ found in the Pauline epistles. The dialogue on the Damascus Road, in all its three versions, does identify the risen Jesus with the Christian Church ('Why do you persecute me? ... I am Jesus, whom you are persecuting' – see 9.4–5, 22.8, 26.15). Thus in the only Pauline passage that bears any relation to the matter, there is, in fact, a trace of 'corporeity'.

There is one other passage deserving careful examination in this connection, namely Acts 4.2, where ἐν is used in a mysterious way. In Acts 4.2, the Sadducees and others are described as pained because the apostles were teaching and proclaiming ἐν τῷ Ἰησοῦ τὴν ἀνάστασιν τὴν ἐκ νεκρῶν. Is this a hint of an incorporative doctrine? On the whole, the answer is that it is less likely to mean 'resurrection for those who are incorporate in Jesus' (the simple proper name, 'Jesus', is in any case unlikely after an 'incorporative' ἐν) than 'resurrection in the case (or in the instance) of Jesus'. And yet, one must admit that the ponderous phrase, ἡ ἀνάστασις ἡ ἐκ νεκρῶν, sounds uncommonly as though it were meant to mean 'the (general) resurrection' (cf. Acts 24.15). We are left in uncertainty; and if – perhaps in spite of himself – Luke has after all here retained a hint of a more corporate understanding of Christ, then it is noteworthy that this time it is placed on the lips of Peter and his colleagues.

It may be appropriate to remark in this connection that there is in any case a further fact to be reckoned with, when one is trying to estimate how far an individualistic conception was normal and how far Paul's corporate sense was exceptional, in the early Church. Although Luke's outlook and perhaps that of most of his sources is in the sense indicated 'individualistic', the fact of baptism in the name or into the name of Jesus implies more with regard to the corporate character of Christ than Luke or the majority of early Christians may themselves have realized or made fully articulate. Paul may have been the only New Testament writer – with the possible exception of John – to make it fully articulate; but Christian practice spoke louder than words.

All in all, the evidence here displayed – unless it has been grossly misinterpreted – seems to show that the Christology of Acts is not uniform, whatever may be said to the contrary. Where Luke's own mentality can be discerned, it is different in certain respects from Paul's or that of the Johannine writings and is nearer, one may guess, to the 'average' Christian mentality than to that of these giants (see Moody 1920). But it is flying in the teeth of the evidence to claim that Luke has uniformly imposed this mentality of his; on the contrary, the number of seemingly undesigned coincidences and subtle nuances that have emerged suggest strongly that Luke either dramatized, thoughtfully and with considerable versatility, in an attempt to impersonate various outlooks,[53] or else used sources. If he did this, he no doubt adapted and arranged them with a free hand, but nevertheless retained their essential character.

Notes

1. *Pace* (e.g.) Conzelmann's assertion of Luke's promiscuous use of titles, 1961, pp. 171 n. 1; 172; cf. 1963, p. 8.
2. This seems to be overlooked, e.g., in Conzelmann's phrase, 'the use of the title *kyrios* even in Jesus' lifetime', 1961, p. 174 n. 3.
3. The same holds good (almost) for John also; 'almost' because in John 20.2, 13 Mary Magdalene is represented as using 'Lord' before she knows that he is risen; and when she does recognize him she uses ‘Ραββουνεί. However, note that John 13.13 and 20.2, 13 throw doubt on the extent to which the Johannine use of κύριος can be pressed as an index of the recognition of 'Lordship' in a Christological sense.
4. Cf. 1 Cor. 1.2.
5. Incidentally, it is not to be overlooked that in a quite secular context it need carry no transcendental meaning whatever: in Gal. 4.1, κύριος πάντων only means 'master of the whole estate', referring simply to the ownership of property.
6. Cf. the same use in Rom. 10.9 with 13; 1 Cor. 1.2.
7. What Aramaic title are we, in fact, to think that Peter might have used, in the kind of context indicated by Acts 2.36? Or is the Hebrew אדן a possibility? See Hahn 1963, p. 114 against this idea. See also *TDNT*, III, pp. 1086–87.
8. See, e.g., Cullmann 1959, p. 19, and literature there cited.
9. See Cullmann 1959, pp. 17ff.
10. Cf. Justin, *Dial.* 76.
11. See Moule 1952, p. 47, 1967, pp. 90f.; Higgins 1964, pp. 143ff.
12. The Revelation use is also in a martyr-context, in the sense that the whole apocalypse is a martyr book; but the question of 'realization' is complicated by the proleptic character of the whole. In another martyr-context and on the lips of another than Jesus, outside the NT, 'the Son of Man' occurs in Hegesippus' account of the martyrdom of James the Just (Euseb., *HE* 2.23).

But here there is the more normal reference to the sitting posture and to a future manifestation: 'Why do you ask me concerning Jesus the Son of Man? He is both seated in heaven on the right hand of Power, and he will come again on the clouds of heaven.' Owen 1954 suggests that in Acts 7.56 Jesus is standing on the verge of returning to earth after his exaltation; and another way of connecting the vision with the return has now been put forward by Barrett 1964: he suggests that Stephen's vision may represent 'a private and personal *parousia* of the Son of man' for the individual as he dies.

13. *Sic*, not 'who rose'. See Braun 1952. But I doubt whether the distinction is, in fact, very important, despite the conclusion that the use of the verb in question carries a subordinationist implication. I am not denying a subordinationist strain in Luke-Acts (as judged – anachronously? – by later Christological controversies); but I question how far this particular set of verbs indicates it.

14. See Robinson 1962[a].

15. We ought rather to say 'exaltation'; there is nothing about going up; it is rather being lifted up.

16. Incidentally, it is surprising what a long career is still being enjoyed by the old suggestion that Acts 17.18 is meant to imply that the Athenians misunderstood Paul to be proclaiming a male and a female deity – Ἰησοῦς and Ἀνάστασις. How could Paul conceivably have used the abstract noun (if he used it at all) in such a way as to suggest this? Luke's summary in the last seven words of that verse would need to be isolated, in order to give rise to so absurd a misapprehension.

17. It occurs in Matt., Luke, John, Acts, not in Mark; Ναζαρηνός occurs only in Mark and Luke; Ναζαρά occurs (*si vera l.*) in Matt. and Luke; Ναζαρέθ (or -τ) occurs in all four Gospels and Acts.

18. E.g. in article 'Nazarene' in *IDB*.

19. *TDNT* IV, p. 877. See further, a bibliographical and critical note in Hahn 1963, p. 237 n. 4.

20. Cf. the terminology of Hahn 1963, e.g. p. 112.

21. Cf., however, Carlston 1963: 'Basically ... the Christology of Acts, though resting on traditional terminology and concepts, is quite consistent with itself, with the Christology of the Third Gospel, and with the author's purpose and situation.'

22. 1956, cf. 1957, pp. 143ff.; cf. van Iersel 1961, p. 65. This theory was apparently misunderstood by Casey 1958 (see p. 261 n. 1). It is not discussed by Hahn 1963, p. 389 n. 2; or by Conzelmann 1963.

23. *Contra* Hahn 1963, p. 385, who takes it to be a formula taken over by Luke from elsewhere.
24. Cf. Smalley 1962.
25. See Lövestam 1961. Or might it be a *double entendre* (cf. Duling 1973–4)?
26. 1959ᵃ, p. 252; cf. 1981, pp. 30, 102.
27. Elsewhere in the New Testament, the specialized use of παῖς, as the Servant of God in Old Testament Scripture, occurs only in Matt. 12.18 (Isa. 42.1); Luke 1.54 (Israel); Luke 1.69 (David).
28. From elsewhere in the 'Servant Songs' (Isa. 49.6) there is a quotation in Acts 13.47, applied not to Jesus but to the apostles.
29. Moule 1952; Hooker 1959. For a very rich bibliography on the subject, see van Iersel 1961, pp. 52f.
30. See Barrett 1959.
31. Note, however, as above, the purely human use of a similar phrase in Gal. 4.1.
32. It is notoriously difficult to believe that James really used an argument depending on the Septuagint in contrast to the Massoretic Text (Acts 15.17) – though even this has been defended as genuine.
33. As this essay is being completed, there appears Martin 1964.
34. Paul uses the other two 'stone' *testimonia*, from Isa. 8 and 28, as does 1 Peter (see Rom. 9.33; 1 Pet. 2.6, 8); but not Psalm 118.
35. For they might (though this would surely be a perverse exegesis) be made to yield an almost *anti*-Pauline sense, by substituting 'is no acquittal' for 'was no acquittal' (taking ἠδυνήθητε, I suppose, as a kind of gnomic aorist).
36. 'Dieser letzteren Rede verleiht Lk am Schluss (13.38–39) eine leichte paulinische Färbung,' Conzelmann 1963, p. 8 (a little grudgingly!).
37. The earlier verses of Psalm 2 occur, in a non-Pauline context, at Acts 4.24ff.
38. See Michel and Betz 1960; van Iersel 1961 (esp. pp. 78ff.); Lövestam 1961.
39. Vielhauer 1966 argues for a radical difference between Acts and Paul in the use of the title: in Acts 13.33 it is 'adoptionist', in Paul it is metaphysical and not connected with Psalm 2.7. But, as Dupont 1964 observes (citing Boismard), Psalm 2.7 is, in fact, evidently in mind in Rom. 1.4 (Michel and Betz 1960. p. 6, associate 2 Sam. 7.12ff. with Rom. 1.4); and the terms 'adoptionist' and 'metaphysical' both belong to a Greek philosophical context which is alien to Paul as much as to Acts. See Dupont 1948, pp. 541ff., and Boismard 1953.

40. Out of the large literature on this subtle problem, see, e.g., Dahl 1953 and Kramer 1963.

41. See the careful analysis in Foakes Jackson and Lake 1920, p. 367. Casey 1958 offers a discussion of the Acts usage; but his summary (p. 261), 'In Acts the usage of the title "Christ" is uniform and cuts across all theories of source-criticism,' is perplexing. O'Neill 1961, pp. 121ff., argued for the comparative lateness of the 'titular' use. His argument does not seem convincing to me; in any case he too ignored the differences just noted when (p. 122) he declared, 'Luke's usage consistently implies that χριστός was a Jewish title with a fixed and definite meaning.' (In the revised edition 1970, this chapter was omitted. See p. xi.) See, on the other side, Smalley 1962.

42. I myself, for instance, made this suggestion in 1959[a] (see pp. 262f.); but I am beginning to wonder whether the Pastorals are not, after all, Lucan. [See now Moule 1981, Excursus II.]

43. There are also, of course, oblique hints to the same effect in the way in which the drama of the birth of Christ is staged by Luke. See Rengstorf 1959, pp. 15f.

44. See BAGD s.v. 2.b, and Haenchen 1961 and Conzelmann 1963, in loc. Conzelmann, on Acts 10.36, cites Epictetus 4.1.12: ὁ πάντων κύριος Καῖσαρ (cf. the discussion of 10:36 above).

45. See Jeremias 1964[a].

46. See Kilpatrick 1945.

47. See Descamps 1950, p. 75, and other authors there cited.

48. It is highly improbable, although this has been suggested, that ὁ δίκαιος in Jas 5.6 is an allusion to Jesus. Much more likely is the meaning 'the just man' (in question), who suffers the injustice without retaliation.

49. Though BAGD, s.v. 3, cites Menander, inscriptions, and Philo for the sense 'have before ones's eyes', and assigns it this sense in Acts 2.25.

50. See the elaborate discussion in Doeve 1953, esp. p. 171.

51. Cf. Jeremias 1964[a], p. 28: 'In earliest times κύριος was used as an eschatological predicate ... Christ was called κύριος as the coming one, as the Lord of the universe in the future consummation. Paul, however, uses the title κύριος primarily as a designation of the *Christus praesens*, the present Lord of His church.'

52. For myself, I would add (1962) that even the Fourth Gospel is closer to the Lucan individualism and to the view of the Spirit as *locum tenens* than some would allow.

53. Cf. Reicke 1957; Doeve 1953, p. 175.

6

JESUS OF NAZARETH AND THE
CHURCH'S LORD

U. Luz und H. Weder (eds), *Die Mitte des Neuen Testaments:
Festschrift für Eduard Schweizer zum siebzigsten Geburtstag.*
Göttingen, Vandenhoeck und Ruprecht, 1983.[1]

All the New Testament writers who treat of the matter at all
accept, as axiomatic, that there is an unseen presence, equally
close to each successive generation, whom they speak of as
'Jesus Christ' or 'the Lord', and that this presence is, in some
sense, continuous with the man, Jesus of Nazareth, who
suffered under Pontius Pilate. This, however, is something that
it is difficult to represent convincingly in terms acceptable to
the modern mind, even if the devout heart is able to feel
something of its meaning. Some presentations of Christian
belief today, therefore, show a tendency to translate what the
New Testament writers think of as the very presence of Jesus
himself into the presence, rather, of the Spirit of God, better
known indeed and better understood because of all that Jesus
once was and did and taught, but not Jesus Christ himself.
Even if, in such presentations, the phrase 'the Spirit of Christ'
is used, or actually 'Christ', yet what is now meant is no more
than an understanding or experience of the Spirit of God
enhanced and conditioned by what Jesus was.[2] This is tanta-
mount to making Christianity a 'founder-religion', looking
back to a great leader of the past, but moving further from
him with each generation.

Another way of rationalizing Christian belief, besides that of
interpreting 'Christ' as the Spirit, is to stress the identity
between Jesus of Nazareth and the Church. There is certainly
a sense in which the Christian community in each generation
represents Christ: he has (it is sometimes said) no hands, no
feet, no voice, but those of the Church. The Church is his
Body, and ministers in his name and represents him: it is
sometimes called the extension of the incarnation. But to

81

resolve Christ without remainder into the Church would, again, imply that there was no more of him himself left than his memory and the movement founded by him or in his name.

If the distinctive characteristics of Christian belief at the inception of the Christian movement constitute the norm by which modern statements of distinctively Christian belief are to be tested (however different may be the language and the analogies they employ), then modern statements along the lines just indicated must be deemed inadequate. The presence of the living Christ is axiomatic for all such New Testament writings as treat of the matter, and to fail to find an equivalent expression for it is to leave out something essential.

But what is the alternative – unless the very words of the New Testament are merely to be repeated without any attempt to give them intelligibility for today? If it is too much to hope for an acceptable answer, this essay – gratefully dedicated to Eduard Schweizer, a scholar-pastor who has constantly sought means of communicating the Christian gospel in contemporary society – attempts at least to locate and identify some of the questions that have to be asked and some of the areas where further thought is needed.

And first, in order to locate what is new in the New Testament, a pertinent question is: How was the divine presence conceived of in Hebrew and Jewish thought up to the time of Christ? It is impossible to reconstruct with complete confidence exactly how the Scriptures were being interpreted at the time of Jesus of Nazareth, because all the extant Jewish interpretative literature except that of Philo and the Qumran scrolls is later – some of it much later. Conjectural reconstruction continues, and it is possible to deduce a good deal from the earliest ingredients in that later literature. Work on the early targums to the Prophets, in particular, has recently yielded striking results.[3] But even without this, we know at least that the Law and the Prophets and the Psalms must have been heard by many when they were read aloud or chanted in Synagogue; and it is not unlikely that many of the rest of 'the Writings', besides the Psalms, were also familiar to devout Jews. Josephus tells us (*Ant.* 10.267) that Daniel was known and popular in his day. The Scriptures themselves, therefore, may be assumed to have provided at least a backcloth of ideas.

In the Scriptures there is a broad spectrum of thoughts about the divine presence. God is ubiquitous. The Psalmist cannot escape his presence (Psalm 139); God fills heaven and earth (Jer. 23.24); Job, groping for God and failing to find him, is yet aware that he cannot escape him either (Job 9; 14; 23). If God is omnipresent, he is also far beyond all 'presence' or location: heaven itself, the highest heaven, cannot contain him (1 Kings 8.27). Yet, there is a persistent belief that there are certain 'focal' points where God may be approached by man and where, at his own behest and on his own initiative, God shows himself (cf. what follows in 1 Kings 8): it is the principle which, in Christian thought, is known as sacramental. Among all the nations there is a people, Israel, in which especially he is found. In Israel there are, from time to time, special localities for theophany – Bethel, Shiloh, Mount Sion. In the sanctuaries at such places there are objects through which God may be met – idols, perhaps, in certain periods (Psalm 84.8).[4] When idolatry is banned, then there are the ark and the cherubim; and there are priests and sacrifices through which the worshipper may communicate with the divine presence. The study of the Torah in the synagogue may, by the time of Christ, have become another recognized 'focus' of the divine presence, along a way paved by such writings as Psalm 119 and developed in later Jewish thought.[5]

When it comes to speaking of that presence, there is a widespread belief that it is fatal for man to see God. It is true that there are exceptions. In Exod. 24.9f. Moses and certain others see God – though in the end nothing is described except the plinth on which his throne is set. In Num. 12.8 Moses, far superior to even the greatest of the prophets, is one with whom God speaks face to face; and in Exod. 34.30 he catches on the mountain top the radiance of the direct confrontation. Yet, already within the Torah, such daring ideas are being contradicted: in Exod. 33.20–23 Moses, after all, sees only the back of God, not his face; according to Deut. 4.12, 15 no Israelites saw God at the giving of the Commandments: they heard him, but saw him not; and later reverential language spoke rather of seeing only God's messenger.

It is striking that, on the rare occasions when God is visually described, it is in terms of the human form. Ezek. 1 was notoriously dangerous. It was used in Judaism by trained mystics to induce 'merkabah' vision (sometimes with devastating results) and forbidden to the untrained reader.[6] It describes the august figure on the chariot-throne as human in form, albeit vaguely delineated and glowing with terrifying glory. In Isa. 6 Yahweh's train fills the Temple, which perhaps suggests a figure in priestly robes; and in Dan. 7 God is The Aged One – the presiding elder in the council of heaven. The very fact that creation stories describe Adam as made in the image of God suggests that God is conceived of as nearer to the likeness of a human being than of anything else known to humans, and that anthropomorphism is the deepest, not the crudest, that can be selected from human analogical language. And even when visual anthropomorphism is not employed, and when 'the face' of God comes to be no more than a dead metaphor meaning, quite non-visually, 'the presence', there are analogies from the other human senses: the arm, the hand, the finger, the mouth, the ear of God.

However, particularly in latter days and in the Wisdom Literature (especially the Greek books), and in Philo, there is a tendency to veer away from the visual and tangible altogether and to use periphrases such as 'the Name' or 'the Presence' (*shekinah*), or non-anthropomorphic analogies such as wisdom, utterance (word, *logos*), and spirit – spirit, that is, in abstract senses: not the breath of God's lips, but his subtle, invisible force. Wisdom is sometimes personified, notoriously in Prov. 8 and in parts of the Wisdom of Solomon, and so is Word – most melodramatically in Wisd. 18.14–16, where God's Word leaps from God's throne in heaven as an armed warrior of super-human stature to deal death in the land of Egypt. Philo makes considerable use of the concept of the *logos* in connection with the relation between the Creator and his creation. Spirit, more often than not, is God's power exerted in and through human persons – leaders, prophets, craftsmen, especially among his people Israel. There is a particularly wide and interesting range of references to the Spirit of God in the Qumran literature (see IQH 7.6f; 9.32, 12.12, 14.13, 16.12).[7] Less often is spirit a creative agent. Even if most versions and early interpretations of Gen. 1.2 make רוּחַ אֱלֹהִים מְרַחֶפֶת a creative agent 'brooding' or 'hovering' over the waters, the Hebrew itself could as well mean a violent hurricane moving to and fro – part of the very chaos to be quelled by the Creator.[8] Scarcely till Judith is creative action attributed directly to the spirit of God. Contrast Judith 16.14:

> thou didst speak and all things came to be;
> thou didst send out thy spirit and it
> formed (ᾠκοδόμησεν) them

with Psalm 32.6 (LXX, 33.6 MT):

> The LORD's word made the heavens,
> All the host of them was made at his command
> (πνεύματι τοῦ στόματος αὐτοῦ).

If this is roughly the shape of ideas in the Jewish Scriptures and related literature, what difference was made by Jesus? One might say that he brought about a dramatic return to anthropomorphism, though on a completely new level. During his ministry, the traditions, critically sifted, seem to show that, wherever Jesus was, there in an unprecedented degree God's sovereignty was seen in action: God was manifested in strength.[9] Where Jesus was, there the sovereignty of God had already 'come' on earth.[10] Even though he taught his disciples to pray for its coming, as something yet to be realized, where Jesus was, there the reign of God has already overtaken them (Matt. 12.28; Luke 11.20); and even the malicious charge of black magic, to which that saying was a reply, is evidence of the exceptional force of the events. If, as seems likely, Jesus made few if any explicit claims to be this or that (Messiah, etc.), and was content rather to speak of his role as that of the loyal martyr-people – the Son of Man of Dan. 7, vindicated only in heaven and on the further side of suffering – yet he exercised, there and then, God's healing and reconciling power: the Son of Man already possesses such authority (Mark 2.10, etc.). The presence of Jesus was seen to be identified with the presence of God in strength.

For most observers, this all fizzled out in a great exhibition of weakness – the abject defeat on the cross. But to his followers Jesus showed himself alive – totally alive with transcendent life, the life of the age to come – confirming his identification with that divinely powerful presence that had been seen in his ministry, but now without the limitations of time and place. To any of them anywhere he came to be known as present with a divine, inclusive presence.

In the earliest datable Christian documents, Paul offers the most articulate account of this conviction. For Paul, Jesus Christ, though still a vividly individual Person, 'who loved me and sacrificed himself for me' (Gal. 2.20), is at the same time larger than individual. He is the very ambience in which Christian life is lived.[11] In the Pauline epistles there are numerous occurrences of the preposition ἐν followed by a name of Jesus, and with a great range of nuances (instrumental, circumstantial, etc.) But four or five are difficult to interpret otherwise than in a locative sense (Rom. 16.7; 2 Cor. 5.17; etc.); which means that Jesus Christ is known as the 'area', the 'environment' in which the Christian people of God find their existence and in which they have been placed by the powerful rescue-operation of God, and that Jesus the Lord constitutes the realm of authority in which their allegiance places them.[12]

Not only are they '*in* Christ' or '*in* the Lord'; it is also in harmony *with* Christ that the Christian life moves: his rhythm is theirs – as is shown by the verbs compounded with συν-: the Christian suffers, dies, is buried, and is to rise with Christ (Rom. 6.3, 5; Gal. 2.20; Phil. 3.10; etc.). Christians are parts and organs of a living organism, which is Christ himself (1 Cor. 12.13): his vital force is theirs.

Conversely, all the graciousness of God which is exercised by him in Christ is with (μετά) Christians.[13] And it is through Jesus Christ as a living Mediator (διά with genitive) that Christians have access to God and offer praise and prayer to him (Rom. 5.1f.; 2 Cor. 1.20). Had New Testament Christians thought of Christ as no more than a founder-figure, they might naturally have used διά with accusative and said, 'Because of Christ, as he once was, we are now able to know God more deeply.' Instead, they said, 'Through Christ we have access to God' – indicating his living presence.

Paul does speak of Christ as in each Christian (Rom. 8.10; Gal. 2.20; cf. Eph. 3.17); but more prominently he speaks of Christians as in Christ. Conversely, although 'in (the) Spirit' occurs often enough, it is seldom in inescapably locative senses (except when Spirit is a realm or 'level' of existence[14]); and more prominently the Spirit is understood as the presence of God or of Christ within each individual.[15] It is the Spirit of Christ in each believer that enables him or her to address God as Christ addressed God: 'Abba!' (Mark 14.36; Rom. 8.15; Gal. 4.6).

Other writers within the New Testament, though differing markedly from Paul in many respects, nevertheless imply a similarly inclusive conception of the person of Christ. Luke-Acts and John conceive of Christ after Easter as still an individual, though exalted and divine. It is in keeping with this that, although the Gospel of John uses the same 'in Christ' language as Paul, it is a distinctly different usage. In John, 'the disciples in Christ' and 'Christ in them' are reciprocal phrases: the interpenetration is that of two individuals: no longer is Christ an environment or a body containing all Christians; and even when he is the vine and they the branches, it is the relation of each branch individually to the vine that is the point, and the vine can be spoken of as 'in' the branches (John 15.4, 5). For both Luke and John, Jesus Christ is a divine individual, exalted to God's right hand in heaven, and represented on earth by the Spirit. So, too, the Epistle to the Hebrews and the Revelation seem to conceive of Jesus as a divine individual in heaven. All this is unlike Paul's thought, which combines the exalted Person in heaven with the 'environment' of Christians; and yet, the belief of these writers in the saving work of Christ is of so universal a scope that it not only accords well with a Christology as inclusive as Paul's, but positively demands it. Paul's account makes sense of these others.[16] Incidentally, there are in the Johannine epistles passages which may possibly be intended to correct false and mechanical interpretations of the 'in Christ'. It is not to be taken as a description of a spiritual luxury – a privilege that exonerates one who enjoys it from responding strenuously: (It is) 'When we keep his commands [that] we dwell in him and he dwells in us' (1 John 3.24; cf. 2.28, 29).[17]

All in all, the New Testament, in a wide range of different approaches and conceptions, reflects a belief in a divine presence, continuous with the historical Jesus of Nazareth, yet now transcendent, inclusive, one with God, and the source, with God, of all the divine mercies and gifts (see the greetings of the epistles). And the presence, which is Jesus Christ, is not identified without remainder with the presence of the Spirit of God. It is true that the functions of Christ and of the Spirit are sometimes identical – conspicuously so in Rom. 8.9–11. But the relation of Jesus Christ to God is not identical with that of the Spirit;[18] nor is Jesus Christ in so many words ever identified with the Spirit, unless 1 Cor. 15.45 and 2 Cor. 3.17 are to be so construed – which is unlikely.[19]

This being so, it is noteworthy also that, of the three terms, spirit, word, and wisdom, which play so important a part in the Wisdom Literature, Christ is identified with the latter two but not with spirit; and conversely the Spirit's function in the New Testament is not cosmic, as Christ's is, but wholly intra-ecclesial.

It follows that it is an over-simplification if a modern restatement speaks of the divine presence as only the ever-present Spirit of God, now known more profoundly because of Christ. The New Testament, through all its varieties of expression, reflects something more subtle and complex. It is probably fair to say that, for Paul, the effect of the presence of Christ is indeed realized and implemented by the Spirit; and, as has already been said, the functions of the Spirit and of Christ are sometimes identical. It is the Spirit that reproduces in believers the voice of Christ. But it is the living Christ himself who is thus present, and it is in his ambience that Christian life is lived. To say less would be to unsay the New Testament's belief in the resurrection and transcendence of Jesus Christ. It would be to revert, ultimately, to a unitarian understanding of the unity of the Deity. It would be to make Jesus Christ no more than a supremely inspired human being and his 'presence' no more than his memory; and if an advocate of such a view challenges this 'no more than', as implying a misunderstanding of the relation between God and humanity, then he is, by implication, obliterating the line between Creator and created which is basic to biblical thinking. The paradox at the heart of Christian belief is precisely that it sees in Christ one who shares the Creator's life-giving function as well as being one with humanity. To ignore this paradox would, again, mean finding in the aliveness of Jesus as his friends understood it – in other words, the resurrection – nothing different from the aliveness which Pharisaic Judaism, followed by Christians, hopes for in the case of all believers, whereas the aliveness of Jesus is, in Paul, a life-giving, a creative aliveness (1 Cor. 15.45) – the very principle of life.

But to acknowledge the paradox of 'incarnation' (in the specialized and distinctively Christian sense of that term) is, of course, to raise a host of questions. One perplexing phenomenon which confronts us is the relation between the individual and the corporate. Jesus, a real person if ever there was one, and the most fully personal person imaginable, begins, after the end of his life on earth, to be perceived by his followers – apprehended, mysteriously yet decisively – as also supra-individual. If it is Paul alone, and near-Pauline writers, who actually articulate this, nevertheless other New Testament writers attribute to Jesus Christ a universal power to release and restore humanity to its true self in relation to God, which could only be his if he were in the supra-individual dimension in which Paul's understanding places him. The risen Christ is, as it were, infinitely capacious: he includes and encloses the Christian Church; he is the place, the environment, the location in which life exists for Christians. Yet he is all this without losing his sharply defined individuality. How can the individual and the supra-individual be thus one, and how can the supra-individual still be fully personal? Louis MacNeice, apostrophizing his fate or his destiny or circumstances beyond his control or (alternatively, and viewed in another light) the very meaning of his life, addresses it, 'O Thou my monster, Thou my guide', and, 'O pattern of inhuman good'; and he exclaims at 'Thy fierce impersonality';[20] and we can understand, perhaps, his feelings. Anything larger than individual may seem a threat to personality, because, on the human level, we experience personality mainly – perhaps only – in individuals. It is precisely when we encounter the more than individual – in crowd-psychology, perhaps, and in a collective 'will' – that we begin to feel afraid, as before something impersonal, irrational, even demonic. Yet, in Christ one whom we may recognize as a known and real person is found to be broadened out to a dimension beyond the individual and yet not contradicting it. The body of Christ contains, so to speak, individual persons within it, as limbs and organs of a larger organism, yet always so as to enhance, not diminish, their personhood, and so as to enlarge, not restrict, their freedom. This is a great (though blessed) mystery.

Is it possible that it is through individuality that we are meant to begin learning what a personal existence means, but that we are also meant to progress in our learning beyond this stage? When Gen. 1 says that Adam was made in the image of God, perhaps that may be taken to imply that the human individual is more like God than anything else we know. Yet God, by definition, transcends the human; and it is his transcending of the human manifestation of personality in an individual that seems to be reflected in Paul's understanding of the risen Christ: it is anthropomorphism raised to a new level. And it is, after all, a Christian principle that, even on the human and individual level, to lose oneself in outgoing service and concern for others is to find oneself (Mark 8.35). The Christian Church is precisely the society in which mutual belonging positively enhances individual freedom and personhood. John Macmurray affirms this principle and applies it to the doctrine of God:

> The more universal a person becomes in his self-transcendence, the more unique does he become in his individuality. There is therefore no ground for hesitation in ascribing personality to God. Absolute personality ... must involve absolute universality and absolute individuality at once, each of these qualities being the condition of the other.[21]

This problem, in its turn, is connected with the perennial problem of the relation of time to eternity and the meaning of creation. If we allow that Jesus, a known individual, turns out to be also in some supra-individual dimension, what does that say about the nature of the eternal being of God? Is there eternally in God both individuality and supra-individuality? If so, what was there new in the appearing of the individual Jesus of Nazareth as God incarnate, and what need was there for incarnation? Alternatively, if the divine individuality was new and had not existed before, does not this land us in the conclusion that something has been 'added' to the Deity that was not there before – a process-theology of a crudity that no process-theologian would be likely to countenance? Perhaps the best that may be said is that, if God is such a God as always to have been approachable by humankind and always to have been knowable by the analogy of human individuality, it is precisely for that reason that he turns out to be such a God as actually to 'become' such historically and creatively, in the course of the progressive creation of the world and the remaking of humankind.

Another problem raised by the distinctive conceptions of the New Testament is the relation between those who are described as 'in Christ' and all other persons (and, for that matter, all other things). If Christ is indeed the eternal Word or creative Utterance of God, then, by definition, all creation must be within his ambit. Yet the New Testament clearly uses οἱ ἐν Χριστῷ only for confessed Christians. Perhaps it is necessary to recognize a distinction between the conscious response to God on the one hand, and, on the other hand, the unrecognized fact of the divine presence. Whereas God's love is offered to all, and his creative power impinges on all, and his presence is absolute, there is a sense in which conscious response to his love and a conscious acknowledgement of his relation as Creator to his creatures brings into being a new situation; and there is a sense in which such response and such acknowledgement made consciously in the confession of Jesus Christ as Lord brings with it a further specific and distinctive situation. There is a difference between a merely latent source of electricity and the flow of the current when the switch is thrown; or between standing before an open door and passing through it.

A further question concerns the meaning of the presence of Christ in Christian experience. Many Christians would agree that there is nothing, in any awareness they may experience of the divine presence, to distinguish the presence of Christ from the presence of God in any other mode.[22] The more formal and orthodox of Christian prayers and hymns are addressed to God through Christ, but many other prayers and hymns are addressed directly to Christ. (Prayer to the saints is another matter.) Is there a difference? If not, does not that mean that it is impossible to experience God as Trinity? The answer is probably 'Yes'. But this does not invalidate a trinitarian understanding of the divine unity, because this stands or falls not with religious feelings but with a Christian Christology. It is the Church's understanding of Christ, to which it was led by all the circumstances of the beginnings of Christianity and its continuance, that lies behind a pluralistic understanding of the unity of God,[23] and this is independent of feelings, as it is of visions seen by individuals, however precious these may be. Many Christians associate the presence of Christ more particularly with the Eucharist, and here, if anywhere, they might claim to be able to call the divine presence by his name. Yet the Christian understanding of God does not stand or fall even with the 'real' presence in the Eucharist.

Finally, what of the pre-existence of Christ and his *parousia* at the end? It would, once again, be logical and rational to attribute pre-existence not to Jesus Christ but to God's *Logos* or Utterance; and to look for the ultimate denouement of God's purposes not in a public manifestation of the personal presence of Christ but in the realization corporately and collectively of all that he stands for. It would 'make sense', that is, to see in Jesus Christ only the historical figure who lived and died as the bearer of the Word but not as himself the Word.[24] But it is, once again, an oversimplification of what is reflected in New Testament religion to resolve the problem so. If the Church's transcendent Lord is deemed, as in New Testament thought, to be continuous with the historical Jesus, does it not follow that the historical Jesus was continuous with the eternal, pre-existent *Logos*? And if it is the Son of Man's – the human figure's – vindication in heaven that is God's verdict on human history, perhaps that verdict cannot be otherwise pronounced than by the one who assumed that role.

No doubt these speculations are rash and crudely framed. They illustrate some of the difficulties that arise if one is dissatisfied with rationalizing expedients. But the fact remains that, if justice is to be done to whatever reality is reflected in the New Testament, and if (as has been argued here) a 'reductionist' Christology is not adequate to this task, then either the Chalcedonian formulae must be somehow rehabilitated or a *tertium quid* must be sought.

Notes

1. This essay, of course, owes much to E. Schweizer's masterly studies on πνεῦμα both in the *TDNT* and in more popular works. But more immediately it springs out of two articles by me (1977[b], 1978[b]). These, in turn, were followed up by me in three lectures delivered in Sheffield at the Sir Henry Stephenson foundation on 8, 9, 10 March 1982, under the title 'The Presence of Christ: New Testament Axiom and Modern Problem', of which this essay is a summary. I here record my gratitude to the Stephenson Trustees for my election to the Lectureship.

2. Frei 1975 is a particularly interesting examination of the conception of the 'presence'. It is a reprint, but with a new preface declaring a change of view, of an exploratory essay, 'The Mystery of the Presence of Jesus Christ', originally published in *Crossroads* (1967). In his new preface, Frei declares that he now believes that the word 'presence' is not satisfactory, and that, 'in the end, it all came to the claim that the specifically Christian affirmation of the presence of God-in-Christ for the world involves nothing philosophically more high-flown than a doctrine of the Spirit, focussed on the Church, the Word, and the Sacrament, and a conviction of a dread yet hopeful odyssey' (ix). But even in the original essay he had written: 'When Christian believers speak of the presence of Jesus Christ now – in contrast to his presence at the time of his earthly life, death, and resurrection, as well as in contrast to his final presence in the future mode – they use the term "Spirit" or "Holy Spirit" ' (p. 155). See also the late Professor G. W. H. Lampe 1972 and 1977.

3. See Chilton 1977–8, 1979; Koch 1978–9.

4. This may originally have read 'they shall see, יִרְאוּ, the God of gods', before it was revocalized into 'he [the pilgrim] is seen, יֵרָאֶה, before God'.

5. See Avot 3.6.

6. See Hag. 2.1; Meg. 5.10; etc.

7. The two spirits of IQS are less relevant here, and more like the יֵצֶר or 'intention' of later Jewish thought.

8. See commentators *in loc*.

9. See Chilton 1979.

10. According to Jeremias 1971, p. 33, to speak of the 'coming' of the kingdom of God was to use language virtually new to Judaism. See ibid. n. 1 for a discussion of such parallels as there are.

11. For details see Moule 1977[a], Ch. 2.
12. For the distinction between the meaning of ἐν Χριστῷ and ἐν κυρίῳ respectively, see Bouttier 1962, pp. 54ff.
13. It is a curious fact that, with few exceptions, the New Testament epistles start with a prayer or a wish for grace, from God (and Christ), *for* the recipients (expressed by the plain dative), whereas they often end with a wish or a statement concerning its remaining *with* them (μετά). 2 John 3 is a rare exception. Presumably it comes naturally for a writer, on taking leave of those to whom he is writing, to pray for God's grace *not* to leave them but to remain with them; cf. the (now old-fashioned) 'Goodbye'.
14. Cf. E. Schweizer, art. πνεῦμα, etc., in *TDNT*.
15. For this distinction between the usage with Christ and the usage with Spirit, see Bouttier 1962, especially pp. 61ff.
16. See Moule 1977[a], Ch. 4.
17. On the community in the Johannine literature, see Schweizer 1959[b] 11a ff. and Eng. trans. 1961.
18. See Dunn 1980, for a very careful analysis (e.g. p. 147); also Bouttier 1962. See, however, Schweizer, art. πνεῦμα, *TDNT* pp. 433–4.
19. 1 Cor. 15.45 seems to contain a double contrast between the first Adam and the ultimate Adam: the first is a *living creature*, the last a *life-giving spirit*; if so, this by no means is an identification of Christ with the Holy Spirit: it means, rather, a life-giving spiritual Being. In 2 Cor. 3.17 ὁ δὲ κύριος τὸ πνεῦμά ἐστιν is best interpreted with reference to the Lord (Yhwh) of Exod. 34, not the Lord Christ. See Dunn 1970, pp. 309ff; Moule 1972.
20. From 'Prayer in Mid-Passage'.
21. From B. H. Streeter, ed., *Adventure*, 193f., quoted by Mackintosh 1929, p. 136 n. 1.
22. See a discussion of this, with reference to L. S. Hunter, 1921, in Moule 1978[b].
23. See Moule 1976, pp. 16ff.
24. Cf. Lampe 1972.

7

THE GRAVAMEN
AGAINST JESUS

E. P. Sanders (ed.), *Jesus, the Gospels, and the Church: Essays in Honor of William R. Farmer*. Macon, GA, Mercer University Press, 1987, pp. 177–95.

The charge for which Jesus was crucified was that he claimed to be King of the Jews. Does this indicate the real reason for his being put to death? If not, what was the real reason? It must seem foolhardy to reopen this endlessly debated question, and over-optimistic to imagine that new light may be thrown on it by a reconsideration of the familiar data. It is my intention, however, to bring to this brief discussion of some of those data two principles which are not always observed. They will become evident in due course. The essay is dedicated with admiration to the recipient of this volume, a friend and scholar who has been conspicuously courageous in his insistence on looking afresh at familiar scenery; and it owes much to the searching challenge contained in the works of another friend and scholar, namely its editor.

A Jewish student, now a rabbi, once asked me what historical thesis would need to be established or destroyed in order to undermine my Christian convictions. Part of an answer to that question might be that it would need to be proved that the death of Jesus was not due to anything in him which threatened the Judaism of his day. The relation of Jesus to Judaism is at the heart of the matter. This is why, in the debate about the death of Jesus, the disputants do, in fact, fall roughly into the two classes of those who deny that conflict with Judaism was a significant factor[1] and those who affirm that it was. Let it be added, in parenthesis, that there is nothing necessarily anti-Semitic in the latter conclusion (to which I subscribe) although it has too often been exploited with anti-Semitic intent.

At the start, there is a certain amount of common ground

between the two opposing views. Probably neither side will doubt that purely prudential considerations were at least among the motives for putting Jesus to death. Even those who believe that the charge of being an aspirant to messiahship (in the popular sense) was a false charge, although undoubtedly the official charge, are still bound by the evidence to recognize that at least it could be made to seem plausible. Herod Antipas, according to Josephus (*Ant.* 18. 118), feared that John the Baptist's influence over the crowds might lead to a revolt, and in the same way Jesus might well have seemed to be a potential danger, even if nothing was further from his own intentions (cf. John 11.48). As Sanders (1985[a]) remarks, 'anyone who claimed to speak for God and who attracted a following would alarm those who wanted to maintain the somewhat precarious *status quo* with Rome' (p. 228). Similarly C. H. Dodd (1938) wrote: 'The Pharisees and Herodians, we are told, formed a coalition against Him (Mark 3.6). No doubt the two parties objected to His proceedings on different grounds, but for both the danger lay in His appeal to lawless and irresponsible elements in the population' (p. 129 n. 1). Whatever may be thought about the suggestion that the Pharisees were involved, the principle holds good – and antagonism from at any rate high-priestly and Sadducean quarters would certainly be likely on such grounds.

Again, it is easy for both sides to the debate to agree that among those who called for the death of Jesus there are likely to have been some who were smarting under the lash of his moral indignation against abuses within Judaism. Outspoken prophets are seldom popular with everyone, least of all at a time when patriotism and solidarity are at a premium. This holds for prophets from Jeremiah through Jesus of Nazareth to that other Jesus, the crazy son of Ananias, who went about shouting doom on Jerusalem during the Jewish war until, ironically, a missile from a Roman ballista silenced him (Josephus, *Bel.* 6.300–309). No Jewish or Christian community can ever have been without its insincere worshippers and its mere ritualists, and attacks by Jesus on such abuses are well authenticated, no matter how much their extent and style may have been exaggerated by later antagonism between Synagogue and Church. The parable of the wicked husbandmen (Mark 12.1–

12 and parallels), with its echoes of Isaiah 5, belongs without much doubt in the context of Jesus' own time and is likely to be substantially authentic. There would be no lack of antagonists among those who were the target of such an attack.

Another by no means negligible factor is the sheer envy that may well have been aroused by the success of an unorthodox wandering healer and by his popularity. This is made explicit in Mark 15.10, Matt. 27.18, and quite plausibly. It is when one asks whether there were not other motives besides those of political diplomacy and of resentment against moral castigation and of envy, that the two main schools of thought part company, one denying that Judaism as such had any substantial complaint against Jesus, the other maintaining that, on the contrary, there is evidence for collision between Jesus and the essential Judaism of his day. In order to maintain the former position, it has to be shown that the relevant conflict-stories in the Gospels are unhistorical or seriously distorted. It has been suggested that the Jewish Christianity of which we seem to get glimpses in, for instance, some of the Matthean material was nearest to the real thing, but that the disciples who were closest to Jesus' own outlook and who might be represented by that strain of tradition were virtually eliminated in the Jewish war, and that the Pauline Christianity that dominates the New Testament represents an atypical, Hellenized, Gentile Christianity very far from the Founder's mind and from historical truth.

Such was the view of S. G. F. Brandon (1957),[2] who proposed[3] that St Mark's Gospel was a deliberate attempt to distance Christianity from its Jewish origins – an attempt occasioned by Vespasian's triumph which brought home to Christians in Rome, with a sudden shock, that their antecedents were uncomfortably bound up with *Judea capta*, and that if they were to escape molestation by the Roman authorities they had better get it believed that Jesus was the victim of Jewish malice, when Pilate wanted to let him off. Hence the conflict-stories and the treatment of the trial narratives by the Evangelists. It is totally unlikely, it is said, that a notoriously brutal prefect like Pilate should be concerned to free Jesus.[4] Whether Jesus was guilty or not, what political harm could his death do? Even violent protest from his followers could easily be dealt with by the army. And what likelihood is there, in any case, of the historicity of the alleged custom of releasing one prisoner at Passovertime?[5] Directly evidenced nowhere but in the Gospels and Acts 3.13f., it sounds like fiction designed to exculpate Pilate and incriminate the Jews. In such ways as this it is sought to eliminate any genuinely Jewish gravamen against Jesus.

It is not my intention here to offer a detailed defence of the conflict-traditions in the Gospels, though I shall underline the case made by others for the authenticity of some of them. What I want mainly to do is to apply to the question about the real gravamen against Jesus two principles. The first is that, to understand a historical situation, its sequel and consequences must be taken into account. This is firmly asserted by E. P. Sanders (1985[a]). He observes that 'with regard to Jesus' intention and his relationship to Judaism,' a good hypothesis 'should meet Klausner's test: it should situate Jesus believably in Judaism and yet explain why the movement initiated by him eventually broke with Judaism.'[6] Again, Sanders believes 'that the evidence shows that . . . there is substantial coherence between what Jesus had in mind, how he saw his relationship to his nation and his people's religion, the reason for his death, and the beginning of the Christian movement' (p. 22). Or, once more,

> . . . [T]he only way to proceed in the search for the historical Jesus is to offer hypotheses based on the evidence and to evaluate them in the light of how satisfactorily they account for the material in the Gospels, while also making Jesus a believable figure in first-century Palestine and the founder of a movement which eventuated in the church. (pp. 166f.)

'Does the persecution of the early Christian movement', he pertinently asks, 'shed light on the opposition to Jesus?' (p. 281).

Applying this principle, Sanders observes, for instance, that there is a total lack of evidence that any of Jesus' followers turned out, after his death, to have cherished a militant nationalism. Jesus was a king, but not of this world: his followers were a messianic movement, but not one looking for territory, p. 294. Perhaps it is significant that this seems to be true even of that very Jewish Christian, James, the Lord's brother.

According to Josephus (*Ant.* 20.200f.), when he and others with him were condemned to be stoned for law-breaking (παρανομεῖν), this offended the strictly observant Jews (περὶ τοὺς νόμους ἀκριβεῖς). That is to say, he had a reputation for being himself observant. But there is no hint of any violent nationalism; and according to Hegesippus (*apud* Eusebius, *HE* 2.23.20ff.), whatever this tradition may be worth, he disappointed the nationalists by refusing to confirm that Jesus was leading the people astray, and by, instead, confessing Jesus as the Son of Man – which I believe stands for passive, not violent, resistance in the name of God.

In the same way, Meyer (1979) appeals to early Christian self-understanding for confirmation of his interpretation of Jesus (p. 239, cf. p. 253); and, in a broader context, Hellwig (1983) follows the same principle when she speaks of the 'attempt to see the past event in the fulness of meaning which its impact on later history has been and still is unfolding' (p. 71).

Following this principle of taking into account the sequel when interpreting the antecedents, I want to call attention in particular to the evidence of the Pauline epistles for interpreting Jesus of Nazareth;[7] and it is there that the second principle to which I referred comes into view. The estimate of Jesus in Paul is a religious estimate; and the second principle is that the religious claims of Christians – in the case in point, these are Christological claims – must not be assumed to be groundless or fictitious merely because they relate to what the historian, as such, cannot investigate; neither ought the historian to overlook the fact that he may find that the hypothesis that such claims correspond to reality enables him to make better sense than assuming their fictitiousness does, of what, as a historian, he can perceive. In other words, what is beyond the purview of a historian as such (e.g., the object of a religious conviction) may nevertheless positively illuminate the scene which, as a historian, he does examine. This is not to deny the danger of religious prejudice;[8] but the danger of the misuse of a hypothesis must not preclude its use. The Jesus of Paul is a transcendent presence: what if it was real, and what if Jesus of Nazareth was that same presence? May a historian not find his strictly historical work illuminated by this hypothesis?

But before the Pauline sequel to the life of Jesus is considered, some recent work on the conflict-stories in the Gospels calls for comment. Sanders (1977, 1985[a], 1985[b]) has demonstrated that some of the reasons for conflict between Jesus and Judaism alleged by many Christian scholars are groundless. It is manifestly false to paint a picture of Judaism as essentially a 'book-keeping' religion that anxiously reckoned up profit and loss in its merit-ledger, and then to contrast this with the glorious freedom of Christianity, and so to claim that the reason why Jesus fell foul of Judaism was that he offered good news of the graciousness of God. On the contrary, a prophet proclaiming the graciousness of God would, as Sanders says, have met with enthusiastic assent. Professor Sanders, indeed, questions whether the main attack launched by Jesus was against self-righteousness in any case.[9] To pursue this point in detail it would be necessary to ask whether Sanders, while correctly pointing to the free grace of God in the belief of Judaism, may not have underemphasized other ingredients in it – for instance, the danger of 'legalism' resulting from the doctrine of staying within the covenant by law-abiding, and the danger of élitism springing from doctrines of the election of Israel. But, be that as it may, he has also exposed other errors in respect of Judaism, into which some Christian writers, insufficiently intimate with the nature of early Judaism, have fallen, such as equating the Pharisees with the *Ḥaberim*, lumping together the *'amme haaretz* with sinners, and imagining that Jesus' concern for ordinary people must have alienated him from Pharisees. In any case it is the chief priests, he points out, and not the Pharisees, who seem to have been the prime movers when it came to action against Jesus (1985[a], pp. 287, 291f.). Sanders has questioned, further, the extent of the evidence that Jesus disparaged the Law, pointing out that this is not reflected, as a principle, among his followers in the sequel (pp. 286f.).

In many respects, then, Sanders challenges what might be called the standard Christian explanation of the clash between Jesus and observant Jews that is depicted in many of the Gospel traditions. But, if he shows that the conflict has often been wrongly located, he does not deny the fact of conflict. Indeed – faithful to the principle of taking the sequel into account – he notes that Jewish persecution of Christians itself points in this direction (p. 295). At certain points he does find well authenticated grounds for serious hostility. Three points in particular are named. Jesus promised access to the Kingdom of God to sinners without first requiring of them restitution (p. 326, etc.); he bade one whom he called to follow him to leave the dead to bury their dead (pp. 252ff.); and he attacked the Temple system (pp. 61ff.). Regarding this last matter, the so-called 'cleansing' of the Temple was nothing of the sort. There was, Sanders maintains, no cleansing to be done, since the traders were only performing services essential to the maintenance of sacrifices, and the charges against their honesty implied in the Gospel narratives find virtually no support elsewhere. Rather, Sanders holds, what Jesus did in the Temple was a prophetic gesture connoting doom to the existing Temple system with a view to its replacement by a renewed Temple of God's making – an eschatological renewal. Among others who have reinterpreted this episode along the lines of a prophetic threat against the Temple are Catchpole (1984)[10] and Borg (1984, pp. 163ff.). The latter maintains that the charge against the traders for turning the Temple into a σπήλαιον λῃστῶν (Mark 11.17 and parallels) does not refer to sharp practice or mercenary-mindedness, but means that the Temple has become a stronghold of the resistance movement, λῃσταί being 'freedom-fighters' (λῃστής, it has been observed, never means a 'swindler'),[11] and resistance to Rome being part of the quest for exclusiveness ('holiness' in that sense), which Borg sees as Israel's disastrous mistake: not exclusive 'holiness' but all-embracing mercy, even towards the Romans, is God's design for Israel. Borg is followed in this respect by Wright (1985).

It is questionable – to pursue the Temple affair a little further – whether any of these interpretations of it is entirely satisfactory. Is it not possible that the charge of mercenary-mindedness is, after all, to be taken seriously (made explicit as it is in John 2.16)? However that may be, that the incident, if it took place, caused deep, perhaps deadly, resentment is, in any case, hard to doubt – resentment that would not be confined to the high priests but would be felt alike by the leaders, the pious, and the populace in general.[12] And that it is not a fabrication is supported by precisely the fact that Jesus' intention is not made altogether clear. The story has neither been suppressed as embarrassing to the Christian cause, nor yet clearly exploited as an attack on the Temple system itself, as it might have been, had it been artificially devised by Christians who had come to believe that the sacrificial death of Jesus superseded the sacrificial system (1 Cor. 5.7; Heb. 10) and that the veil of the Temple had been rent (Mark 15.38 and parallels, Heb. 10.20), and, indeed, the Temple made redundant (Acts 7.48; Rev. 21.22).[13]

As for the saying 'let the dead bury their dead' (Matt. 8.22; Luke 9.60), there seems to be little doubt that this must have been grossly offensive. Hengel, in his monograph on the theme (1981), makes a good case for its being a signal instance of something highly distinctive and disturbing in Jesus' style of leadership. There are, Hengel finds, no close parallels to this style in Judaism:

> ... Jesus' relationship to his disciples simply cannot be derived from the analogy of the teacher-pupil relationship such as we find it among the later rabbis. And, despite stronger points of contact with the apocalyptic prophets of his day than with the rabbis, Jesus is also fundamentally different from them too ... Neither the misleading term 'rabbi' nor the designation 'eschatological prophet' ... can adequately characterize his activity.

Hengel finds a similar lack of parallels among the Greek philosophers and teachers. Accordingly 'Jesus' "charisma",' he continues, 'breaks through the possibilities of categorization in terms of the phenomenology of religion. The very uniqueness of the way in which Jesus called individuals to "follow after" him is,' Hengel concludes, the expression of an 'underivable' authority (p. 87). Sanders (1985[a]), with knowledge of Hengel's observations, deems that the incident shows that 'at least once Jesus was willing to say that following him superseded the requirements of piety and the Torah' (p. 255). Similarly Rowland (1985) speaks of 'the harsh saying to repudiate an important religious obligation (to bury a corpse, Nazir 7.1) ...' (p. 144).

Regarding the fraternizing of Jesus with tax collectors and others who were reckoned as blatant sinners, Sanders may well be right that Christian commentators have assumed too readily that this itself must have been offensive to observant Jews. 'If Jesus, by eating with tax collectors, led them to repent, repay those whom they had robbed, and leave off practising their profession, he would have been a national hero' (1985[a], p. 203, cf. p. 272). (The story of Jesus' doing this in the case of Zacchaeus, Luke 19.1–10, is regarded by him as a secondary construction.) He concludes that Jesus' practice was offensive to Pharisees not because he was ready to associate with sinners, but only because he offered sinners access to the Kingdom of God without requiring formal restitution. Even his followers, he believes, did not maintain this practice (pp. 209, 323f.).

Without denying the scandal, it is important not to interpret failure to require statutory restitution as failure to require repentance. There are convincing indications in the Gospel traditions that Jesus did not always insist on formalities. He does appear to have sat loose to conventional religious practices. 'Indeed,' writes Rowland (1985), 'there is a case to be made for regarding Jesus' teaching as a kind of eschatological Torah, whose emphasis on the inward motives may find its antecedent in the prophetic hope of the new Law written on the heart . . .' (p. 143). It is true that Jesus is shown directing a leper to secure the statutory authorization of his cleaning (Mark 1.44 and parallels; Luke 17.14), but this might be for the leper's sake; otherwise, as Bowker (1978) puts it, 'Jesus was claiming that relatedness to God depends on the condition of faith, not on the conditions in the covenant' (p. 161). But none of this means that he did not call the sinners to repentance. Moreover, while it may be true that in theory an observant Jew would see nothing wrong in accepting table-fellowship with a sinner, if it was with a view to bringing him to repentance, how much evidence is there that Pharisees did in fact go out after sinners and take the risk of consorting with them with evangelistic intentions, without any prior guarantee of their intention to repent, and that they would not have suspected the integrity of one who did?[14]

It seems to me that there are good grounds for believing that observant Jews would have regarded Jesus' behaviour as irregular, even if, as seems to me overwhelmingly probable, he did summon the sinners to repentance, if not to the conventional signs of it; but whether his practice in this respect would, by itself, have led to an attempt on his life is another matter. What does seem to be clear is that, taken together, the incidents thus far reviewed constitute a very strong case for the unacceptability of Jesus to the Judaism of his day.[15]

But I believe that it was on a deeper level that the fundamental gravamen lay. Does Sanders perhaps hint at this when he alludes to Jesus' extraordinary self-claim,[16] and when he sees the disciples' belief in the resurrection of Jesus as decisive for launching the sequel and recognizes that this could not have happened in a vacuum?[17] That is to say, however dramatic and unexpected the phenomenon of the birth of the Easter-belief was, to be convincing the belief had to be congruous with what the disciples knew of Jesus himself. The transforming belief was not just belief in a resurrection, but belief in the resurrection of the Jesus they knew. However, Sanders draws a line at this point. He grants that 'in the Anglo-Saxon world it has often been argued ... that something about Jesus could be inferred from, in fact was necessitated by, the faith which sprang up among his disciples' but he declares that, for his part, he does 'not consider it likely that the link between Jesus and the consolidation and persecution of his followers lies in a common view of his *person*'. It is enough, he thinks, that Jesus 'was God's spokesman, knew what his next major action in Israel's history would be, and could specify who would be in the kingdom' (1985[a], pp. 12, 280). The basic question, round which not mere ideas but specific issues revolved, was 'who spoke for God?'[18]

I believe, however, that Paul's understanding of the 'person' of Jesus is relevant to the inquiry about the circumstances of the death of Jesus. The Jesus of Paul, I have said, is a transcendent presence: what if Jesus of Nazareth was the same? Consider the facts. Paul of Tarsus is our earliest datable witness to the sequel to the life of Jesus. Those who object to treating the letters of Paul as primary evidence for that sequel are not justified in deeming him either ignorant of Judaism or not interested in Christian origins. Even if one ignores Acts 22.3 (the claim that he was trained by Gamaliel the Elder) as secondary, there are his own statements in Gal. 1.13f. and Phil. 3.4–6 about his training in Pharisaic Judaism; and there is the evident conflict of loyalties reflected in Rom. 9.11 and elsewhere;[19] while, for his concern for Christian tradition, there is clear evidence in Gal. 1.18ff. (in a context where it was not to his advantage to acknowledge dependence on tradition) and in 1 Cor. 7.10, 11.23ff., and 15.1–11. It cannot be denied that Paul is rooted both in Judaism and in early Christian tradition.

What light, then, do the Pauline epistles throw on the causes of the crucifixion? On the external level, the earliest known reference to it anywhere is in 1 Thess. 2.15f., which attributes it to the bitter antagonism of certain Jews. That passage contains a venom that is almost unparalleled in the Pauline corpus (though Phil. 3.2ff. is not far off) and it was evidently written in the heat of anger; but it is difficult to believe that the charge could at any stage and in any circumstances have been gratuitously invented by one who was subsequently to write the passionately patriotic Rom. 9–11. Besides, in attributing the death of Jesus to certain Jews, Paul is only saying what non-Christian Jews were later to say in the much-quoted *baraitha* in b. Sanhedrin 43a, before it became popular to claim that Jesus was turned into an embarrassment to Judaism only by subsequent Christian falsification.

This makes it initially difficult to believe that Jesus gave no offence to Judaism; but the nature of the offence begins to become visible only when one takes into account the remarkable fact that Paul, and with him practically all the other writers in the New Testament, assume the transcendent figure of their religious experience to be continuous with the historical figure, Jesus of Nazareth. Even discounting the 'I am Jesus' of the heavenly vision in Acts 9.5, 22.8, 26.15, it is Paul himself who can speak of mystical union with one of whom, in the same breath, he speaks historically (using aorists) as 'the Son of God, who loved me and sacrificed himself for me' (Gal. 2.20). The one whom Paul found in his religious experience was assumed by him to be continuous with the one who was known as a historical individual, crucified in Judaea only the other day. The historian can observe, within the limits set by the data, both the historical figure and the symptoms of the subsequent religious experience; but if he is both properly inquisitive and honest, he is bound to pay attention also to what is implied by the religious symptoms, although this itself belongs outside the strictly historical purview.

Of course, nothing is simpler than to dismiss the implied claims as the product of fantasy. The historian's instinct, and indeed his duty as a historian, is to see whether he can rationalize the continuity between the historical figure and the transcendent Lord in the mind of the Christian worshipper by assuming that it is the spurious result of religious imagination. Given time and enthusiasm, a euhemeristic process of evolution can produce a god out of a hero easily enough. But in this instance there are considerations that tell against this instinctive explanation.

One is that the understanding of Jesus as a transcendent presence appears full-blown in the earliest datable documents available. Some of the deductions, such as that Jesus is divine, may wait to be spelt out explicitly by later writers;[20] but all the implications are there from the first, in the Pauline epistles. There is not, in the New Testament documents, the progressive development that an evolutionary theory would expect. Even when Rowland (1985) adduces evidence for more 'deification' of heroes within Judaism than one might expect in so monotheistic a tradition,[21] it still remains very remarkable that a contemporary figure, recently crucified, should have been viewed as Jesus is viewed very early in the development of New Testament devotion.

Assuming, for the time being, that the continuity deserves serious attention as perhaps reflecting reality, not fantasy, it is relevant to the present quest to inquire how Paul understands the relation between Jesus and Judaism. Paul says that Jesus was put to death by Jews. Is there any light thrown, in Paul's understanding of Jesus, on the reasons, for this? One matter at least immediately presents itself in reply. The Jesus of Paul's experience is understood to have inaugurated a new covenant that superseded the Mosaic covenant. It is true that Paul never speaks of Israel itself as superseded: 'new Israel' is a term that occurs nowhere in Paul or, for that matter, in any part of the New Testament. Neither does Paul or any other New Testament Christian, unless it be those represented by Stephen (Acts 6, 7), explicitly propose to disregard the Mosaic Law.[22] But Paul does see the new covenant as superseding the Mosaic covenant, and says so clearly in 2 Cor. 3, as the writer to the Hebrews does also with almost brutal explicitness in Heb. 8.13 (and *passim*). Whatever Paul meant by τέλος νόμου in Rom. 10.4,[23] that he regarded the covenant inaugurated by Jesus as transcending the Mosaic covenant is clear not only from 2 Cor. 3, but from the polemic contained in Galatians. Paul is there passionately opposing the requirement that uncircumcised Christians be circumcised, and the reason for so heated a repudiation seems to be that the requirement would impugn the sufficiency of Jesus Christ as what might be called 'the covenant area'. That is to say, in Paul's belief, a Gentile who has been baptized 'into' Jesus Christ is *ipso facto* within the covenant: nothing further may be required of necessity to make him a member of God's People. Conversely – such appears to be the logic of the situation – a circumcised Jew who does not, in addition, confess Jesus as Lord (and, no doubt, submit to baptism in his name, cf. Acts 2.38), while he certainly cannot cease to be an Israelite, has not yet gone forward into the full destiny designed by God for his People – into 'God's Israel' (Gal. 6.16).

That, no doubt, is deeply offensive to a Jew; but it seems to follow from Paul's understanding of Jesus. Jesus fulfils and transcends the Mosaic covenant and includes and transcends Israel-of-the-old-covenant, fulfilling Israel indeed, rather than superseding it, but doing so by inaugurating a new covenant which does positively supersede the old. Jesus, rather than Torah, is seen by Paul to be now supremely the way into covenant with God. Christian life is lived 'in' Christ, as in a magnetic field of energy. Grace, mercy, and peace come from God-and-Jesus – an astonishing formula for a monotheistic Jew to use.

It is easy to understand that if Jesus of Nazareth was, all along, in such a relationship with God – not necessarily (indeed, probably not) proclaiming it in so many words, but simply occupying such a position, in relation to God and to Israel – he must have been felt by many observant Jews to be intolerable and to constitute a blasphemy. If the Jesus of New Testament devotion corresponds with reality, and is not fiction, and if his continuity with the historical Jesus of Nazareth represents fact, not fantasy, then conflict between that historical figure and the Judaism of his day becomes as inevitable as conflict was for Paul who understood Jesus in this way, even if Jesus' attitude was not explicitly hostile to the law, and even if his behaviour had not been as unorthodox as it seems, in certain respects, to have been.

Returning, then, to the Synoptic Gospels, it is possible to see numerous indications of just such a situation. Jesus is often portrayed as evincing a startling immediacy in his relation to God. Sanders speaks of 'Jesus' extraordinary self-claim'.[24] Bornkamm (1960) speaks of 'the character of unmediated presence' (p. 62). Fuchs (1960) writes, 'Jesus dares to make God's will effective as if he himself stood in God's stead' (pp. 154, 156). Dodd (1970) wrote: 'There must have been something about the way in which Jesus spoke and acted which provoked' the charge of blasphemy (p. 78). Such impressions are based, not on the questionably historical statements that he actually made the sort of claims that (by 'hindsight', perhaps) he is represented as making in the Fourth Gospel, but on Jesus' quiet assumption, unmediated by appeals to Scripture or tradition, that he knew God's mind and was doing God's work.

Admittedly, it is well enough known that Judaism did recognize as authentic a certain degree of such intimacy with God. To claim to be spokesman for God was not, in itself, generally offensive.[25] If the average devout believer sought access to God's mind and will through the Torah and its traditional interpretation, through prayer and, while the Temple stood, through sacrifice and the mediation of the priestly system, yet there were the prophets and the charismatics who claimed more direct access to God, who had stood in his council (cf. Jer. 23.22, etc.) and overheard his words, and who might even evince a startling familiarity with God. Vermes (1973) has familiarized us with this last phenomenon, when he adduces (p. 81), for instance, the cases of Honi the Circle-Drawer (a saint of the first century BCE) and Rabbi Hanina ben Dosa (a wonder worker of the first century CE). Such charismatics, he says, showed an 'informal familiarity with God and confidence in the efficacy of their words' which was 'deeply disliked by those whose authority derived from established channels'. But at least Judaism knew about them and did not put them to death. Vermes concludes that Jesus belonged 'in the venerable company of the Devout, the ancient Hasidim'. He 'did not belong among the Pharisees, Essenes, Zealots or Gnostics, but was one of the holy miracle-workers of Galilee' (p. 223). Rather similarly, but less precisely, Lapide (1983) places Jesus in the category of the great spiritual leaders of Israel.

But even these charismatic figures had to be subject to tradition, as Rowland (1985) points out (p. 228), whereas Jesus, at least on certain occasions, seems to have flouted it. Still more striking is the vast difference between the jocular, 'Don Camillo' style of intimacy with God which characterized these Jewish charismatics and the Abba-prayer of Jesus (Mark 14.36) which combines intimacy with total devotion and reverence. Jesus does not really match any of the suggested parallels. 'Even within the characterization ... of an "eschato-logical charismatic",' writes Hengel (1981), 'he remains in the last resort incommensurable, and so basically confounds every attempt to fit him into the categories suggested by the phenom-enology or sociology of religion' (p. 69). Perhaps the nearest analogy in pre-Christian Jewish thought is in the Scriptures themselves. In Num. 12.8 Moses is placed in a class far above that of a prophet, by reason of his unique closeness to the Almighty in face to face confrontation. The passage is taken up by Philo in *Leg. All.* 3. 103 and *Her.* 262 (the latter citing also Deut. 34.10); and Rowland (1985) cites Sifre on the passage (p. 177), where the analogy is used of a king's agent who is virtually identified with the king. 'In all his utterances' says Josephus of Moses, 'one seemed to hear the speech of God Himself' (*Ant.* 4.329; Loeb translation). But was such a phenomenon as is described in Num. 12.8 anything more than theoretically conceived? It is hard to believe that any devout Jew would have remained unshaken if he had actually encoun-tered such immediacy of access to the divine in a contemporary at close quarters, bringing what Bowker (1978) calls the 'effect' of God into disconcerting proximity. 'Jesus', writes Bowker,

insisted, first maybe on the edges, but then at the very centre of Israel, eventually in the Temple itself, that what he knew, and what could be discerned in his life and work, of the nature and effect of God, was an authentic representation of that nature and its effect in the world of God's creation. (p. 129)

The Fourth Gospel makes explicit the position of Jesus in this respect which was implicit in his life and words. In the end, it is a choice between Moses and Jesus. Sanders (1985[a]), categorizing Christian authors who, in effect, declare that Jesus died 'for the truth of the gospel' defines one group among these as believing that Jesus died 'for his own christology ... because he set himself at least by implication above Moses...' (p. 331). I accept that as a description of my belief, and I think that it is dictated by the evidence, and not by Christian prejudice. In none of the traditions in the Gospels does Jesus appeal to any human authority, unless it be in John 5.33, where it is revoked in the next verse. The appeal to the baptism of John the Baptist (Mark 11.30 and parallels) is best interpreted as an appeal not to the Baptist's authorizing Jesus, but to the divine commissioning which was evident in the Baptist's case, and – so Jesus implies – is a parallel to the origin of his own authority. Jesus, with no authentication from the orthodox sources, simply pronounces what he assumes to be God's words and does what he assumes to be God's deeds – and his words and deeds 'succeed'. He does not use a prophetic formula such as 'Thus says the LORD': he says 'I say...' He pronounces forgiveness (Mark 2.5 and parallels), and appeals for evidence of its validity to the visible cure that follows. It is true, of course, that absolution may be effectively pronounced in the name of God by any minister of God formally authorized or even authenticated by his personal standing (cf. Matt. 16.19);[26] and Luke 7.48 (if it is interpreted in line with vv. 41ff.) shows that the Evangelist knew what was meant by the confirmation of a pardon already bestowed by God. But the incident in Mark 2 and parallels seems to be intended to represent a declaration made by Jesus as straight from God.[27]

There are at least two further matters that seem to imply an exceptional character in what Jesus does and says. These are the Son of Man sayings and the traditions of the Last Supper. I have written at length on 'the Son of Man'[28] and need here only state my conclusions. The fact that, almost without exception, the sayings-traditions, whether of Jesus, of Stephen (Acts 7.56), or of James the brother of Jesus (Euseb. *HE* 2.23.20ff., these two both alluding to Jesus), present the phrase with the definite article is difficult to explain unless, in the Aramaic originals of these traditions, there was some locution which was unambiguously deictic (probably not, therefore, *bar naš*' but rather some unambiguous phrase), and which meant 'the (well known) Son of Man'. If so, the most likely object of reference would have been the human figure – 'what seemed a son of man' – of Dan. 7, for Daniel was known and popular at the time (Josephus, *Ant.* 10.267). Daniel's figure, in its turn, in some way represents (whether as a symbol or as a heavenly champion) the loyal, observant Jews who were prepared to part with their lives rather than transgress the will of God as they understood it. It is plausible, therefore, to conclude that Jesus used Daniel's human figure as a symbol for his vocation of total obedience, and for the vocation of those whom he summoned to share it – the vocation to be the very heart of true, renewed Israel, with the confident expectation of vindication ultimately in the heavenly court. But, if so, Jesus is himself always assumed to be the heart of that heart. Whereas he chooses a symbolic Twelve to represent renewed Israel but does not include himself within the number, standing, instead, over and above them, with the Son of Man a similar supremacy is expressed by his holding a special quintessential position within and at the very heart of the symbol. In the Synoptic traditions of the Sanhedrin trials, Jesus is equated with the Son of Man as vindicated before the heavenly tribunal. Sanders (1985[a]) rightly observes that 'the claim to be the Son of man, or to know that he was coming, is not blasphemy' (p. 55); but here is the use of the claim with a differ- ence. Independently of whether or not the Sanhedrin trial is historical, and independently of the debated question whether 'the Son of Man' is in any way messianic,[29] the Son of Man sayings seem to reflect the affirmation of an obedience to the design of God of a quality which, because of its absoluteness, is not surprisingly called blasphemy.

The other set of traditions that must be mentioned as reflect- ing something of Jesus' extraordinary self-claim is that belonging to the Synoptic accounts of the Last Supper.[30]

These of course belong to what was private to the disciples, and subsequent liturgical developments have no doubt left their mark upon them. But there is every reason to believe in the authenticity of the tradition that, in the upper room, Jesus claimed to be inaugurating a new covenant. Indeed, there seems to be no plausible explanation, otherwise, of the fact that the new covenant is, as we have seen, a significant factor in Paul's thinking.

Here, then, is evidence, additional to the impression of 'immediacy' already discussed, for two startling claims that Jesus was destined by his death to enter upon the eternal kingship referred to in Dan. 7 as given in heaven to one like a son of man, and to have inaugurated the new covenant of Jeremiah 31. No doubt the Fourth Gospel makes explicit, by 'hind-sight', much that was only implicit in the words and deeds of Jesus; but when that Gospel locates the gravamen against Jesus in a claim to oneness with God that seemed blasphemous (5.18, 10.30ff.), this appears, in the light of the evidence, to be a fair summary of the implications of his presence; and what is reflected in Paul's epistles and other parts of the early Christian writings seems to match what may be gathered from a critical sifting of the traditions about the life of Jesus. If one disallows either of these, one causes difficulties for both. As Sanders (1985[a]) asks (referring to what Jesus himself seems to have stood for),

> Unless the entire scheme – which is a complete scheme, including a Messiah and extending to the final act, the inclusion of the Gentiles – was imparted via the resurrection appearances [an option which he justly questions], where did it come from? (p. 129)

Meyer (1979), at the end of his book, remarks that 'it is above all in the tradition generated by Jesus that we discover what made him operate in the way he did...' (pp. 252f.). Something similar may be said, if the argument of this essay is on the right lines, about discovering what caused Jesus to be crucified.

The conclusion of this essay amounts to a distinctively Christian understanding of Jesus; and that, of course, relates to matters outside what a historian, as such, can investigate.

But the question the essay is intended to pose is whether the hypothesis that this Christian estimate corresponds with reality does not make better sense of a larger number of data such as a historian can investigate, both in the traditions of the life of Jesus and in the evidence for the nature of its sequel, than a more 'reductionist' estimate does: in other words, whether it is not right and proper to hold the historical and the 'trans-historical' together in a single continuum, albeit without any blurring of the respective limits and frontiers of the two.[31]

Notes

1. Bibliography in Bammel 1984.
2. '. . . the Jerusalem Church fell together with the Jewish nation in the catastrophe of AD 70, because the Church in its principles and the loyalties of its members was essentially one with the nation' (p. 180). Till then, the authority of the Jerusalem Church, Brandon thought, had successfully surmounted the Pauline movement (which aimed to transcend the barriers of nationality), as is shown by hints in the Synoptic Gospels, Josephus and Hegesippus. For a critique of Brandon, including his 1967, see Hengel 1969, pp. 231–40, and 1971; and Bammel and Moule 1984.
3. Brandon 1960–61; cf. 1967, pp. 221ff. *Contra* Bruce 1984.
4. A recent brief restatement of this opinion is to be found in Watson 1984–85.
5. See, for instance, Merritt 1985, arguing that, whether or not the Evangelists have created two persons out of one (for some hold that 'Barabbas' was another name for Jesus of Nazareth), they have invented the episode on the basis of comparable customs known elsewhere in the ancient world (Babylon, Assyria, Greece, and perhaps Rome). For a critique of attacks on the plausibility of the Johannine portrayal of Pilate and of the offer of amnesty to a prisoner, see Robinson 1985, pp. 254ff.
6. P. 18, referring to Klausner 1925, p. 369.
7. The significance of Pauline Christology for interpreting the origin of early Christian belief is pursued in more detail in Moule 1977[a]; and the question of Paul's relation to Judaism, in Moule 1987.
8. Sanders 1985[a], pp. 278f.
9. 1985[a], p. 281. It must not be forgotten, however, that the 'book-

keeping' mentality is not absent from Jewish literature (or, for that matter, from Christian literature). Snodgrass 1986 names some instances, n. 48.

10. Catchpole 1984, pp. 319–34: 'the action of Jesus in the Temple is an anticipatory sign carried out in prophetic fashion' (334) – anticipatory, that is, of an eschatological order of the future associated with Zech. 14.21. Cf. Derrett *apud* Sanders 1985[a], p. 367, n. 46.

11. Harvey 1982, p. 132 and notes, *apud* Sanders 1985a, p. 66. It is, however, coupled with *kleptēs* in John 10.1, 8.

12. Sanders 1985[a], pp. 287f.

13. Ibid., p. 86. Since the publication of my essay, publications relevant to the subject include: Bauckham 1988, Hooker 1988, Neusner 1989, Buchanan 1991, Bockmuehl 1994 (pp. 72–74).

14. For Jewish attitudes to proselytism, see Bowers 1980, pp. 316–23 (320 n. 7).

15. On the question how far the message of Jesus included a national call to repentance, see Caird 1965. Sanders 1985[a], pp. 108, 112f., 116, is inclined to estimate the evidence for this as less convincing.

16. For references, see index of Sanders 1985[a], under 'Jesus, self-claim'.

17. Ibid., pp. 21, 240, 320, etc.; 129, cf. 95.

18. Ibid., pp. 280, 281, cf. 288. For a summary of this and other views see Davies and Sanders, forthcoming 1999.

19. See Sanders 1983, p. 80, etc.

20. Certainly Rom. 9.5 is no sound basis for a contrary conclusion.

21. P. 38. Cf. Ezekiel the Tragedian's picture of Moses as ruling from heaven, cited by Charlesworth 1985, p. 85.

22. This point is insisted on by Sanders 1985[a], pp. 268f.

23. For a recent discussion, see Sanders 1983, pp. 38f. See now also Barrett 1994, p. 96.

24. See n. 16 above.

25. Sanders 1985[a], p. 271.

26. Ibid., p. 240. But he also allows (p. 301, cf. pp. 273f.) that 'If Jesus pronounced forgiveness of sins (Mark 2.9–12), he might also have been arrogating to himself the prerogatives of the priesthood.'

27. I am indebted to Dr W. Horbury of Corpus Christi College, Cambridge, for notes and references on this question. He believes that what provokes the verdict of blasphemy here is that one who had no formal authorization spoke thus confidently.

28. E.g., 1974 (= 1982), and below, pp. 205f.
29. See, e.g., Horbury 1985; Bittner 1985.
30. Cf. Sanders 1985[a], p. 324.
31. Wright 1996 must now be added to the literature relevant to the theme.

Part Three

The Holy Spirit

8

THE HOLY SPIRIT
IN THE SCRIPTURES

The Church Quarterly, 3 (1971), pp. 279–87.

This theme is not only too high and tremendous for anyone to attempt successfully in a short article. It is also extremely difficult to organize, in view of the wide variety of viewpoints within the Bible. The most objective method might have been to make no attempt at a general account, but simply to display the various conceptions of the Spirit of God in each successive writing. But, since this might be dull and inconclusive, another method is here adopted, namely, to take certain specially significant aspects of the subject and attempt to illuminate them from the Scriptures, particularly those of the New Testament.

Spirit and Creation

It may come as a surprise that the words for 'spirit' are, in the Bible, rarely connected (as they are in many other religious vocabularies) with creation generally. In the Bible, 'spirit' sometimes means that which animates – the life in a living thing; more often, it is some manifestation of divine power in a human being; but very seldom does it stand for the activity of actual creation or for the divine element in the non-human world. Naturally one thinks of Genesis 1.2, where the evocative phrase 'the Spirit of God moved upon the face of the waters' (AV) conjures up a tender, brooding image of the Creator Spirit, especially when one knows that the same verb is rendered by 'flutter' in its only other Old Testament occurrence (in Deut. 32.11, referring to a bird). But what if 'the Spirit of God' really means 'a mighty wind' (as perhaps it may, in Hebrew idiom), and what if it 'swept over the surface of the waters',[1] as it does in the NEB version?[2] The key verse for the notion of the Creator Spirit then becomes at least open to question. So it is, for one reason and another, with most of the other candidates for consideration,[3] though an exception may, perhaps, be found in Job 33.4; in the Apocrypha, Judith 16.14; and among the Pseudepigrapha, 2 Baruch (the Syriac Apocalypse of Baruch) 21.4.

In general, then, the Spirit of God is scarcely associated with the actual making of the material world. Instead, it is sometimes associated with the introduction of life into what is already made (though for this, another word for breath is also used besides the word usually translated 'spirit' or 'wind');[4] but, more often, God's 'spirit' is God's mighty action among human beings – and especially in and through the outstanding leaders of his own people, Israel – Judges, Kings, and others.[5] In Ezekiel, again, it is God's Spirit that gives to 'God's frozen people', dead and ossified, new life and a will to return to him (Ezek. 37.1–14). In the New Testament, the Spirit is never associated with creation, unless the stories of the virgin birth should be treated as an exception (Matt. 1.20; Luke 1.35); and it is invariably confined to the Christian communities, with the sole exception of Jesus himself and participants in the infancy-stories (the Baptist's and the Lord's family and circle). Of course it is fair to ask, but who else, in the scope of the New Testament, is a possible candidate? And, admittedly, there is not a great deal of scope for references beyond these confines. But there is some: the Holy Spirit might have been described as moving the hearts of those who listened to the preaching of the gospel (e.g., Lydia, Acts 16.14), or those who helped Paul from outside the Church (e.g., the 'Asiarchs' of Acts 19.31), or those who are prayed for beyond the limits of the Church (e.g., 1 Tim. 2.1, 2.). Yet, in none of these cases is his agency, in fact, mentioned. Whatever the reason for this limitation, perhaps it is not irrelevant to Christian belief in an intense concentration of God's self-expression in Jesus Christ.

Holy Spirit

Another surprise is that the adjective 'holy' is by no means as a matter of course attached to 'spirit' in Jewish religious literature before the New Testament. In the whole Old Testament, whereas the word for spirit is common enough, the phrase with the adjective, 'Holy Spirit', occurs in precisely two passages, Psalm 51.11 (Heb. verse 13) and Isaiah 63.10, 11. In the Jewish apocryphal books there are a few examples (e.g., Wisdom 9.17); it becomes fairly common in the 'Manual' and Hymns of the Dead Sea Scrolls, in the (related) Damascus Document, and in rabbinic writings, though in the last it is said to be confined mainly to the theme of the inspiration of prophets or of Scripture.[6] In the New Testament, by contrast, '[the] Holy Spirit' is a standard term, and is not confined to any one aspect of the experience – though the Spirit is, as we have seen, mentioned (with only the rarest exceptions) in connection exclusively with Christian experience. The reason for this may well be simply that current usage by that time favoured the adjective, while Christian experience had both widened and intensified the meaning of Spirit. But it is possible that another factor contributing to the frequency of the phrase 'the Holy Spirit' in the New Testament was the consciousness of the early Christians that they were called to be the very quintessence of the people of God. Perhaps it is significant that the adjective 'holy' used as a noun – 'the holy [ones]' – is used, in Hebrew and Jewish documents, to describe loyal Israelites, only in what may be sectarian writing. Generally, 'the holy ones' means angelic powers.[7] But the use of the term for human beings, God's loyal people, appears in certain parts of Daniel,[8] once or twice in the Psalter, and perhaps in the so-called Damascus Document, related to the Dead Sea Scrolls.[9] But in the New Testament 'the holy ones', οἱ ἅγιοι, is the commonest of descriptions for Christians. Might it not be, then, that a group who thus described themselves should find it natural also to say 'Holy Spirit', when they thought of God's Spirit in connection with their own special dedication?

However that may be, the most remarkable thing about the Christian use of the adjective 'holy' – whether for Christians or for the Spirit – is that, through Jesus Christ, it has been revolutionized and turned inside out. Instead of connoting separation with a view to safety from contamination, it now meant consecration to take the light, healing, and cleansing of God's Spirit to the dark and dirty corners of the world: it meant having to soil the hands, not being anxiously concerned to keep them clean. 'The saints', οἱ ἅγιοι, are not to live segregated, like the Jewish Essenes; they certainly do not call themselves 'holy' because they imagine themselves 'holier than thou'. It is simply because they know themselves dedicated to be, in society at large, what Jesus and his disciples were during his ministry. That is what holiness means when it is communicated by the Holy Spirit through Jesus Christ.[10]

Human Beings and the Spirit of God

Both in the Old and New Testaments, the word 'spirit' sometimes denotes some aspect of a human being; but seldom without some indication that it is really the Spirit of God, on loan, as it were, to humankind. This is not at all the same as the idea (commonly associated with Hellenistic and Stoic thought) that a human being necessarily contains an indestructible spirit, an unquenchable spark of the divine fire or a seed of the all-permeating principle of reason. It is much more theistic than that. It means that, if God pleases, he may bestow his Spirit on humankind; but, equally, God can withdraw the Spirit. It is no inalienable right of man as such. Consequently, it is often difficult, in an English version, to know whether to make the initial 's' small or capital: 'spirit' or 'Spirit'.

Take Psalm 51.10, 11, NEB:

> Create a pure heart in me, O God,
> and give me a new and steadfast spirit,
> do not drive me from thy presence
> or take thy holy spirit from me.[11]

In more ordinary usage, the first instance of the word has a small 's' and the second a large one. In the New Testament, the human spirit and the Spirit of God appear side by side, in much the same way, in 1 Corinthians 2.11, but are represented in the NEB by a small and a large 's' respectively:

> Among men, who knows what a man is but the man's own spirit within him? In the same way, only the Spirit of God knows what God is.

This passage is instructive not only because of the collocation of the two uses of the word, but, still more, for Paul's conception of the relation between human beings and God, and of how revelation takes place. He seems to be saying that, when the spirit of a man or woman is somehow in touch with the Spirit of God, then that person's self-knowledge or self-consciousness acquires (if one may dare to follow the apparent direction of Paul's thought) God's self-knowledge or self-consciousness: he or she, as it were, is enabled to share the mind of God – to 'think God's thoughts after him'. But it is probably only because of this daring parallel that Paul here uses 'spirit' at all, to describe an aspect of a human being; by verse 16, he has reverted to his more usual term νοῦς, or 'mind': 'we possess the mind of Christ'.[12]

This brings us to Paul's more usual language. Perhaps it may be said (though one can never reduce the torrential thinking of Paul to complete consistency) that Paul generally conceives of an individual as viewable in two aspects, or operating on two levels – on the one hand, that of νοῦς, 'mind', the level on which God's Holy Spirit may enter and be welcomed in: 'mind' in a much more than merely intellectual sense – the person's understanding, his faculty to apprehend; and, on the other hand, that of σάρξ, 'flesh' – his physical and instinctive level of existence. If you like, σῶμα, 'body' (to introduce a third term), often means the whole man or woman – a person; and this person operates both on the level of the understanding and responsible choosing (νοῦς), and on the physical level of instinctive feeling and appetite (σάρξ, 'flesh'). If, now, he or she lets in sin through 'flesh-gate', as it were, by yielding blindly to self-interest and mere appetite without consulting the will of God, he or she begins to become a sensual person, σῶμα σαρκικόν (or σάρκινον) – a 'fleshly body'. If, on the other hand, the Spirit of God is let in through 'mind-gate', νοῦς (sometimes, though rarely, called πνεῦμα, the 'spirit'), he or she becomes σῶμα πνευματικόν, a spiritual person. To let oneself become 'sarkik', merely sensual (or what Paul sometimes calls ψυχικός – possessed, that is, of no more than mere ψυχή or animal life), is to be heading for death. To become 'spiritual' (πνευματικός) is to be beginning to be transformed by God's Spirit into the capacity for an eternal quality of life with God. These processes are hinted at in such passages as Romans 8.1ff. (where, however, Paul uses not νοῦς but the language of attitude or outlook, φρονεῖν and φρόνημα) and 1 Corinthians 2.6–3.3, 15.44–9. In a famous passage in Galatians 5.16ff., 'the deeds of the flesh' (meaning, the upshot of surrender to self-concern) are contrasted with 'the crop yielded by the Spirit', which constitutes Christian character on the deepest level.

The Spirit as Pledge of the Future

And this explains why the presence of the Holy Spirit in a Christian individual or in a Christian community is often described by New Testament theologians as 'eschatological' in meaning: it is an anticipation and an assurance of what God will ultimately achieve in his people. The Pauline epistles use vivid images for this idea: the Spirit's presence is a pledge of God's good faith; it is God's seal or stamp on what belongs to him; it is like the ritual 'first fruits' representing something larger still (Rom. 8.23; 2 Cor. 1.22, 5.5; Eph. 1.13, 14, 4.30). Moreover, joint-participation in the Holy Spirit leads to close fellowship between believers, so that the presence of the Holy Spirit begins to create the ideal society of God.[13] We have already seen that, in the New Testament, the Holy Spirit of God is spoken of almost without exception in relation to Christians only. This is not to say that the New Testament does not think of God as active outside the Church: of course not – μὴ γένοιτο! as Paul would say. There is clear teaching in the New Testament about God as Creator (Mark 10.6; 2 Cor. 4.6, etc.) and about Christ as the agent of creation (Col. 1.15ff.; Heb. 1.2, etc.), and as God's λόγος or self-expression active in all the world (John 1.1ff.). But this 'extra-ecclesial' activity of God is simply not described in terms of Spirit. Of this, more later.

The Gifts of the Spirit

Returning to the subject of the Spirit of God as received by a man or woman in the processes of becoming Christian, we may now add this. If the acceptance of the Holy Spirit is a *sine qua non* of being Christian at all, this is not to deny that, in addition to this basic gift possessed by all Christians as such, there are special manifestations of the Spirit issuing in special capacities and gifts – χαρίσματα ('free gifts'), as they are often called. Much is said about these in 1 Corinthians 12–14, where Paul's intention seems to be both to exhort his friends to a mutual recognition of their various specialized capacities, and to warn them against indulging in the exercise of one particular gift – the spectacular gift of 'tongues' – in Christian assemblies, regardless of whether or not it was valuable to the assembly as a whole.

Revivals of Pentecostalism in our own day have greatly intensified the study of this phenomenon. The modern Pentecostalist claims that a manifestation of 'tongue-speaking' is a sign that the believer has advanced beyond his or her baptism in water to baptism in Spirit, and further and richer relationship with God: it is the so-called 'second blessing'. J. D. G. Dunn (1970), in his stringent examination of the relevant New Testament passages, has put a strong query against the Pentecostal claim to find this doctrine in Scripture. If Dr Dunn is right, this is certainly not to deny that an outburst of tongue-speaking may indeed be a sign of a new release and freedom in the Christian life. It is only to protest against the claim to scriptural authority for the necessity of 'the second blessing' for full Christian existence. Such a doctrine may jeopardize the close association of the Spirit with water-baptism which the New Testament seems to indicate and can lead to a disastrous exclusiveness. It is true that, according to Paul, nobody is a Christian who has not the Spirit (Rom. 8.9); but the phenomenon of 'the second blessing' is not the only criterion of having the Spirit.

However, it is not only in Pentecostal circles that a wedge is driven between water-baptism and Spirit-baptism. The practice of baptism in infancy with confirmation at years of discretion has tended in the same direction. Confirmation is *par excellence* a rite of the Holy Spirit; and, in teaching about confirmation, appeal is often made to Acts 8.14–17, as scriptural authority for a special rite, distinct from water-baptism, for conferring the Holy Spirit; but it is precarious to build so much on this one incident. In Acts 10.44 the Holy Spirit comes to Cornelius and his company before baptism. Water and Spirit evidently must not be regimented in a rigid system, when the experience of becoming a Christian is so rich and complex.[14]

Either way, by a Pentecostal emphasis on 'the second blessing', or by focusing the Holy Spirit on confirmation at the expense of baptism, something is lost of the New Testament recognition that entry into the Church is by baptism in water-and-Spirit (cf. 1 Cor. 12.13).[15]

The Spirit and Inspiration

The inspiration of Scripture is another controversial matter. Strictly speaking, this doctrine is almost unknown to Scripture itself. Once only is the adjective 'inspired' (θεόπνευστος, 'God-breathed') applied to Scripture (2 Tim. 3.16), though there are passages in the Epistle to the Hebrews where the written words seem to be identified with the Spirit's utterances (3.7, 9.8, 10.15–17). In the main, the Holy Spirit, God's 'breath', is conceived of as residing not in inanimate things but in human persons. The Spirit, essentially a personal manifestation of God, finds his sphere of action in personality. The prophets may be said to speak under the influence of God's Spirit.[16] But if their words, when written down, are called 'inspired', that is only by a kind of derived usage; more strictly, they are words once spoken by inspired people, and if the voice of the Spirit is to be heard again through them, it can only be by the re-creation of a personal situation; the readers will themselves need to be inspired (cf. below pp. 211ff.). In 1 Corinthians 14.26–33 Paul describes a Christian assembly in which God's will is made known through various sorts of human utterance, and it is interesting that the congregation's discrimination (verse 29) is part of the process by which the utterance of God is received from the voice of the Christian speaker. The Spirit is not actually mentioned in this passage; but God's message conveyed through human channels is the essence of inspiration; and in this description of Christians in assembly the process is seen to be a joint, congregational concern on a fully personal level. More explicitly, the Holy Spirit is the source of divine guidance according to the 'Paraclete' sayings in John 14–16. The 'Paraclete', the Spirit of truth, represents a continuation of Jesus' own teaching after Jesus' earthly ministry is over; and it is on the personal level, among the friends of Jesus, that the Spirit operates. The teaching, revealing – as we might say, inspiring – work of the Spirit is essentially through persons and in the context of the Christian community, even when the result (John 16.8–11) is that the world at large is convicted.[17]

The Spirit and Christ

The 'farewell discourses' in John 14–16, mentioned at the end of the preceding section, are relevant also to the theme of the present section. In those chapters, the Holy Spirit is called, in the original Greek, the Paraclete. The force of this term is much debated: there is a full-length discussion of it in Johnston (1970). But, in brief, it is fair to say that if one dominant aspect is to be singled out from what is no doubt intended to be a term with a multiple meaning, that of 'advocacy' or 'championing' is a strong candidate. Παράκλητος, is, quite literally, the Greek for what in Latin is *Advocatus*; and the Holy Spirit is going to 'vindicate' or 'champion' the work of God in Jesus Christ, continuing and extending it, although no longer in the visible presence of Jesus. It is very much the same conception of the Spirit's work as one finds in the Acts. The Holy Spirit is doing for and in the Church what Christ was doing in his earthly ministry: witnessing to the truth, convicting of sin, vindicating loyal tenacity, helping his friends forward into new insights, providing the driving force for missionary expansion.

Thus, a relationship between the Spirit and Christ is indicated in terms of identity of function but at least some measure of distinguishability (though, notoriously, the Johannine farewell discourses oscillate between identity and distinction).[18]

Even deeper and more suggestive is the understanding of the relationship in Paul's use of 'Abba'. It is the Holy Spirit, he says (Rom. 8.15; Gal. 4.6), who utters, in believers, the cry of intimate trust and absolute obedience, 'Abba! Father!' which was exemplified in Jesus Christ himself (cf. Mark 14.36). The Holy Spirit is the Spirit of God's Son, and it is this Spirit who compasses our adoption as sons: that is, the distinctively Christian experience of the Spirit of God is as the Spirit of Jesus the Son of God, reproducing in Christians the sonship which, in a unique sense, was his. They now know God 'through Jesus Christ' and find the Son–Father relationship which exists between Jesus and God beginning to become a reality to them. If, according to Paul, each Christian individually and Christian congregations collectively are 'in Christ' or 'in the Lord' – incorporated in him, as organs or limbs are incorporated in a body – then, conversely, the Holy Spirit of Jesus Christ (that is, God's Spirit received and experienced because of what Jesus Christ has done and is) is in believers. It is the merit of some recent studies of the 'in Christ' formula[19] that, with more precision than hitherto, they recognize this difference. Although there are exceptions, and Paul's usage is not wholly consistent, nevertheless there is a discernible tendency not to say indifferently 'we in Christ' and 'Christ in us', but to speak of Christians as in Christ and of the Holy Spirit as in Christians. To be a Christian is to be incorporated in Christ and to have the Spirit of Christ within oneself. It is true that Johannine usage is much more reciprocal: 'we in Christ and Christ in us' (e.g., John 15.4f.). But even here, it is clearly not possible actually to sustain so complete a reciprocity, for the vine cannot be 'in' the branches in quite the same sense as the branches are in the vine. The Fourth Gospel, with more individualistic tendencies than Paul (see Moule 1962 and 1970[c]), allows such reciprocal phrases, but their very setting provides a qualification. Paul himself tends to avoid them, speaking less often of Christ than of the Holy Spirit as in Christians, but speaking of Christians as in Christ rather than as in the Spirit.

This is a pointer towards the conclusion that at least Paul, if not other writers, is feeling his way towards formulations that distinguish between Jesus Christ and the Holy Spirit. This is sometimes denied. It is alleged that, for Paul, there is virtually no difference between the risen Lord and the Spirit. But this is difficult to sustain, and it is certainly not legitimate to appeal to 2 Corinthians 3.17, 'now the Lord is the Spirit', for the more plausible interpretation of that much-quoted phrase is to refer 'the Lord' to the LORD (Yahweh) in the passage from Exodus 34 on which 2 Cor. 3 is a 'sermon' (cf. Dunn 1970). It seems possible, indeed, that the closing words of the chapter mean that the LORD of the Moses-story is now present (in the Christian era) as Spirit – that is, in the new experience of the constant presence of the Spirit, through Jesus Christ, in the Christian Church; and that the Christian, accordingly, is able to reflect God's glory with increasing intensity: that is what comes of the LORD (Yahweh) being present as Spirit (2 Cor. 3.18) (See Moule 1972.) 'Spirit', in this passage, describes a mode of the divine presence; and, although it is because of Christ, that does not make Spirit identical with him (see above, pp. 81ff.).

It is, of course, possible to draw up a considerable list of parallel passages from the New Testament in which, if one does not pay too much attention to the meaning, but merely counts the words, it might appear that the same or similar activities are ascribed to Christ and to the Spirit.[20] But even where identity of activity is established, and where the parallels are not merely verbal, identity of activity is still not necessarily absolute identity; over against such passages, there are also the converse passages where God, Christ, and the Holy Spirit are mentioned side by side and therefore distinguishably.[21]

The Spirit and the Church's Mission

The fact would seem to be that Christians looked back, through their traditions, to a Jesus who was himself vividly conscious of God as his Father, with whom he held dialogue, and of the Spirit of God with him and within him, sustaining and strengthening him in his ministry of deeds of power;[22] and that they found themselves, broadly and generally, using a correspondingly 'triangular' mode of expression. The Jesus of the Gospels is endowed with Spirit in a special way: the coming of the Spirit upon him at baptism sealed an intense realization of his relation to God and his vocation in God's service, as a Son responding to a Father; but it was not until this filial relationship had been consummated by death that Christ was able to pass it on to others. It is unlikely that this is intended by the phrase (unusual though it seems to be) in John 19.30: 'he ... gave up his spirit' (NEB; literally, 'he handed down the spirit'); but that the transmission of the Spirit takes place only after the 'glorification' of Christ which is his death, is explicit in John 7.39; and the bestowal is described in John 20.22, and, in a different way, in the Pentecost story of Acts 2. In both cases, it is closely linked with mission. To receive the Spirit means to be 'sent' on Christ's mission. This is written into the whole texture of the Acts, where every forward step is guided and powered by the Spirit; but, equally, passages in other writings such as 1 Cor. 2.4, 1 Thess. 1.5, and Heb. 2.4 reflect the consciousness that effective evangelism is always achieved by the power of the Holy Spirit. Thus Jesus, unique bearer of the Spirit himself, and uniquely fulfilling the implications of the relationship which the Spirit establishes, becomes thereby uniquely the bestower of the Spirit on others. In this, as in many other ways, the Gospel traditions about Jesus in his earthly ministry are linked with the life of the Church after Easter. Jesus himself is the only example of the perfect and complete reception of God's Spirit and of the perfect filial relation and the complete and absolute implementation of his being 'sent' by the Father; but, through his death and resurrection, it becomes possible for 'Abba! your will be done' (the Lord's own prayer) to be uttered by the Spirit of God within his friends, and for the Spirit in his friends to carry on the mission of God's Son to the end.

Thus, in sum, the whole biblical doctrine of the Spirit of God, from the mighty blast of mysterious divine potency up to the even more mighty and revolutionary power of the name of Jesus is summed up in one Aramaic word – and that the word of a child: 'Abba'!

Notes

1. See e.g., Galling 1950, who interprets the phrase not as 'Spirit hovering', but as 'wind moving to and fro' and notes that 'wind' instead of 'Spirit' was the interpretation also of several ancient writers here.
2. So text. Margin has: 'the spirit of God hovering'.
3. E.g., Ps. 33.6.
4. The word normally translated 'wind' or 'spirit' is *ruach*, while 'breath' is *neshamah*; but *ruach* can also mean 'breath'.
5. See Judges 3.10, 6.34, 11.29, 13.25, 14.6, 19, 15.14.
6. See a weighty note in Bowker 1969, p. 44, n. 3; and for some examples of its actual use, see ibid. pp. 151, 239, 240, 257, 260, 266.
7. E.g. Ps. 89.5 (Heb. 6), 7 (Heb. 8); Job 5.1; Zech. 14.5.
8. Although the 'angelic' use is also found there, e.g. 4.13 (Heb. 14); 8.13.

9. See Dan. 7.21. 22, 8.24; Pss. 16.3, 34.9 (Heb. 10); CD 20.8. But Vermes 1962 and some others interpret this last in the 'angelic' sense.

10. See Neill 1960.

11. And cf. Ezek. 36.26, 37.14.

12. See Scroggs 1967, p. 54 n. 1.

13. The Greek word κοινωνία, often rendered by 'fellowship', means, strictly, 'participation'. In 'the grace' (2 Cor. 13.14), the meaning, probably, is 'participation in the Holy Spirit' (not fellowship in the sense of 'companionship'). But joint-participation in the Spirit does create a community or fellowship.

14. For an important discussion, see Lampe 1951.

15. See now Turner 1996[a], 1996[b].

16. See Micah 3.8 (but the reading is uncertain); Isa. 61.1; 2 Pet. 1.21.

17. In all likelihood, 'the sword of the Spirit, which is the word of God', in Eph. 6.17 means utterance given to the Christian confessor when on trial (cf. Mark 13.11; Acts 6.10), or the Christian's obedience to God's command.

18. E.g., John 14.18, 'I will not leave you bereft; I am coming back to you'; but 15.26. '... your Advocate ..., whom I will send ...'.

19. E.g., Neugebauer 1961; Bouttier 1962.

20. Christians are 'justified' in Christ (Gal. 2.17) and in the Spirit (1 Cor. 6.11); sanctified (1 Cor. 1.2, 6.11; Rom. 15.16), 'sealed' (Eph. 1.13, 4.30), and 'circumcised' in both (Col. 2.11; Rom. 2.29); and in both they have joy (Phil. 3.1; Rom. 14.17), faith (Gal. 3.26(?); 1 Cor. 12.9), love (Rom. 8.39; Col. 1.8), and 'communion' (1 Cor. 1.9; 2 Cor. 13, 14). See Kirk 1928.

21. See Rom. 8.9–11; 1 Cor. 12.4–6; 2 Cor. 13.14; Gal. 4.4–7; Eph. 4.4–6; 2 Thess. 2.13, 14; cf. 1 Pet. 1.2.

22. For the relation of the Spirit to the Kingdom of God in the life of Jesus and beyond, see Dunn 1970.

Part Four

The Eucharist

9

THE SACRIFICE
OF CHRIST

London, Hodder and Stoughton, 1956.

In launching this slight essay on the sea of however small a group of readers, I am very well aware that I am courting shipwreck on the rocks of scholarly criticism if not on some others of an even sharper kind. The informal lectures, of which it still virtually consists (for they have been only very slightly touched up), were originally delivered to a friendly group of ordinands.[1] And the only excuses for sending them further afield are two: the first, that some of the original hearers were kind enough to suggest it and the Publishers most kindly furthered the project; and the second, that the present time [1956] seems favourable, as I have said in the lectures, for the ventilating of the subject. Perhaps never before has there been so much mutual understanding – or at least desire for it – between the different traditions of the Christian Church. I cannot resist quoting from Fr Hebert to illustrate this. The following words (cited by Dr Massey H. Shepherd in the Minneapolis addresses) would only need to be very slightly altered, near the middle of the quotation, to serve as a summary of what I try to say in these talks:

The eucharistic Sacrifice, that storm-centre of controversy, is finding in our day a truly evangelical expression from the 'catholic' side, when it is insisted that the sacrificial action is not any sort of re-immolation of Christ, nor a sacrifice additional to His one Sacrifice, but a participation in it. The true celebrant is Christ the High-Priest, and the Christian people are assembled as members of His Body to present before God His Sacrifice, and to be themselves offered up in sacrifice through their union with Him. This, however, involves a repudiation of certain mediaeval developments, notably the habitual celebration of the Eucharist without the Communion of the people; or the notion that the offering of the Eucharist is the concern of the individual priest rather than of the assembled church; and, above all, any idea that in the Eucharist we offer a sacrifice to propitiate God. We offer it only because He has offered the one Sacrifice, once for all, in which we need to participate.

It may be, then, that even so ephemeral and tentative a discussion as this may prove to be some small contribution to the healing of our divisions: a little tract for the times.

It is only one individual trying to think aloud about a perennial problem. And to any who are patient enough to listen, he wishes to say two more things before he begins. First, pride bids me anticipate criticism by saying that, if there is any realm in which I can claim some experience, it is in biblical exposition. Outside it – and especially in the disciplines of philosophy, history, and liturgy (where much of the following discussion lies) – I am the merest amateur and pretend to be no more. My justification, if any, for trespassing has already been offered. Second, anxiety for goodwill compels me to say also that I hope that those Evangelicals with whom I have joined issue will be ready to believe that, in regard to essentials, I am with them still. If we must use labels, I am proud to call myself an Evangelical.[2]

Introduction

The subject which is offered for discussion here is a familiar one, but so great and deep a mystery that we can hardly think about it too often. It is the strange paradox which lies at the very heart of our faith, and which arises from the finality and yet constantly repetitive nature of salvation – the finished work of God in Christ, over against his continued work in the Body of Christ which is the Church. It is the tension set up by the distinction, yet union, between Christ as an individual and the corporate Christ in his Church. It is the restless question of the relation between the sacrifice on Calvary and (as some would put it) 'the sacrifice of the Mass'. Imagine somebody who has little or no theological background, but who is a really serious inquirer into the Christian faith. Suppose that, in studying the New Testament, he encounters these two strands of its texture in quick succession. First he reads the cry of finality and achievement, the 'It is finished' in the Fourth Gospel's story of the cross; or reads these equally absolute phrases in the Epistle to the Hebrews: Christ 'has no need, like those high priests, to offer sacrifices daily, first for his own sins and then for those of the people; he did this *once for all* when he offered up himself' (7.27); or:

> Nor was it to offer himself repeatedly, as the high priest enters the Holy Place yearly with blood not his own; for then he would have had to suffer repeatedly since the foundation of the world. But as it is, he has appeared *once for all* at the end of the age to put away sin by the sacrifice of himself (9.25f., RSV).

And then our inquirer, having done his best to grasp and come to terms with this 'scandal of particularity', this astonishing claim that the eternal and final and absolute is in some sense fastened at a moment in the flux of time, goes on to find himself after all confronted with the famous words of St Paul in Col. 1.24 about the continuation and completion of the work of salvation in the Christian Church: '... who now rejoice in my sufferings for you, and fill up that which is behind of the afflictions of Christ in my flesh, for his body's sake, which is the Church'. What would you say to such a person if he asked you in perplexity just what this meant? It is not easy to give a fair answer; and too often the answers stated or implied are lopsided. And this brings us at once to frankly controversial territory.

The Protestant tends to stress the 'once for all', the ἅπαξ, clinging resolutely to the precious good news that salvation is complete and Christ's finished work sufficient. The Roman Church, while wholeheartedly acknowledging this, would also (I think it is true to say) stress the frequentative and the repetitive aspects of salvation. Similarly, the Protestant emphasis falls upon the uniqueness of Christ and his historical past, while the opposite wing, again accepting all that, will pay more attention to the Church as the Body of Christ contemporary with every age – the continuation of his presence. Arising in part from these contrasts is another pair of antitheses: it is

notorious that on the whole the Protestant tends to individualism in religion (though many qualifications need to be added
to that rash generalization), while the opposite emphasis is
upon its corporate nature. Eucharistic doctrine naturally
follows the same main divide, and that in many respects; but
the most obvious is the matter of sacrifice. At one end of
thought, the act of offering is relegated – or appears to the
outside observer to be relegated – to a secondary or lower
position, while representatives of the opposite end may not
stop short of speaking of the offering of Christ at each Mass; or,
at the very least, thinkers on that side of the divide will wish to
bring the act of offering up into a position of prominence. The
position of the Prayer of Oblation in the 1662 Prayer Book is
often interpreted as standing for the Protestant emphasis – the
reluctance to associate the idea of offering with the main
action of the service, and the preference for mentioning it only
as a consequence, not as a part, of the sacrament itself.

I take some examples of these different stresses in eucharistic
thought and practice from some recent comparatively incidental writings. First from *The Fulness of Christ* (1950). This, it will
be remembered, was the Evangelical Anglican member of
that trilogy of replies to certain questions formulated by the
Archbishop of Canterbury, the other members of which were
Catholicity (1947), from the opposite side of Anglicanism, and
The Catholicity of Protestantism (1950), from the Free Churches.
In *The Fulness of Christ* (p. 32) came these words about the
eucharistic offering:

> The Eucharist is the divinely instituted remembrance of
> Christ's sacrifice, and in it God gives and the Church receives
> the fruits of that sacrifice, the Body and Blood of Christ. In
> virtue of this, and only so, the Church is enabled to make that
> offering of praise, thanksgiving, and self-oblation which
> (apart from the alms) is the only sacrifice actually offered in
> the Eucharist. Only as united to Christ in his death and resur-
> rection through receiving the Body and Blood of Christ is
> the Church able to offer itself acceptably to the Father.

Canon Alan Richardson (1951), in a review which in the main
was very friendly and appreciative, took up this point vigor-
ously when he wrote:

In implying . . . that the bread and wine are *not* offered in the Eucharist, they deny the primitive (second-century) conception of the Eucharist as a sacrament of Creation as well as of Redemption, through the offering up of the 'first-fruits' of the created order under the forms of bread and wine. In the early Church every Lord's Day was a Harvest Festival as well as an Easter Sunday. Furthermore, they deny the primitive symbolism of the offering of the sacramental elements as representing the worshippers themselves – 'There you are on the altar, there you are in the chalice', said St Augustine to his congregation at the Eucharist. They destroy the whole symbolism of the 'People's Offering', now so widely practised in Anglican churches, with the precious note of realism which it introduces into the liturgy as the worshippers come to offer to God not only themselves but all the labours of their hands, represented under the forms of manufactured articles, the bread and wine of the eucharistic offering. There is lacking the sense of grandeur and mystery in the eucharistic oblation, which Christ, true priest at every celebration, offers to God as He presents his body the Church already – eschatologically – made pure and spotless, a living sacrifice, holy, acceptable to God. But the Church (*Laos*) is one with Christ as Offerer as well as with him as offered; the priesthood of the *Laos* derives from the eternal high priesthood of Christ.

I must be allowed to say in parenthesis, as one of the signatories to *The Fulness of Christ*, that I am sure that none of us in fact intended to 'deny the primitive symbolism of the offering of the sacramental elements as representing the worshippers themselves', still less to 'destroy the whole symbolism of' the People's Offering (a symbolism in which I for one habitually join with the greatest of profit). But it is perfectly true that the two emphases – one on receiving and the other on giving – do serve as symptoms of a difference. Here, next, are a couple of instances of an extreme antisacrificial position from Anglican writers of the Evangelical school (a position which I, though proud to be of that school, cannot myself accept unqualified). One writer in *The Churchman*, (1954, pp. 233f.) says: 'The Atonement is something wholly other than ourselves. We have nothing to add to the Atonement, nor can we add anything to the Sacrifice of Christ upon the Cross, *least of all by joining in His self-offering*'. Another in a review in the same journal (1954, p. 255) repudiates 'all views that suggest that the eternal Son of God is continually offering Himself in order to secure our acceptance with God'. Returning back from this to illustrate the opposite stress, here is a very important observation made by my friend Mr Roland Walls of Corpus Christi College, Cambridge. In Clare College Chapel, Dr Robinson, the Dean, has introduced in a very impressive form the People's Offering (which I said just now I had myself found so profitable), and several other similar features, embodying them in a manual which is aimed at helping the worshipper to participate, not as an isolated individual, but as an active member of the community. Reviewing this manual most appreciatively, Mr Walls (1954–5, p. 316) adds:

> The book leaves one thing unsaid or unstressed and that is the age-old belief of Christians that in the Holy Communion the family of God have an opportunity of joining in and pleading the offering to the Father of the one perfect sacrifice of the Son of God. Something like the words of William Bright's hymn, now to be found in the hymnbooks of free-church and presbyterian traditions, needs to be given on the left-hand page [that is, the part of the manual devoted to comments and aids to prayer]:

> > And now, O Father, mindful of the love
> > That bought us once for all on Calvary's tree,
> > And having with us Him who pleads above,
> > We here present, we here spread forth to Thee
> > That only offering perfect in Thine eyes,
> > The one true, pure, immortal sacrifice.

For the moment I make no comment on this: we shall have occasion to return to it. But I have simply quoted these varying viewpoints in quick succession, taken not from considered works of doctrine such as Dr Mascall's *Corpus Christi* (1953) or, before him, Gore's *The Body of Christ* (1901), but from current and comparatively incidental and ephemeral writings, just in order to remind ourselves of the welter of opinion, even about this one question of the eucharistic sacrifice, let alone the related problems.

Where different branches of the Church advance opposite views or stress opposite ends of a series, there is generally something precious in both insights. And it is not so much the mean between the two that we must seek, as the common root from which these two different growths shoot up; and it is my belief moreover that in this particular instance there is real hope of common ground being discovered by our both being willing (if one may press the metaphor a little further) to dig down deeper than we generally do towards that root. I have been particularly impressed over the last few years by the richness of the unity that I have been able to find at the deeper levels of this controversy, both in the reviewing of Roman Catholic works on the New Testament, and in discussions, and in common worship with Christians of varying standpoints.

It is for this reason that I venture to offer these informal talks about the sacrifice of Christ, believing that if they lead us to study together in the context of worship the Gospel of Salvation which we hold in common, we shall, by God's grace, have taken a not unimportant step forward into that mutual understanding from which God can build a stronger and more united Church. In the three sections which follow, therefore, I shall ask you to consider first, the uniqueness and finality of the sacrifice of Christ and all the precious truth which has been guarded with especial care by the Protestant emphasis on the once-and-for-all security of our salvation. This is the ground of all Christian confidence: the objective, finished work of Christ – achieved, unalterable. Second (that is, in the third section) we shall come to the correlative truth contained in the New Testament phrases of repetition ('I fill up that which is lacking of the afflictions of Christ') and is implicit in the doctrine of the coinherence of believers and Christ. The doctrine of the Church as the Body of Christ carries in it the corollary that in some sense the sufferings of the limbs are the sufferings of the Head, and vice versa. Finally, in the last section, we shall try to think about the implications of all this for eucharistic doctrine.

If some suggestions may be allowed by way of pointers to appropriate readings and thinking in this connection, first, the

Epistle to the Hebrews, which is one of the key documents in regard to both poles of our paradox, should be read and re-read as a background to these short sections. Second, it is profitable, I suggest, for us to try to rethink, not only the relation between Christ and his Church – an obvious priority in our discussion – but also the relation between baptism and Holy Communion. Both of them sacraments of the death-and-life of Christ, both reproductions of the whole gospel of salvation – wherein are they distinct? Why has baptism not been called a reburial of Christ, on the analogy of the Eucharist being claimed as a sacrifice? Third – a point which will have to be taken up in the last section – what is the relation between the Eucharist, as the 'focus' of obedience, and all 'foci' of obedience throughout our lives – all sacraments and quasi-sacraments, all actions, in short, which are performed in Christ in obedience to God's will, and into each of which is cast the whole obedience of our lives? Are all these to be designated by terms similar to 'the eucharistic sacrifice'? Martyrdom counted as baptism: do lesser acts of obedience also partake of the nature of these great sacraments of obedience? Finally, it is vital, to my mind, that we should often reconsider the meaning of the terms sacrifice, priesthood, and intercession when they are used with reference to the relation between man and God or Christ and God. How often, let us ask ourselves, does the New Testament use a phrase like 'Christ offered a sacrifice to God'? How far are terms of propitiation legitimate in this context? How, and in what circumstances, is Christ's intercession mentioned? How far is it true that God is the subject rather than the object of these actions? And how far, if at all, is it legitimate in such contexts to separate the actions of the Son from those of the Father?

The Finished Work of Christ

Every section of Christian opinion unites to affirm the uniqueness and finality of the sacrifice of Christ. Yet it is well, for completeness' sake, that we should consider what the New Testament says about it. Besides, Christians who live for a time, as some of us do, chiefly within a circle of like-minded believers may too easily forget what a monstrous claim this seems to the outsider – how puzzling, how naive perhaps. It is in a vehement form the 'scandal of particularity' – this claim that an obscure man, put to death like two other condemned men at the same execution, and like, alas, millions of poor wretches at one time or another, achieved by his death something of such potency that its effects stretch infinitely far (if one may put it so) both backwards and forwards – backwards so as to take all past history into its embrace, forwards to the length of the human race that is to be. How can one individual conceivably be placed in such a position? Living in an unimportant corner of the Roman empire, under a second-rate provincial governor, virtually ignored by secular historians of the next and many generations – how can this person be claimed to occupy the very centre of history and of whatever lies outside and beyond history? That is the question asked hopelessly and incredulously by many earnest people who sincerely admire Jesus as a good man and a great man and a martyr.

Yet this is what all Christians from the very earliest days have persistently affirmed, in many different ways and from a variety of angles, but always with the same conclusion. Let us not allow the unanimity of this conviction to blind us to its extraordinariness.

My purpose is now to remind you of some of the variety exhibited by the New Testament writers in their presentation of this conviction, and of the correspondingly impressive unity of their central agreement as to the uniqueness and finality of what God in Christ has done. I said that the Christian claim was that Jesus achieved by his death something of such potency as to embrace the whole of history, past and future. But the stress on the death in that very phrase 'achieved by his death' ought to remind us of some shades of difference in the way that achievement is described. For sometimes the spotlight is indeed sharply focused on the death itself. Here for instance are passages in which the cross is the focus of redemption: 'We proclaim Christ crucified, to the Jews a cause for stumbling, and to the Greeks folly, but to those who are summoned, whether Jews or Greeks, Christ the power of God and the wisdom of God' (1 Cor. 1.23); '... but now he has reconciled you in his physical body through his death' (Col. 1.22; cf. Eph. 2.16); '... who himself carried away our sins in his body to the cross' (1 Pet. 2.24). Sometimes, on the other hand, the stress is on the resurrection: 'If Christ has not been raised, your faith is futile: you are still in your sins' (1 Cor. 15.17); 'All praise to the God and Father of our Lord Jesus Christ, who of his great mercy has begotten us anew into a living hope through the resurrection of Jesus Christ from among the dead!' (1 Pet. 1.3). In fact, however, taking the larger context into account, salvation is seen as really the two together in an inseparable unity.[3] 'The New Testament as a whole', wrote Gore (1901, p. 258), 'refuses to allow us to separate the death from the life to which it leads up.' But it remains true that these varieties of approach or emphasis do exist. Sometimes, again, it is the whole incarnation rather than its culmination in the death and resurrection which is viewed as the decisive act. And again, when the death in particular is considered, it is sometimes in ritual terms as the perfect cleansing sacrifice; at other times rather as the great outgoing act of personal generosity, as of a Father giving himself to reconcile his children. Readers will have already recognized in these latter allusions various types of writing within the New Testament – the Epistle to the Hebrews, of which Professor Alexander Nairne said that it met the need of those who feel the stain rather than the chain of sin, the Pauline epistles ('God was in Christ reconciling the world unto himself'), the Johannine writings ('In him was life . . .')

Take first the primarily sacerdotal, sacrificial approach. The Synoptic Gospels, of course, give us the two great sacrificial sayings of Jesus – 'his life a ransom for many' and the words of institution; but in this matter of the finality of that sacrifice, they have a further startling thing to say. They say that at the expiring cry of Jesus the veil of the Temple was torn in two:[4] that is to say, something terrific, something decisive happened to the centre of worship in Judaism. I find it difficult to believe that any of the Evangelists thought that that literally happened. Friends of mine with whom I have discussed this are prepared to believe that St Mark did take it to be a literal fact. If so, I can only think that this Mark was remote from the ways of Judaism. Can you conceive of so shattering an event passing without stir or comment? But whether or not the Evangelists believed that it happened literally, at all events what they describe was a symbol of something dramatically new and revolutionary in the relations between God and man: a quite new way of approach – an open access to God. Sacerdotally speaking, approach to God had hitherto been by specially prescribed means – the manipulation by the accredited priests of the blood of animal victims. Now (for this seems to be what the symbol of the rent veil is saying)[5] the way into the inner sanctum stands open; and that, because a Jew named Jesus from the Galilean town of Nazareth had died on a cross outside Jerusalem on a spring day in about AD 30.

So far these Gospels. The writer to the Hebrews, intensely concerned with the finality of the work of God in Christ and with its contrast with the incompleteness of the Levitical system, seized hold of that tradition about the rending of the veil, and wrought it in his poetical way into a highly charged, allusive symbol. The way into the sanctuary, he says, was not yet opened (9.8) during the previous era. But now, 'brethren ... we have confidence to enter the sanctuary by the blood of Jesus, by the new and living way which he opened for us through the curtain, that is, through his flesh' (10.19f., RSV). I know that Westcott maintained that we should translate 'a new and living way through the veil – that is the way of his flesh', dissociating the veil from his flesh. But, although one differs from Westcott at one's peril, this does seem to be one of the points at which the weight of New Testament scholarship had tended against him. The veil, the curtain, the writer seems to be saying, was in a manner of speaking Christ's own body. In one sense, indeed, the incarnation is the bridge between heaven and earth. But it is not until Christ's body is pierced and torn upon the cross that the curtain is ripped down and a new way opened into God's presence – access via that human person who was put to death.

And this tremendous fact – the final abolition of the barrier – corresponds with the complete supersession of all the apparatus of approach that went with it. (In passing we may remind ourselves that this supersession is viewed in Eph. 2.14f. as having led to the abolition of that other barrier, the wall of legal observance[6] which separated Jew from Gentile.) Once access is open to God without the limited apparatus of approach, the way is equally open for the Gentile believer. But to return to the writer to the Hebrews, the animal victims of the Levitical system, he says, could at best never be more than a repeated reminder of our need, a symbol of man's conviction that, guilty, he needed some remedy for his guilt:

> For since the law has but a shadow of the good things to come instead of the true form of these realities, it can never, by the same sacrifices which are continually offered year after year, make perfect those who draw near. Otherwise, would they not have ceased to be offered? If the worshippers had once been cleansed, they would no longer have any consciousness of sin. But in these sacrifices there is a reminder of sin year after year. For it is impossible that the blood of bulls and goats should take away sins. (10.1–4, RSV)

The very fact that sacrifices were constantly repeated bore witness to their inability to be finally efficacious: the repetition of sacrifice is its own indictment.[7] And it is in contrast to this that the writer describes Christ's sacrifice. The animal victims were ineffective gestures. The very essence of Christ's self-offering is that it is once and for all. If it had not been effective absolutely it would have had to be repeated. But it is in fact final. As soon as he comes who instead of offering an animal victim offers himself, body and will, forthwith a new era opens and the old is outmoded:

> Consequently, when Christ came into the world, he said,
>> 'Sacrifices and offerings thou hast not desired,
>> but a body hast thou prepared for me;
>> in burnt offerings and sin-offerings hast thou taken no pleasure.
>> Then I said, "Lo, I have come to do thy will, O God,"
>> as it is written of me in the roll of the book.'
> When he said above, 'Thou hast neither desired nor taken pleasure in sacrifice and offerings and burnt offerings and sin-offerings' (these are offered according to the law), then he added, 'Lo, I have come to do thy will'. He abolishes the first in order to establish the second. And by that will we have been consecrated through the offering of the body of Jesus Christ once for all. And every priest stands daily at his service, offering repeatedly the same sacrifices, which can

never take away sins. But when Christ had offered for all time a single sacrifice for sins, he sat down at the right hand of God, then to wait until his enemies should be made a stool for his feet. For by a single offering he has perfected for all time those who are consecrated. And the Holy Spirit also bears witness to us; for after saying,

'This is the covenant that I will make with them
after those days, says the Lord:
I will put my laws on their hearts,
and write them on their minds,'
then he adds,
'I will remember their sins and their misdeeds no more.'
Where there is forgiveness of these, there is no longer any offering for sin. (10.5–18, RSV)

The same kind of language is also used by 1 Peter. Verses 2.21ff. admittedly, use the language of Isa. 53 which is not so clearly sacrificial in the Levitical sense. 'Aνήνεγκεν means 'removed', I think, rather than 'sustained' (still less, 'offered'). Indeed I doubt if the idea of redemption by sheer 'sustaining' is anywhere to be found in the New Testament. But 1 Pet. 1.2, 19, 3.18–20 are in the same sacerdotal cast and there is the same affirmation of finality with an implied contrast to the repetitive nature of the Levitical offerings: it is ἅπαξ, once for all. But as soon as one begins to inquire upon what grounds the efficacy of Christ's sacrifice is recognized as final, immediately, I think, one begins to move out from the sacerdotal analogies into something bigger still. It is not enough to say merely that the sacrifice of Jesus was perfect, for in sacrificial terminology 'perfect' simply means conforming precisely to the Levitical requirements, and for this a perfect sheep or bullock might do. No: the moment one gets off mere analogy and asks a basic Why? one is transported into the great realm of the dealings of a personal God with his children. The answer to the question why Christ's sacrifice is effective in contrast to the Levitical victims is twofold. First, that it is the offering not of a reluctant beast but of a voluntarily surrendered human personality. That is very clearly expressed in the passage we have just read in Heb. 10: it is an offering of willing obedience. But not a few noble men had already offered such a sacrifice – notably the Maccabaean martyrs, who are evidently in the writer's mind at the end of Chapter 11. The obedient self-offering of a personality was not a unique event. What is it, then, that marks out Christ's self-giving as a full, perfect and sufficient sacrifice? The answer to this second question is in Christology. Christ is a priest of an eternal order offering the eternally valid sacrifice:

> The former priests were many in number, because they were prevented by death from continuing in office; but he holds his priesthood permanently, because he continues for ever. Consequently he is able for all time to save those who draw near to God through him, since he always lives to make intercession for them. For it was fitting that we should have such a high priest, holy, blameless, unstained, separated from sinners, exalted above the heavens. He has no need, like those high priests, to offer sacrifices daily, first for his own sins and then for those of the people; he did this once for all when he offered up himself. Indeed, the law appoints men in their weakness as high priests, but the word of the oath, which came later than the law, appoints a Son who has been made perfect forever. (Heb. 7.23–end, RSV, with paragraphing omitted)

Thus, Christ is both perfect and representative Man and also the eternal Son of God. And this act of will is therefore not only the one perfect response of Humanity to the will of God but also it is the will of God going out to man in yearning love. This writer uses the term Mediator, I think, only metaphorically: Jesus is the negotiator of a new covenant (8.6, 12.24; cf. 7.22). But he might well have used it Christologically, as it is used in 1 Tim. 2.5. Christ is for him both the Man and the eternal effulgence of God's glory. That is why he bridges the gap between man and God. That is why in him acceptance is complete. That is why through his torn body, surrendered in obedience to God's love for those who tore it, the way lies open for access.

Thus almost unwittingly we have been lifted off the analogical level of ritual acts on to the level of personal dealings; and Son is the term that marks the transition. We find Jesus as representative man fulfilling that destiny of obedience and harmony with God from which Adam by transgression fell. And here we are immediately in touch also with the thinking of St Paul. Indeed there is a striking parallel between Heb. 2 and Phil. 2.6ff. In Heb. 2 the ideal for man, described in Psalm 8, is contrasted with man's present sorry state of defeat and frustration. But, says the writer, there is one in whom we see man's destiny completely realised – Jesus who because of his obedience in death has been crowned with the glory and honour due to man.[8] In Phil. 2 similarly we find the pre-existent one coming and wholly sharing the lot of man, obedient absolutely, even to the very limit of death itself; and accordingly realizing the destiny of glory which is God's design. It is, as has often been suggested, a reversal of Adam's pride and fall. This, in contrast to the story of the Fall, is humility and exaltation – and that, on behalf of all mankind. I believe also that Phil. 2.6ff. is virtually a Son of Man passage. Here is the eclipsed and suffering Son of Man (σχήματι εὑρεθεὶς ὡς ἀνθρώπος, 'being found in human form', RSV) ultimately vindicated and exalted (as in the clouds of heaven) and given the title of Lord.

But now that we are on Pauline territory, let us take one step back and then one step further forward. Stepping back, we can notice that St Paul, no less than the writer to the Hebrews, is capable of viewing the incarnation in terms of a new dispensation – a superseding of the old. The era of 'faith' succeeds that of 'law'; man 'comes of age'; Christ is both the goal and the end of the old era (Gal. 3.23—4.7; and Rom. 10.4). The step forward is into a kind of explanation of forgiveness in terms of the unique event. For we have looked at the finality of the death of Christ in terms of the absolute sacrifice, superseding all the victims of the Levitical law. We have seen also how Jesus, as perfect man, is man rendering obedience to God; and how, as the Son of God, he is also God working in man for reconciliation. And now we can add that he is the final explanation (so far as that word applies to such mysteries at all) of forgiveness. There was full recognition of the fact of forgiveness in the Old Testament, not only in the sacrificial system which, nominally at least, only applied for the most part to ritual sins, but in the plain straightforward proclamation of pardon. David said 'I have sinned against the Lord'; Nathan said

'The Lord also hath put away thy sin'. 'The sacrifices of God', says the Psalmist, 'are a broken spirit.' God's free forgiveness had often been proclaimed before the incarnation. The free graciousness of God was no new idea. But it was proclaimed unexplained, in uneasy tension with the conviction of God's righteousness. How could it be, when you came to think of it, that the holy and righteous God could forgive? That was an absolutely insoluble problem until it was seen that the holy God himself met the sin, accepted its entail, entered into its costliness, suffered redemptively in his own Son. Then at last it became clear – however mysterious and unsearchable God's ways must always remain to us – that here was no overlooking of guilt or trifling with forgiveness; no external treatment of sin, but a radical, a drastic, a passionate and absolutely final acceptance of the terrible situation, and an absorption by the very God himself of the fatal disease so as to neutralize it effectively:

> ... whom God put forward as an expiation by his blood, to be received by faith. This was to show God's righteousness, because in his divine forbearance he had passed over former sins; it was to prove at the present time that he himself is righteous and that he justifies him who has faith in Jesus. (Rom. 3.25f., RSV)

There for once St Paul does step aside from his essentially activist, practical preaching of the fact of salvation, to say a word about its how and why. And his explanation turns on the finality and uniqueness of Christ. For a different purpose, and in quite a different context, the absolute priority of the Son over creation is linked in Colossians also with the finality of his salvation – the new creation: 'He is ... the first-born of all creation; ... the first-born from the dead ...' (Col. 1.15, 18, RSV). He is uniquely Man – 'Adam' is applicable to Christ in a new and absolute sense (1 Cor. 15.45). The Man Christ Jesus: here is the heart of the mystery. Whatever angle you approach it from, you always reach this centre: in Jesus God is at work uniquely, with incomparable intensity. The incarnation is something absolute and final because of its unique quality: an act of creation only comparable to God's initial creation.

The Johannine writings, in their own special idiom, tell the same story. The Word of God is manifested in some degree in all God's creation. But when the Word became flesh and dwelt among us that was the crowning, the unique event: we beheld his glory, the glory as of the only begotten of the Father – the Father's unique Son – full of grace and truth. That is the Pauline πρωτότοκος, first-born, set in an even wider context of thought. This unique Word of God, the convergence of all God's words, this life and light and love absolute, this Son who is subject to the Father and, by virtue of this subjection, one with him: he it is alone who at the crown of his achievement, reigning from the tree, can cry the τετέλεσται, 'it is finished'. And although very broadly it may be true that whereas for St Paul Christ saves by his death, for the Fourth Evangelist it is by his life, yet for the Fourth Evangelist too the death is the decisive thing. The Good Shepherd lays down his life; 'I if I be lifted up . . .'; 'except a grain of wheat fall into the ground and die . . .'

We need not labour the finality of Jesus of Nazareth further: it is clear enough, though many more examples might be quoted. Sometimes in a deliberately theological way, sometimes as though it were narrative – a 'documentary' – the 'scandal of particularity' is ruthlessly forced upon us by the New Testament wherever we turn. Even if in the most theological of the Gospels it is said that Abraham rejoiced to see Christ's day, yet it is still that Christ who is uniquely manifested under Pontius Pilate. It is this Lamb alone who removes the sin of the whole world; he alone whose death is to be available for the whole world. It will be for the next section to inquire how, despite this anchorage in time, the saving work of God also runs continuously through history like a perennial stream of blessing.

But meanwhile, one further observation. If we speak in terms of sacraments, it is baptism which provides the 'focus' for this once-and-for-all aspect of redemption. Both baptism and the Holy Communion are sacraments of the death of Christ; but baptism especially represents the finality and unrepeatability of it. For any one individual it is once and for all in a life. It is the sacrament *par excellence* of the once-and-for-allness of salvation. As Christ's incarnation, his death, burial and resurrection, are the world's baptism (as recent writers have been reminding us)[9] so each person's baptism is the point of contact with that final achievement. Hence, of course, the problem of post-baptismal sin which may have begun to show itself in Heb. 6 and 10; though for my part I believe that, at least in Chapter 10, the Eucharist also can be detected, and that the crux is not post-baptismal sin as such, but apostasy – changing sides from that of the Crucified to that of the crucifiers.

To that passage we shall have occasion to return later, if only for a moment and for another purpose. For the present, we break the matter off on this unresolved chord – the separateness, the finality, the stark uniqueness of the incarnation: the centrality for all Christian thinking of the Jesus of history.

The Work of Christ Continuing

In the last section we were reminded of the striking unanimity of the New Testament regarding the finality and uniqueness of God's work in Jesus Christ – a unanimity the more striking because of the obvious differences of approach in the various writers, and their freedom from dogmatic regimentation. Nothing could be clearer than that the Christian gospel refuses, as long as it is true to itself, to surrender this 'scandal of particularity'. Once and for all at a given time in history God visited and redeemed his people. Nothing can add to the completeness and finality of that declaration.

And yet it is more than a declaration. That is an axiom for Christians and it carries important corollaries. It is the approach of the living God – the personal approach of the living God – to man. And a personal approach to persons is by its very nature something which cannot be confined within a statement, or limited to a proposition. St Paul may, on a rare occasion, step aside contemplatively (as we have seen) to say that the death of Christ, as one with God, explains how God was able to forgive: it was because he was that sort of character – one who was ready to suffer, one who deals realistically with sin, not (as it might have appeared) passing it over, but sacrificially expiating. But much more commonly St Paul, like the other writers of the New Testament, is concerned with the practice, not the rationale, of evangelism: with the gospel as power rather than as demonstration: not with explaining so much as with applying the gospel. For it is the power of God leading to salvation – leading, that is, to total soundness, completeness and integrity of personality. Like the miracles of Jesus, it is more than a manifestation: it is a deed of power.

If, then, the gospel is more than a declaration, if it is something which we do not merely know about but experience, essentially God's action to reconcile estranged man to himself, then it follows that the uniqueness and finality of his action in Jesus Christ is not the uniqueness of discontinuity, nor the finality of a dead and static thing. There can never be an end absolutely to this reconciliation, for it is the living God at work and it is part and parcel of the fellowship which issues from his work and in which it is perpetuated. And thus it was that the physical body of Christ, given up to death and raised from death, brought with it that fellowship which we call the Church, the Body of Christ. 'Destroy this temple, and in three days I will raise it up again.' He spake of the temple of his body. And in a sense, too, the Church was continuous with the People of God of the old dispensation. The unique incarnation, for all its uniqueness and finality, is found to be the centre of history – not discontinuous; a great flowing stream, not a separate draught of water; the apex of a pyramid, not an unattached point in mid-air. Or, better, it is the point of intersection of the two lines which, narrowing as the faithful remnant showed itself to be a minority, and converging to vanishing point when the remnant came to be one perfect Man, yet diverge again as that one Man becomes the growing point of a new society.

Final, absolute, unique; yet not static nor discontinuous. No diagram that one can invent to represent the position of Jesus in history can detach him from it. Here is a profoundly important matter for a doctrine of the Church; and it is part of the universally agreed doctrine of the Person of Christ. If in any sense the incarnation is continuous with the People of God before it, then in some sense redemption must be continued in the Church after it. What does this mean?

As we stand on the brink of great doctrines, easily perverted into great heresies, let us with childlike simplicity recall ourselves to that most perfectly drawn of human analogies, the story of the prodigal son, to use it simply as a picture of the reciprocal quality of reconciliation. In trying to find my way through matters which are too difficult for me, I constantly take refuge in this human analogy. And such refuge, I think, is not a retreat from reality. On the contrary, it provides a salutary touchstone of our soundness. For after all, there are no higher, no profounder categories known to us than the personal; and the reconciliation of a son by and to a father provides surer terms than the most elaborate sub-personal analogies of ransom, bond or sacrifice, or the most abstruse abstracts of metaphysics, however valuable they are as contributory explanation. What then can we find in this homely analogy that may help us in relating God's once-and-for-all to our repetitive needs? The father's act of running out to meet his returning penitent is datable and tangible, and to that extent complete. We could say, that is the spot in the road where they met; here they flung their arms round one another, here the tears fell. It was at such and such a time, on such and such a day. Done! Once and for all that reconciliation had taken place. The boy could see, as he looked at his father, what suffering had gone into that reconciling love, how costly it had been. But it is done; and there is joy unspeakable. What is more, it is done by the father's forthgoing initiative. The son came home, true; but the father it was who alone could initiate the offer of restoration.

Yet no reconciliation is one-sided. Because it is between persons, not automatic, not mechanical, it has to be both received and reciprocated. The son progressively responds. First the amazement – the difficulty in believing it; then the gradual acceptance, the picking up of loose threads, the recovery of lost ground: a process. And then, the sorest test of all; the resentful, censorious elder brother. His attitude is so easily intelligible, and yet so hard to accept. Psychologically we can easily understand that outraged elder brother's feelings; but how difficult the younger brother is going to find it to accept him, and make allowance for him, and forgive him. Here is the test: can the younger brother sacrificially enter into his father's conciliatory attitude? Can he align his will with his father's will for the wholeness of the family? Can he humbly accept censure, gently meet coldness with love, win and woo and accept the pain? In a sense it all depends now on him. Once and for all, the father's attitude speaks reconciliation: can the younger brother cast away his *amour-propre* into that great pool of love and self-giving, and throw in his lot with this reconciling power? The family's completion depends on that. If the parable, originally, in all likelihood, about pious and self-righteous Jews in contrast to the disreputable, came soon to be applied to Jewish Christians over against Gentiles welcomed into the Church, it became poignant indeed: can Gentiles in their new-found access to God – such as we were considering in the previous chapter – be sacrificially gentle and understanding towards their resentful elder brothers in Christ?

I need not pursue the analogy: you see the point. Acceptance of forgiveness and transmission of it – these are not merely addenda to the Father's reconciling love. However much the initiative is his, yet these, too, are a part of it. The process is a living, personal, organic one and must be a growing and expanding – a continually expanding – one. That helps us, I think, to read Col. 1.24 with understanding. St Paul rejoices that his sufferings help to complete what is lacking of the afflictions of Christ. This seems to mean two things. First, that the Christian's sufferings (in this case the Apostle's) are a share in Christ's sufferings, because the Christian and Christ are somehow connected. To be in Christ is of course to share Christ's sufferings, and there are always more of them in the future for each of us. Secondly it means that there is a quota of sufferings which the whole Church, the corporate Christ, has to exhaust before God's plan of salvation is complete; and the Apostle rejoices to take his share – or more than his share – of these. Thus 'the afflictions of Christ' are both Christ's historical sufferings, mystically shared and entered into in each Christian's sufferings, and the corporate Christ's, the Christian Church's afflictions. The two are in that sense one. There is plenty of evidence that the Christians took over the Jewish apocalyptic idea of the messianic woes; and there was a certain quota of these to be completed before the end could come. So the afflictions of the (corporate) Christ, the messianic community, were a necessary prelude to the consummation, and their endurance was cause for rejoicing. But also

155

there is the more mystical conception of sharing Christ's Cross. A. R. George, in his admirable book *Communion with God in the New Testament* (1953, p. 184), says:

> Paul does not mean merely that the Christian experiences the sufferings of Christ after Him in thought, imagination, or sympathy, nor merely that his own actual sufferings are endured with Christ or for the sake of Christ (though all these ideas are present), but that *his own actual sufferings are a real participation in Christ's sufferings, suffered by virtue of his communion with Christ.* (My italics.)

In any case, the Church has more to suffer. The corporate Christ's afflictions have yet to be completed. But in no case does the incompleteness lie in the divine power or source of redemption – only in the accepting, entering into, implementing, and transmitting of it. The prodigal son is called upon to respond; the family has to enter into the realization of the reparation. This seems to be the sense – a carefully safeguarded and qualified sense – in which Christ's sacrifice can be spoken of as constantly renewed. And we are bound to add that the sufferings of those who lived before Christ must also be gathered up and reckoned in the process. If the Church's sufferings are in this sense a sharing of Christ's sacrifice, so are Israel's sufferings an anticipation of it. If the Eucharist is in any sense a sacrifice related to Calvary, so was the obedience of Abraham. Since Christ is the centre of history and, though a real individual, is yet more than an individual, he gathers up into himself all the God-ward activities of all his people and creatures, past, present and future: he is one with mankind and with creation.

We have now returned from the consideration of the reciprocal nature of redemption to the question of Christ and the Trinity. I often revert in this connection to Helen Waddell's story of Peter Abelard (1933). Abelard and Thibault hear a sudden cry. It is a poor little rabbit in a trap, and when they reach it, they are just too late.

> It lay for a moment breathing quickly, then in some blind recognition of the kindness that had met it at the last, the small head thrust and nestled against his arm, and it died.

It was that last confiding thrust that broke Abelard's heart. He looked down at the little draggled body, his mouth shaking. 'Thibault,' he said, 'do you think there is a God at all? Whatever has come to me, I earned it. But what did this one do?'

Thibault nodded.

'I know,' he said. 'Only – I think God is in it too.'

Abelard looked up sharply.

'In it? Do you mean that it makes Him suffer, the way it does us?'

Again Thibault nodded.

'Then why doesn't He stop it?'

'I don't know,' said Thibault. 'Unless – unless it's like the Prodigal Son. I suppose the father could have kept him at home against his will. But what would have been the use? All this', he stroked the limp body, 'is because of us. But all the time God suffers. More than we do.'

Abelard looked at him, perplexed.

'Thibault, when did you think of all this?'

Thibault's face stiffened. 'It was that night,' he said, his voice strangled. 'The things we did to – to poor Guibert. He –' Thibault stopped. 'I could not sleep for nights and nights. And then I saw that God suffered too. And I thought I would like to be a priest.'

'Thibault, do you mean Calvary?'

Thibault shook his head. 'That was only a piece of it – the piece that we saw – in time. Like that.' He pointed to a fallen tree beside them, sawn through the middle. 'That dark ring there, it goes up and down the whole length of the tree. But you only see it where it is cut across. That is what Christ's life was; the bit of God that we saw. And we think God is like that, because Christ was like that, kind, and forgiving sins and healing people. We think God is like that for ever, because it happened once, with Christ. But not the pain. Not the agony at the last. We think that stopped.'

Abelard looked at him, the blunt nose and the wide mouth, the honest troubled eyes. He could have knelt before him.

'Then, Thibault,' he said slowly, 'you think that all this,' he looked down at the little quiet body in his arms, 'all the pain of the world, was Christ's cross?'

'God's cross,' said Thibault. 'And it goes on.'

'The Patripassian heresy,' muttered Abelard mechanically. 'But, oh God, if it were true. Thibault, it must be. At least, there is something at the back of it that is true. And if we could find it – it would bring back the whole world.' (pp. 289ff.)

No doubt there *is* heresy there if it is stated without counterbalance; but there is more than 'something at the back of it that is true'. Here we have been driven again to face one of the most arresting and important of all Christological terms, the inclusive Christ as the Second Adam, the New Man, the beginning of God's new creation. That Jesus was a man, not merely mankind, has been strenuously and rightly re-affirmed by the late Dr D. Baillie (1948): he protested against the depersonalization of calling Christ 'Man' instead of 'a man' – 'Humanity' rather than an individual, Jesus of Nazareth (pp. 86f.). That I am sure is right. But the fact remains that if to call Christ Humanity is to call him by too abstract a term, to limit him to an individual is equally to fail to do justice to the facts. For his individuality is somehow inclusive: he is representative Man; he includes mankind and in fact fulfils the destiny of man, as those New Testament writers saw who applied to Jesus the ideal picture of man in Psalm 8, and who likened him to Adam. Therefore Christ's obedience is man's obedience. And if man, as a result, begins to obey, that may be called Christ's obedience in man. There *is*, then, a continuity in some sense between Christ and man, and between man's obedience derived from Christ's, and Christ's perfect, underived holiness.

And this real element of continuity may help to explain the sense in which, elsewhere in the New Testament, terms of intercession are used of the atoning work of Christ. We must think more about this in the next section, but meanwhile we recall that in Rom. 8.27, 34 the Spirit and Christ are said to plead for us; in Heb. 7.25 the Great High Priest lives continually to make intercession; in John 14—16 the Spirit is our Paraclete or Vindicator, and so, in 1 John 2.1, is Christ again. The work of

Christ – God's work of reconciliation in him – achieved once and for all, is, so to speak, a standing intercession, for it is Man as he ought to be. Its efficacy remains continually active, just as the father's act of welcome to the returning Prodigal Son – a single and datable act, but one which was only the 'focal' point of a long-formed character and constant activity – is a standing intercession (if you like), all the time realistically facing sin's entail, saying all the time 'It was meet that we should make merry and be glad: for this my son was dead and is alive again, he was lost and is found.' The father's character is the real continuum. He is that sort of father: that is why reconciliation can take place. God is a self-incarnating God: that is how man is related to him.

Thus the one, final, definitive act of God in Jesus Christ is also his continuous act. It is, in terms of Greek grammar, like the combining of an aorist tense – he saved us, ἔσωσεν, with a resultant perfect – we are saved, σεσωσμένοι, and, indeed, with a present tense of process – we are being saved, σωζόμενοι. But Christ is never, I think, actually spoken of as continuing to suffer with us (unless you count Heb. 4.15, 'we have not a high priest who is unable to sympathize with our weaknesses' – and even there the past is prominent – 'but one who ... has been tempted').[10] Still less is he described as offering himself or being offered again, or as being crucified with us or dying with us. St Paul is crucified with Christ; but in the only place in the New Testament where recrucifixion of Christ is mentioned (Heb. 6.6) it is a description of apostasy, not (as such) of the work of redemption. Yet, because we are incorporated in Christ, the work of salvation is in a sense actually continuing among us: it is not ours, but it is Christ's in us. That is what is meant perhaps by his continued intercession.

Thus the Church is not the source of salvation, but it is the transmitter of salvation and the sphere in which God's saving work continues. It is not strictly speaking the extension of the incarnation, for incarnation by long usage means God's fulness, πλήρωμα, in flesh; and the Church, although indwelt by God the Holy Spirit, is not all-divine as an incarnation on that showing must be, any more than the great men and prophets before Christ, though indwelt by God, were incarnations. Or else, if God be called incarnate in the prophets, then *a fortiori* the Church is the extension of the incarnation; but then the moment we say this and use 'incarnate' so, we are blurring precisely that uniqueness of Christ which was the theme of the previous section. We must not try to have it both ways in our use of 'incarnation'. Not yet does God's fulness, his πλήρωμα reside in us as it does in Christ; the Church is not co-equal with God as Christ is; there is no absolute *communicatio idiomatum* between Christ and his Body the Church. Thus it seems to me impossible fully to identify an act of obedience in a Christian (including his participation in the sacrament of obedience) with the absolute and perfect act of obedience by God incarnate in Christ. Each Christian act of obedience is indeed Christ's obedience in us; but not therefore identifiable with his own one-hundred-per-cent obedience in his own person. Hence Dr C. H. Dodd's phrase 'in solidarity with him we have died and risen again' seems more faithful to the New Testament than Dr E. F. Scott's 'a repetition in the believer of Christ's death and resurrection'.[11] It is that the believer is present at Christ's death rather than that Christ is present at his: Paul taught not so much that the believer *repeats* Christ's experience, as that he is *with Christ* in Christ's experience.

But on any showing Christ is closely concerned in the activity of his Church: the Church's sufferings are his. And the Church, if not fully an incarnation, is destined to grow up in all things into Christ's full stature, and who can say what may not some day be? Is it possible (one shrinks from so daring a speculation) that the Church of today may be to the Church of the End – the coming Great Church – what the prophets of Israel were to Christ? Is it that one day God will become incarnate again, but this time not as a perfect individual, Jesus of Nazareth, but as his Holy Spirit incarnate in the perfect society, the Bride? Is that the Day of the Lord?[12]

The Eucharistic Sacrifice

In the two preceding sections I have tried to formulate successively, first the Christian conviction of the absolute uniqueness and finality of what God incarnate in Christ had done, and second the equally strong conviction that in a sense that final and completed act is yet being implemented in the life of the

Church which is the Body of Christ. The body of his flesh is so related to his Body the Church that the Church's afflictions are the implementing of his Passion under Pontius Pilate. And indeed the afflictions of the Old Testament people of God – and of the true and upright everywhere – must in some way be woven into the texture of that Passion. Though unique, it is not altogether discontinuous, just as Christ himself, while unique, was not discontinuous with the Law and the Prophets before him. God incarnate in the form of an individual man is somehow related to God dwelling corporately within a society, though an incarnation (using that word in the stricter, narrower sense) of this corporate sort has never yet been seen. Perhaps it is yet to come.

Baptism, as I said, is the sacrament *par excellence* of the once-and-for-all finality: it stands for the finished work of Christ as it is applied to each individual's life. Holy Communion, so far as it may be contrasted with baptism, is different in precisely this respect that it essentially represents repetition. Within any given individual's life, there can be no repetition of baptism. Where there is sacramental repetition of the gospel, it is in the Eucharist. Thus, of the two, the Eucharist is the more particularly connected with our second theme – the implementing, the repetition, the continuation. And, the mode of this continuation being a theologically difficult matter, it is hardly surprising if Holy Communion has, alas, become the battleground on which many a champion of one insight or another has fought desperately against the opposite. That, no doubt, is partly due, not only to sheer sin and selfishness, but also to our inevitable human limitations which make it almost impossible to get one part of the truth sharply into focus without finding that the remainder looks blurred and repellent and arouses our antagonism.

> Ever since the sixteenth century, [wrote the late Dom Gregory Dix (1945, pp. 613f.)] we Anglicans have been so divided over eucharistic doctrine, and we are today so conscious of our divisions, that there is scarcely any statement that could be made about either the eucharist or our own rite which would not seem to some of one's fellow churchmen to call for immediate contradiction on

conscientious grounds. It is quite understandable. These things go deep behind us. Two archbishops of Canterbury have lost their lives and a third his see, in these quarrels. One king has been beheaded and another dethroned; many lesser men have suffered all manner of penalties from martyrdom downwards on one side and another. These things have left their traces, tangling and confusing our own approach to the matter in all sorts of irrelevant ways. Besides the conscious inheritance of differential intellectual and doctrinal positions from the past, and inextricably mingled with it, is another inherited world of unconscious misunderstandings, prejudices, assumptions, suspicions, which are only accidentally bound up with theological terms and which yet come into play instantly and secretly and quite irrationally with their use. To spring the word 'transubstantiation' on the company without preparation in certain circles (or the names 'Tyburn' or 'Barnes' in others) is to invite a reaction which springs much more from emotion than from reason.

So we need not, perhaps we must not, agonize over much about the sin of dissension on such holy ground, sinful though it is. And at least we can give wholehearted thanks for the privileges of the present generation, in which the Spirit of God is putting into our hands instruments for mutual understanding such as our fathers never possessed. In view of this, I hope you will agree that we can profitably consider so controversial a matter as the meaning of the eucharistic Sacrifice without violating the devotional attitude appropriate to it: indeed, pray God, it will be for the deepening of our devotion.

I venture to ask, then, at the outset: do we sacrifice at all in Holy Communion? Is this a sacrifice we are performing? I have tried in my own thinking to reckon with Dr E. L. Mascall (1953), and through him with De la Taille (1930) and Vonier (1925). But I am not attempting now to argue the matter scholastically. All I am going to try to do is to explain my convictions and why I hold them, as a contribution simply to mutual understanding. This is just an individual thinking aloud, for what it is worth, in the company (as he hopes) of friends, even if at points they will think differently. You will remember the comments I cited in the first section. One of them urged the importance of emphasizing the fact that at a Eucharist the Church offers the whole of the material world to be dedicated to the service of God – all that the offertory procession expresses. Another stressed the aspect of pleading – pleading before God the efficacy of Christ's sacrifice. A third wished to wipe out all idea of sacrifice, except in the sense that the worshippers, receiving the benefits of Christ's once-and-for-all sacrifice, then offer themselves in devotion as response. We could have multiplied voices, conflicting, complementary, modifying, at endless length. What then are we to say? What do we do at Holy Communion? Let me in part anticipate my own conclusions, and then discuss them a little.

We do offer sacrifice at Holy Communion. Starting from the less controversial, at least we offer (as the Prayer of Oblation explicitly says) the sacrifice of ourselves, our souls and bodies, of our praise and thanksgiving. The whole Church offers up her praise and her obedience to God; and with it (in the vein of Romans 8 and of all that is implied in the Christian doctrine of man) is offered the whole creation of which man is the representative: 'Man the High Priest of Nature'. The New Testament certainly uses terms of sacrifice for this offering of praise and obedience: Rom. 12.1; Heb. 13.15f.; 1 Pet. 2.5, are examples, and the Prayer of Oblation deliberately echoes such language.

But can we say more? Do we hereby offer up not only ourselves, but Christ's obedience, or rather does he through us offer up his own obedience? Well, any obedience which we can offer is imperfect, derived, secondary – a result only of Christ's perfect obedience; but, with these limitations and to that extent, it is Christ's obedience in us: in that sense, our sacrifice is Christ's sacrifice in us. *In that sense* who could deny that the Eucharist is Christ offering himself?

Yet, to my mind the New Testament's usage which we considered in the last section – as a rule distinguishing between what Christ did and what Christians do, reluctant to speak of Christ doing these things in us, far more ready to speak of our doing them in Christ, of our participating in Christ's sacrifice, and death, and life – is a pointer to the importance of maintaining the perspective in which the uniqueness and special nature

163

of Christ's perfect offering is clearly visible. I would therefore sooner speak of the Eucharist as a uniting of our offering with Christ's, and that in virtue, and as a result, of our first receiving from him the gift which he alone can offer.

But before we can get any further, it seems to me that one misconception must at this point be faced and cleared away. Priestly terms have frequently been used in our discussion – necessarily, since we are discussing New Testament doctrine, and terms of priesthood, sacrifice and intercession occur in the New Testament. But in what sense are these words to be understood? Not – let us be clear at the outset – in a propitiatory sense. The sacrifice of Christ was not, according to the New Testament, propitiatory – still less, then, is there anything propitiatory about any derived or related sacrifice of the Church. It is a grave misfortune that the misleading word 'propitiation' has got into the English Scriptures at Rom. 3.25 and 1 John 2.2, and so into the Prayer Book. It has been to my mind conclusively shown that the remarkable thing about the words ἱλαστήριος and ἱλασμός used in those verses is precisely that, whereas their secular use was indeed of propitiating an alienated deity or person, in the Bible generally, and certainly in the New Testament, the amazing revelation of God's redemptive dealings with man has spun the word round face-about, and has compelled it to have, as its object, not God but sin. It is not that Christ or man tries to propitiate God, but that God in Christ expiates sin: God – marvel of marvels – suffering in order to neutralize man's sin. The very initiative is God's: how then can God be said to be propitiated? He is the subject of the verb, no longer its object.

In the New Testament, then, the idea of a propitiating of God on any showing never comes into view. Terms of intercession or pleading are, it is true, associated with Jesus as though he had to plead man's cause before an alienated Judge. But can we possibly press even this figure in such a way as to allow that conclusion? In Romans 8.34 it does not look like it. In Hebrews it is of course bound up with the whole analogy of the Day of Atonement ritual, and, as we shall see, it is Christ's vindicated humanity which pleads. Thus it must be a vivid way of saying that what God incarnate has done is so realistic a dealing with sin that his morality is inviolate when he forgives us, when he clears the guilty. So in 1 John 2.2. We simply cannot allow these juridical terms – part of the apparatus of 'theodicy' – to drive a wedge between the Persons of the Trinity. If we use the figure, it must be held firmly as an internal dialogue – God's own self-sacrifice meeting his justice.

> The modern conception, [wrote Westcott in his great Commentary on Hebrews (1889, p. 230)] of Christ pleading in heaven His Passion, 'offering His blood' on behalf of men has no foundation in the Epistle. His glorified humanity is the eternal pledge of the absolute efficacy of His accomplished work. He pleads, as older writers truly expressed the thought, by His Presence on the Father's Throne.

I must add here that for myself I remain wholly unconvinced by the attempts to make the *anamnesis* ('this do in remembrance of me') mean that God is here reminded of what Christ has wrought: 'Do this to remind God of me.'[13] Reminding God of man's deserts is indeed a conception not absent from the Old Testament; but I cannot find room for it (or for the adapted form – reminding God of Christ's merits) in the New Testament. Nor do I think the linguistic arguments for doing so are at all persuasive.[14]

And all this is what makes me a little uncomfortable even with that familiar verse of Bright's extremely beautiful hymn already quoted:

> We here present, we here spread forth to thee
> That only offering perfect in thine eyes.

Of course it can be justified in terms of that internal dialogue within the Godhead – God's mercy pleading with his justice. It can be justified in terms of Christ's obedience being inherent in every act of man's obedience. But both because of my hesitation in identifying those two obediences, and because of my fear of propitiatory language, I feel a reluctance about such phrases.

At any rate, you will, I am sure, agree with me that it is vital to remove from our minds any crudely propitiatory conception of the sacrifice of Christ. Yet in the same breath we must now add that the realistic dealing with sin which I suppose it is the chief purpose of that language of propitiation, mistakenly so translated, and that language of vindication, to safeguard, is intensely important and as vividly present in the Eucharist as can be. Christ's glorified humanity, representing the costly obedience of mankind – God's own costly obedience to his own laws, incarnate in mankind – is of absolute efficacy. Nothing could be clearer than that the gospel, focused in the Lord's Supper, is a gospel of God's final and effective and infinitely sacrificial and costly dealing with sin: a gospel of obedience to the will of God achieved within man, sin's entail met in man by maintaining perfect obedience in the face of the worst that man's sin could do.

But is this obedient humanity? Is not this the point at which we return to the question of our offering at the Eucharist? It is true, admittedly, that never except in Jesus Christ has mankind assumed its proper attitude of obedience to the Father; and that it is through this obedience of the perfect Man alone that sinful humanity can approach the Father. Or, putting it in unitarian terms, it is through the divine Father's initiative alone that we, the prodigal sons, can come back into our Father's home, and through no merit of our own. Yet, as we have been at pains to see, some active response is necessary. Unless, in the parable, the father's initiative and gracious for-giveness so move the son that he responds with all the obedience at his command – wholeheartedly so far as his heart is his to give – he cannot in the nature of the case come in; or at any rate he cannot stay inside the home. Unless his obedience is laid on the altar with the father's sacrificial love, there is small hope of the elder brother being won. In short, it is in fellowship with the father – in a union of will with him – that the son (still speaking in terms of the parable, not in trinitarian terms of the Persons of the Godhead) can be his true self and make his contri-bution to the wholeness of the family. And it is in communion with God in Jesus Christ that we are caught up into his work. The key to any understanding that may be given us of what happens when man is born into God's activity in Jesus Christ is this κοινωνία, 'fellowship',[15] this being ἐν Χριστῷ, 'in Christ'. Our own obedience is at best a derived, imperfect obedience. But in union with Christ's perfect obedience it is offered to God; and may it not be said that every imperfect offering of our obedience is both derived from, and again joined in the stream of Christ's obedient love which flows continually to the

Father? For it is a stream of continuous flowing; and one of our difficulties is precisely that, in rightly affirming the unique and once-and-for-all nature of Christ's offering, we yet have to find some way of doing justice to its continued movement: the tree-trunk is sawn through only at one particular point; yet the marks which it there reveals in fact run continuously throughout its length. It is this dilemma, the dilemma of man as the Great Amphibian, living in history, yet aware of the beyond, that Dom Gregory Dix (1945) so clearly illuminated, when he showed that, when once the redemptive action was limited to the cross, then the Eucharist had to be conceived of either as in some way a repetition or iteration of the redeeming act of Christ, or else, with the Reformers (who stressed the finality of the cross), as only a remembering of the past:

[T]he practical confining of the redeeming action of Christ (into which the eucharist enters) to Calvary [he wrote] led to serious and unnecessary difficulties. Being wholly within history and time, the passion is wholly in the past – the only moment of redemption which is so wholly confined to the past. The church at the eucharist can only be conceived to enter into a wholly past action in one of two ways, either purely *mentally* by remembering or imagining it; or else, if the entering into it is to have any objective reality outside the mind, by way of some sort of *repetition* or iteration of the redeeming act of Christ. Thus the way was not so much laid open as forced upon the church to that general late mediaeval notion of some *fresh* sacrifice of Christ, and His immolation again at every eucharist. There was no other way by which the reality of the eucharistic action could be preserved on the mediaeval understanding of it; yet the unbroken tradition of liturgy and theology alike insisted on this reality. And since the eucharistic action was now viewed as the act of the priest alone – though the liturgy itself continued to state a different view ('We Thy servants together with Thy holy people offer unto Thee...'), there was no escaping the idea that the priest sacrifices Christ afresh at every mass. However hard they tried to conciliate this view of the matter with the doctrine of the Epistle to the Hebrews of the one oblation for sins, perfect and complete (so far as history and time are concerned) on Calvary, the mediaeval theologians, and the party of the old religion at the English Reformation, never quite got away from the necessity of defending the reality of the eucharistic sacrifice as in some sense an iteration of the sacrifice of Christ at the hands of the priest, even though they insisted that it was not a *new* sacrifice.

The Reformers, on the other hand, likewise carrying on the mediaeval insistence on the passion as the whole redeeming act into which the eucharist enters, took the other alternative. Since the passion is wholly in the past, the church now can only enter into it purely mentally, by *remembering* and imagining it. There is for them, therefore, no real sacrifice whatever in the eucharist. The external rite is at the most an acted memorial, *reminding* us of something no longer present . . .

All that constitutes the eucharistic action on this view is the individual's reception of the bread and wine. But this is only a 'token'. The real eucharistic action (if 'action' is not a misleading term) takes place mentally, in the isolated secrecy of the individual's mind. The eucharistic action is thereby altogether deprived of its old corporate significance; it is practically abolished even as a corporate act. The external action must be done by each man for himself; the real eucharistic action goes on separately, even if simultaneously, within each man's mind . . .

Even the external rite is no longer a *corporate* rite integral to the performance of the real eucharistic action, but a common preparation for it, designed only to prepare each communicant subjectively to perform it for himself. . . . There is no possibility of pleading the eucharist for one another, or for the dead in Christ; though we may pray together *at* it (not *by* it) as we intercede at other times . . .

All this is a strictly logical and inevitable development from the protestant basis, and the proof of this is that it was the development everywhere followed by later protestantism, in spite of the hesitations of the Reformers. They would gladly have saved more of the primitive and mediaeval devotional estimation of the eucharist, if they could. But I ask attention for the fact that it is the logical development along one line of something which in itself is Latin and mediaeval, the practical restriction of the significance of the eucharist to the passion, as the historical element in the redeeming act, seen apart from its supra-historical elements in the resurrection, ascension and eternal priesthood. Given that restriction, there is no way of entering into Christ's action but by a repetition of it however guarded, or by a mere mental remembering of it, however vivid and devout. Fifteenth-century catholicism, in effect, took the one line; protestantism, to safeguard the sovereign efficacy of the sacrifice of Christ, took the other. As regards the eucharist they are not complementary in their ideas, but strictly alternative developments of the same idea. The one can never comprehend the other. (pp. 623–25)

I should wish, greatly daring, to challenge Dix's virtual identification of the inward and the mental with that which is individual (as though the external were the only corporate). But for the moment let that pass. It is his clearly drawn dilemma that we are concerned with. Once limit redemption to Calvary, and you must either *repeat* or else only *remember*. There is, I think, a resolution of this dilemma only when we give full value to 'the mystical union that is betwixt Christ and His Church' as a union of fellowship, distinguishing it at the same time from a union of identity. By κοινωνία, by being ἐν Χριστῷ, we in some way enter into his obedience; and accordingly, every offering of our obedience is both derived from, and caught up into, his obedience. Our obedience is derived from his and dependent upon it; and in the perennial stream of his obedience it goes to God. But it is not identified with it. Westcott (1889, p. 229) referring to the high-priestly work of Christ in threefold terms as intercession, as bringing the prayers and praises of his people to God, and as securing access to the Holy Place, writes:

These three forms of Christ's work shew under the conditions of human experience what He does for humanity eternally. Our fellowship with God will grow closer, more perfect, more conscious, but still our approach to God, our worship, our spiritual harmony, must always be 'in Him' in Whom we have been incorporated.

Thus whenever we approach God it can only be in Christ or in the Spirit. Every virtue we possess and every victory won, and every thought of holiness, are his alone. But every act of derived obedience on our part, though not identical with it, is yet really joined with Christ's own obedience. And in a sacrament which is a focal point of obedience the two obediences – Christ's and ours, Christ's in ours and ours in Christ's – are offered to God together. The New Testament 'with' and 'fellowship' words, the συν- and κοινων- and ἐν Χριστῷ, are not phrases of identification-mysticism but of fellowship-mysticism. God forbid that we should countenance what Gore (1901) calls a view of which it is exceedingly difficult to bear the statement: a view 'which involves in each mass in some real sense a re-sacrificing of Christ' (p. 179, cf. Dix as just quoted). Incidentally if we did assert this of the Mass, would not consistency demand that we proclaimed every baptism a re-burial of Christ? A baptism is a real sharing of Christ's death and burial, and thus equally liable to be called a re-enactment of it. In each baptism, at least as really as in the Easter sepulchre, Christ is buried and rises again. But this is clearly, in the case of baptism, in a derived, limited and specialized sense. How then can the so-called re-enactment of the death of Christ in the Eucharist be otherwise understood? As we saw in the last section, the present tenses in the New Testament are mostly of verbs applied to the Church, not to Christ: it is the Church with Christ, rather than Christ with the Church. We cannot speak, then, of re-sacrificing. The only New Testament passage which speaks of recrucifying Christ relates to apostasy (Heb. 6.6). St Paul is crucified with Christ; he does not speak of crucifying Christ. He and his fellow-Christians are offered as a sacrifice; he does not speak of offering Christ, or even of Christ continually offering Himself.

Yet the sacrifice of Christ, complete and perfect, is nevertheless the historical focus of a continual obedience: the obedience of Christ which must be in all suffering accepted in his name and in all praise and worship and self-dedication whatever. And since this is derived from, focused, and caught up in Christ's sacrifice, it is possible (though only with careful safeguards) to speak *in that sense* of such offerings as a constant reproduction of it – a part of it, and not merely a remembering of it. In Rev. 7.14 there is mention of those who have washed their robes and made them white in the blood of the Lamb. This, of course, is applicable to all Christians as such: we all owe our cleansing to that blood. But if, as is sometimes held, this passage refers specially to martyrs, then I suggest — though this is only a guess — that it is possible that we are confronted with a striking example of the way in which Christ's once-and-for-all sacrifice might be, in certain circumstances, spoken of as repeated in each act of human obedience joined with his. The martyrs' own blood, shed in faithfulness to the Lord, turns out to be the blood of the Lamb. When their blood flowed, behold it was the blood of the Lamb. Their sacrifice was united with his — not as though theirs were independently redemptive or added anything to his, but in the sense that, being united, believer and Lord are, in that sense, one: his blood their blood, their blood his. The blood which is the sacrament of obedience is the Lord's blood: the wine which is the sacrament of obedience is, *in that sense*, the Lord's blood.

The dangers that need most strenuously to be guarded against (to repeat this once more) are, as it seems to me, the dangers of allowing any trace of a doctrine either of human merit or of propitiatory sacrifice to creep in. Christ's sacrifice is not propitiatory, but it is God's absolutely effective and final meeting of sin. Man's sacrifice is neither propitiatory nor in its own right effective or final. The Church is not identical with Christ, and its sacrifice is simply derived, as all that we have is derived, from Christ. But being thus derived, and being united with Christ's, it becomes *in this sense* a continuation of what Christ has wrought. It is (although, as we have seen, the New Testament is very chary of such expressions, and they need to be carefully qualified) Christ in us, Christ within humanity, Christ expressing man's obedience to God's loving purposes, Christ's once-and-for-all sacrifice being implemented in us. And every Eucharist is a 'focal' point of that; not a mere recalling to the mind, nor yet a re-enactment; but an entering into what Christ has done — just as indeed is every symbol of obedience. For this too must be faced. It is theologically false, I am convinced, to segregate the gospel sacraments and the ecclesiastical sacraments in any essential way (apart from degrees of authoritative institution) from all those quasi-sacramental 'focal' points of obedience in life – the tangible, datable implementations of our will to serve God. The convert at the penitents' bench, the repentant person making restitution – these are using sacramental acts as channels for their acceptance of God's gift of forgiveness. All these are tangible, datable: hand-holds in the rock face of our life's ascent in time and space, points at which we grasp the once-and-for-all achievement of God's redemption. Every time a Christian or a group of Christians does something for the Lord's sake, whether it is (positively) giving a donation of blood at a transfusion centre, or going to a house to visit someone in need, or rendering some service as a community; or whether (negatively) it is refusing some pleasure because it appears to hinder the Lord's work; and whether it is an external action or a secret transaction of the soul – at all such points the stream of the sacrifice of Calvary is still seen flowing. It is (if, guardedly, we use a dichotomy of language) the Lord's obedience in us being offered up to God. 'Inasmuch as ye did it unto one of the least of these my brethren, ye did it unto me' is, surely, also capable of being extended into 'Inasmuch as ye did it unto God the Father, ye did it as adopted sons, united with his only Son'.

William Temple (1924, pp. 238f.) wrote:

> The sacrifice of Christ is potentially but most really the sacrifice of Humanity. Our task is, by his Spirit, to take our place in that sacrifice. In the strict sense there is only one sacrifice – the obedience of the Son to the Father, and of Humanity to the Father in the Son. This was manifest in actual achievement on Calvary; it is represented in the breaking of the Bread; it is reproduced in our self-dedication and resultant service; it is consummated in the final coming of the Kingdom.

That seems to me a marvellously comprehensive and measured statement; and for my part I would only wish to qualify or to explain, in the manner I have already tried to indicate, the word 'reproduced'. *Mutatis mutandis*, the same applies, from my point of view, to this, from the same context (pp. 241f.):

> The Eucharist is a sacrifice; but we do not offer it; Christ offers it; and we, responding to His act, take our parts or

shares in His one sacrifice as members of His Body. The Bread which the Church, by the hands of the priest, breaks and gives is the Body of Christ, that is, it is the Church itself ... Christ in us presents us with Himself to the Father; we in Him yield ourselves to be so presented; or to put it in other words Redeeming love so wins our hearts that we offer ourselves to be presented by the Love that redeems to the Love that created and sustains both us and all the universe.

The only phrase there which, it seems to me, goes beyond the very words of the New Testament is 'Christ in us presents us with Himself to the Father'; but even that is (as I have tried to show that I recognize) implicit in the New Testament idea of Christ as the New Humanity, the Second Adam, representative Man, offering representative obedience to the Father's will. And it is to be noticed that Temple was careful to guard against a false dichotomy in his description of the Love that redeems making an offering to the Love that creates.

Thus, looking back over the themes we have pondered together, it is certain that all Christians alike agree that at Holy Communion we declare and acknowledge what God in Christ has done once and for all: we declare his finished work of redemption. We declare it, moreover, expectantly: till he come. We shall all agree, necessarily, that we also penitently and gratefully receive for ourselves this finished work: we stretch out our hands to take the proffered pledges of his love; we assimilate, by faith, the Son of God who loved us and gave himself for us. We feed upon him: we eat the Bread of Life. We agree, further, that these pledges of his love are also pledges of our obedience: they are our fealty, offered up to God, representing all creation dedicated to the Creator. We agree that this offering is the result of Christ's perfect obedience – made possible alone by him; and that it is offered in communion with him, in the fellowship of his sufferings: in Christ, our offering becomes a part of his.

Where we may differ, at least in emphasis or degree, is on the question of whether this is, therefore, a repetition of Christ's offering: whether he offers himself or whether the present tense can only strictly be used of us *in* him. And the varying emphases here – arising, I think, from the crippling limitations of our finite minds – are of value because each stands for some great facet of the single, supremely mysterious truth.

For my own part, I feel, at present, the great importance of stressing the once-and-for-all uniqueness of Christ's sacrifice and the utterly dependent and derived character of ours. I am therefore inclined still to welcome the 1662 position of the Prayer of Oblation. Burkitt (1927) (a six penn'orth of wisdom greater than many more costly volumes) said that what he wished to change in Cranmer's plan was the rubric *Or this*, between the Prayer of Oblation and the Prayer of Thanksgiving. *And this* was Burkitt's amendment.

But most of all I am concerned to preserve the precious truth embodied in the *personal* categories of our religion (and 'personal' means not 'individual' only: corporate also, but personal), using the sub-personal categories only as aids and illustrations, not as controls. If we call upon God as Father, I do not see how we can find room in our worship (any more than the New Testament found room) for terms of propitiation, but rather for the infinitely greater and more marvellous gospel of the 'expiation' of sin by God himself who, in Christ, was reconciling the world unto himself – submitting to the consequences of our disobedience. And it is by entering into communion with him, by κοινωνία, in his Son Jesus Christ, that we are united with that reconciling act by the response of sons. 'Communion' or 'fellowship' (κοινωνία[15]), 'together with' (συν-), and 'in Christ' (ἐν Χριστῷ) – these, as I see it, are the keys to the meaning of the Eucharistic sacrifice; and they express a union not of identity but of fellowship. Organic terms are precious and illuminating; but, as Dr Dillistone (1951) reminds us, they are complementary to the terms of Covenant and Communion.

We have only scratched the surface of a fathomless mystery. Even to do that much is to realize its awfulness and wonder and supreme complexity. God enlighten us, and lead us forward together by his mercy into the mystery of his love as Creator, Redeemer, indwelling Spirit of Obedience!

Notes

1. They were the Holy Week Lectures at Cuddesdon College in 1955, by kind invitation of the Principal [the Reverend, and since 1960 the Right Reverend, E. G. Knapp-Fisher]. I owe very warm thanks to him, his Staff, and his men for their kindly welcome.

2. Perhaps it is worth while now (1997) to observe that when these talks were delivered 'an Evangelical' still meant one who, whether conservative or not regarding the authority of the Bible, insisted that the Church of England was not only Catholic but reformed, who recognized the value of the Reformation (much though this is now questioned), and who tended to judge 'catholicism' by the norms of the apostolic age reflected in the New Testament.

3. Rom. 4.25 (cf. 8.10) is possibly a distinguishing of the two, but more probably the combination of them. See also 1 Pet. 3.18, 21f.

4. I say 'at the expiring cry' following Mark and Matt.; Luke places the last word from the cross after the rending of the veil.

5. There were other interpretations: the Temple rending its garments, or the egress of God from the Temple, etc. But access seems by far the most likely. It would be interesting to know how soon the transition was made from this phrase to the Te Deum's image 'Thou didst open the kingdom of heaven'.

6. Whether or not the phrase is an allusion to the wall across the temple court. See the discussion in Charles Masson's commentary (1952).

7. Since writing these lectures, I have come to realize that a reader of the Epistle to the Hebrews might justly counter this particular point (though not the main contention) by asking, Why, then, is the Christian Eucharist a repeated rite? May not the Levitical sacrifices, equally, be seen as repeated sacraments of the eternal forgivingness of God?

8. I think that it is much the most telling exegesis of this passage to take verses 6–8 (the Ps. 8 quotation) as applying not specifically to Christ but to man as he is meant to be. The reference to Christ then comes in verse 9 with great force.

9. See Cullmann 1950 and J. A. T. Robinson 1962[a].

10. NB Rom. 6.10, where the tenses are significant: he *died* once and for all; but he *lives*.

11. See Best 1955, p. 46 (quoting from the Moffatt Commentaries on *Romans*, by Dodd, and *Colossians*, by Scott).

12. For a good discussion of the limitations of the idea of the Church as the extension of the incarnation, see Newbigin 1948, Ch. 5.
13. See the discussion in Jeremias 1955, pp. 162ff.
14. See Jones 1955.
15. Since this was written, it has become clear to me that κοινωνία in the New Testament almost always means, not 'fellowship' but 'joint-participation'. Campbell 1932, etc. had been too little heeded – and are still forgotten by many.

Part Five

Jesus-Traditions

10

THE FUNCTION OF THE

SYNOPTIC GOSPELS

E. Grässer and O. Merk, (eds), *Glaube und Eschatologie: Festschrift für Werner Georg Kümmel zum 80. Geburtstag.* Tübingen, J. C. B. Mohr, 1985, pp. 199–208.

The object of this essay is to question an assumption widely made by New Testament scholars. It is offered, with gratitude and admiration, to one who has a grasp, probably unique in its extent, of the assumptions and speculations of his fellow-scholars and a gift for incisive criticism. The essay will not escape that critical scrutiny any more than the rest; but the verdict, adverse or favourable, will be that of a good friend: and that is enough.

First, the assumption which is to be questioned. It is probably fair to say that the majority of interpreters assume that each of the Synoptic Evangelists is presenting, more or less completely, his own version of the Christian faith and that of the community which he is assumed to be representing. In other words, each Gospel contains the kerygma, the Christian proclamation, as it is understood by the writer, albeit in narrative form rather than in credal or declaratory form, and presented by hints and allusions rather than by direct statement and explicit exhortation. This assumption is even extended to the hypothetical source Q and the community which it also is supposed to represent, so that – to take one recent instance – J. D. Kingsbury (1981, p. 5) can refer to Q's 'distinctive understanding of Jesus, of discipleship, and of salvation'. Thus it is quite normal to treat the Synoptic Gospels as a comparatively late form of an earlier proclamation of the Christian gospel – an indirect, narrative form of the apostolic kerygma which earlier had been delivered more directly. H. Merkel is right when he says: 'It is generally recognised that the Gospels are of a kerygmatic nature' (1984, p. 131; cf. 1981, p. 209). E. Käsemann, in a celebrated lecture delivered in 1953 (1964,

p. 21), deemed it 'strange' (in the light, that is, of the paucity of historical references in the rest of the New Testament) 'that we encounter in the New Testament *any* writings like the Gospels'. Käsemann had to find a special reason for the emergence of the Gospels. He explained it by the need to maintain the tension and connection between the 'once upon a time' of history and the 'once for all' of eschatological reality.

Others, still assuming that the contents of the Gospels represent the full Christian kerygma, have associated one or other of the Synoptic Gospels primarily with Christian worship. E. Trocmé (1983) has suggested that the early Passion narrative, on which he believes Mark drew, originated in the worship of Jewish Christian pilgrims assembled at Jerusalem for the Jewish festivals, especially the Passover; and there have been plenty of proposals for associating entire Gospels with worship.[1]

All those speculations about the function of the Synoptic Gospels work on the assumption that each represents more or less the full creed of the writer and of the community for which he speaks. If this assumption is correct, then there is a great difference between Christianity according to Paul and Christianity according to Mark. Where Paul proclaims salvation by incorporation in the Body of Christ, crucified and risen, through faith in Christ, Mark presents a way of discipleship: the ideal that he holds up (if he is assumed to be holding up an ideal) is that of abandoning self-interest and following the Master – or, if not literally following him, then being a follower of his teaching and ideals. Whereas the death of Christ and his resurrection are at the heart of Paul's gospel of the redemptive love of God, in Mark there are only two passages where it is interpreted redemptively, namely, in the ransom-saying (10.45) and in the words of institution. And if, as many believe, the Gospel was intended to end abruptly and dramatically at 16.8, then Mark does not even describe any sort of encounter with the risen Christ, let alone faith in him or salvation by union with him. If Mark is presenting his version of what it means to be a Christian, then it is what Johannes Weiss called a 'Jesus of Nazareth religion', as contrasted with an 'exalted Christ religion' (1909, pp. 4ff.)

Corresponding observations are made (as we have seen) of the good news according to Q and its presumed community;

and so with Matthew and Luke. Each of these two Evangelists is interpreted as presenting his particular sort of Christology and soteriology, different from those of Mark and Q, but nearer to them than to Paul or to the authors of the other epistles, except the Epistle of James. Students of the Synoptic Gospels, assuming that these Gospels are intended to present the full Christian message, ask what their readers or hearers were meant to understand and learn from this hint or that, from the juxtaposition or order of two bits of tradition, from a silence, or from a riddle. Always, the Evangelist is assumed to be preaching.

But why these assumptions? Certainly, there is every reason to see St John's Gospel as kerygma in narrative form, since its Christology and soteriology and pneumatology are (with only certain reservations) openly of a post-resurrection and confessedly Christian sort. For John, life is by faith in Jesus and by union with him. The much-debated sentence in John 20.31 expressly declares a fully Christian intention, whatever the doubts about which tense represents the true reading. But why should the reticent and comparatively inarticulate statement of the Synoptic Gospels be assumed to represent the full, post-resurrection faith of their writers? Is it not at least as plausible an assumption that these Evangelists, writing what is designed to be ancillary to but not the whole of the kerygma, are intending their narrative to be what it purports to be – a reconstruction of what Jesus seemed to be to his contemporaries before his death – and that they are consciously refraining from expressing the full, post-resurrection faith which they themselves entertain? Not unnaturally, they are by no means wholly successful in avoiding anachronisms. Sometimes, parables and sayings assume a form appropriate only to the post-resurrection Church. Often, Jesus is explicitly shown as fulfilling Scripture and exhibiting God's design in his life and ministry.[2] Notoriously, Matthew insists on the messiahship of Jesus, multiplies the incidence of doing obeisance (προσκυνεῖν) to him,[3] and eliminates certain phrases that might seem derogatory to his power. But no attempt is made (as it is in St John's Gospel) to formulate a fully Christian confession (unless 28.19 must count as such), to give a distinctively Christian answer to the question: 'What must I do to be saved?', or to preach the whole of the resurrection faith. This is not to question the suitability of the Synoptic Gospels or comparable material for use in Christian worship. Justin, 1 *Apol.* 67 (cf. 66), provides evidence that such material was so used; and, whether or not one is persuaded by lectionary theories, such as those of P. Carrington for Mark and G. D. Kilpatrick for Matthew,[4] there is no need to doubt that the Synoptic Gospels could have fulfilled a liturgical function. In the same way such material was used also in explicitly Christian preaching and continues to be so used. But the question remains whether this was their primary purpose.

In the light of this query, a query may be placed against the assumptions normally attached to the use of the 'dissimilarity criterion'. In Gospel research, use is constantly made of the 'dissimilarity criterion'; that is to say, elements of the tradition which are evidently out of tune both with the Judaism of the time (so far as it may be established) and with the interests of the early Church (as established by independent evidence) are recognized as having a strong claim to originality and authenticity. These elements are usually assumed to have survived because they were too well established in the tradition and too firmly resistant for the Evangelist to be able to alter them or reject them to suit the fashion of his own day. But if the primary purpose of the Synoptic Evangelists was to reconstruct the story of the ministry of Jesus, might it not be justifiable to reverse the emphasis and ask whether the Evangelist's anachronisms and 'contemporizings' are there only because they were too well established in his Church for him to resist?

One of the factors that have contributed to ignoring the assumption that the Synoptists were aiming to tell a historical story is the assumption that the early Christians did not distinguish between history and interpretation, that they were not interested in the past, and that they completely assimilated sayings of Christian prophets in the name of the risen Christ with traditional sayings of the historical Jesus, so that, in their minds, there was no difference between the two. J. Breech (1983, p. 7) asserts without offering evidence:

> Since the early Christians did not distinguish between the risen Lord Jesus and the earthly Jesus – in their experience

he was one and the same person – they also did not distinguish between the words of the risen Lord and the sayings of the earthly Jesus.

In the preceding paragraph he blandly assumes, without discussion, that 1 Cor. 7.10 (Paul's reference to an injunction of the Lord, which Paul carefully distinguishes (verse 12) from his own opinion) refers to a saying of a Christian prophet in the name of the Lord. It is surprising, if so, that Paul does not reckon his own opinion, equally, to be an inspired utterance of the risen Lord. There is something to be said (though even here it is not a foregone conclusion) for interpreting 1 Thess. 4.15 (τοῦτο γὰρ ὑμῖν λέγομεν ἐν λόγῳ κυρίου) in this sense; and there are those who wish to take 1 Cor. 11.23 (ἐγὼ γὰρ παρέλαβον ἀπὸ τοῦ κυρίου) in a similar way. But the opposite case is arguable; and, in any case, 1 Cor. 7.10 is not formulated like these passages. At any rate, there is no ground for the pure assumption that the early Christians did not distinguish between historical tradition and prophetic revelation.[5] No doubt post-resurrection convictions did sometimes come to be represented as sayings of the earthly Jesus. It is difficult, for example, to believe that Matt. 18.20 is not an instance of this. But it is a considerable leap from the recognition of this to the conclusion that Christians were oblivious of the difference and unconcerned about it.

Nor is there evidence that they were not interested in history. It is time that scholars give up deducing from the paucity of references to the historical Jesus in the Pauline epistles that Paul was not interested in him. Some arguments from silence are justified; but if ever there was an unjustified argument from silence, it is this; for the epistles are addressed to those who had already been evangelized and were already believers, and they have no occasion to recite the whole story or to reiterate Paul's initial evangelism. There may be one or two passages in the epistles where we, with the particular selection of the sayings of Jesus given us in the Gospels, might expect a saying to be quoted. Ought Rom. 14.14 to have been fortified by what we know as Mark 7.18ff.? Or is indeed Paul's ἐν κυρίῳ a reference to dominical tradition (as a friend suggested to the writer long ago)? Conversely, in Acts 20.35 a saying not known from the Gospels is quoted – though Luke 6.20 (cf. 12.33) is not unlike: why does not the saying occur in Luke's Gospel? We know too little for such silences to be conclusive; but it is significant that, on the two occasions when Paul does hark back to the beginning, in 1 Cor. 11.23ff. and 15.1ff., the material becomes uncommonly like Gospel narrative.

It is equally fallacious to argue from 2 Cor. 5.16 that Paul was not interested in the earthly Jesus. In that much quoted phrase, εἰ καὶ ἐγνώκαμεν κατὰ σάρκα Χριστόν, ἀλλὰ νῦν οὐκέτι γινώσκομεν, it is well established that κατὰ σάρκα qualifies γινώσκειν, not Χριστός. (The locution is not τὸν κατὰ σάρκα Χριστόν.) Besides, κατὰ σάρκα there does not mean 'with reference to flesh-and-blood historicity'. It is a worldly, rationalistic knowing that Paul is renouncing, which is by no means the same as declaring the new way of knowing to be independent of historical events. He declares that he no longer knows anybody in the κατὰ σάρκα way; but that is not the same as saying that he does not care whether they exist.[6]

It is pure assumption that early Christians neither distinguished the Jesus of history from the risen Christ nor were concerned with the historical facts; and it is actually demonstrable that at least one of the Synoptic Evangelists consciously distinguished between the Christological estimate of Jesus before his death and that of the post-resurrection period. If the Acts is by the same author as the Gospel of Luke (as most allow), then that author is not presenting in the body of his Gospel the same Christology as he presents in the last chapter and in the Acts. It is well known that in Luke's Gospel the Evangelist himself refers to Jesus as ὁ κύριος. But this is part of his own, editorial language when he is speaking for himself, as the narrator. When he is reporting how Jesus' own contemporaries spoke during the ministry, ὁ κύριος is almost never on their lips. The vocative, κύριε, does not count. All the Evangelists represent Jesus' own contemporaries as addressing him so; but, although it is likely enough that the Evangelists themselves did hear in that vocative some of its distinctively Christian and post-resurrection overtones, it need not in itself carry any special meaning, since it is the commonest of respectful addresses in Greek. An old-fashioned English schoolboy would politely address 'Sir' to a master; but that is very different from the use of 'Sir' in cases other than the vocative. (Not all schoolmasters are knighted.) Luke, then, allows the *dramatis personae* of his story the use of ὁ κύριος as a title for Jesus almost never. Luke 1.43 (Elizabeth saying 'How comes it that the Mother of my Lord should come to me?') is an exception. Luke 1.76 (in the Benedictus, anarthrous) might be a *double entendre* for Christian readers, while 19.31 (cf. verse 34) where Jesus refers to himself as the κύριος of the colt, is hardly to be counted: with the possessive genitive, it could mean 'owner', as οἱ κύριοι αὐτοῦ in verse 33 certainly means 'its owners'. Otherwise, it is only on the lips of supernatural beings – the angels addressing the shepherds (2.11). But as soon as the resurrection has taken place, from Luke 24.34 and right through the Acts, the writer freely represents the disciples as using the title. Now, whether this is historically correct or not (and, if it is, what locutions might have lain behind it in Aramaic tradition) is not the point. The point is that it demonstrates that the Evangelist who himself called Jesus ὁ κύριος (7.13, etc.) refrained from representing others as doing so until the resurrection: proof positive that at least one Evangelist deliberately kept his narrative from Christological anachronism, at least in that respect. Incidentally, it is interesting that, although the fourth Evangelist makes no attempt to maintain historical reserve in his Christology, he does observe virtually the same rule as Luke with regard to ὁ κύριος. Unless one reckons John 13.13 (ὑμεῖς φωνεῖτέ με ... ὁ κύριος on the lips of Jesus), only John 20.2 is anachronous. This it is, though it is after the resurrection, since Mary is represented as using ὁ κύριος before she knows about the resurrection. The fourth Evangelist observes a similar reserve with regard to the use of 'Christ'. Except in 1.17 and 17.3 χριστός is used, with the article, not as virtually a proper name for Jesus but as a Jewish title (cf. Robinson 1985).

There are other features about the Christology of Luke's Gospel as compared with the Acts that point in the same direction. But the case of ὁ κύριος is the most clearly demonstrable (see above, pp. 51ff.). And now E. E. Lemcio is suggesting that something of the same historical consciousness may be seen when, in Mark's Gospel, the Christology of the Evangelist in his editorial capacity is distinguished from the traditional material which he is reporting.[7] He points out that the very first words of Mark, 'Αρχὴ τοῦ εὐαγγελίου 'Ιησοῦ Χριστοῦ (υἱοῦ θεοῦ), represent a post-resurrection Christology and a post-resurrection conception of εὐαγγέλιον quite distinct from τὸ εὐαγγέλιον τοῦ θεοῦ on the lips of Jesus in Mark 1.14. He notes that the phrase τὸ εὐαγγέλιον ... Χριστοῦ is unique in the New Testament, as is the whole phrase that contains it – 'Αρχὴ τοῦ εὐαγγελίου 'Ιησοῦ Χριστοῦ. My own belief following a suggestion made by others is that, actually, the phrase may belong to a much later Christian than the Evangelist. If the autograph of Mark, or a very early copy, was in codex-form, and the bottom leaf was somehow lost, then simultaneously the beginning and end of the Gospel would be removed. A subsequent scribe, asked to copy an exemplar thus mutilated and finding that it began with nothing but a relative adverb, καθώς, might well have prefixed, *faute de mieux*, 'Here begins the Gospel of Jesus Christ the Son of God' using his own, post-resurrection Christology. Arriving at the end and finding ἐφοβοῦντο γάρ, he either gave it up in silence or added a pastiche from later traditions.[8] It is true that the earliest manuscript evidence shows no trace of a longer Gospel. But mutilation so early as to have already established the manuscript tradition is, *pace* K. Aland (1969, 1979, pp. 246ff.), not unthinkable. But, in any case, the point is that this Christology, whether of the Evangelist or of a later scribe, is different from that of the narrative itself.

Relevant to the same question is William Wrede's theory of the Messianic Secret, which sees the secrecy-motif as a theological construction imposed on the earlier traditions by the Evangelist or his predecessors. If this were true, it would reinforce the theory, contrary to the one here expressed, that the Evangelist is accommodating the story to his own situation, in such a way as to make it warn his Christian hearers about the elusive character of the title Christ in Christian understanding. But Wrede's theory is wide open to criticism. He expressly refused to distinguish between secrecy over messiahship strictly so called, and secrecy over other aspects of Jesus' person and ministry. He believed that such distinctions belonged to modern scholarship and not to the mind of the Evangelist.[9] One can only beg to differ. Is there any reason why Mark should not have been conscious of the difference between 'Messiah' and 'Son of God', or between Jesus' seeking to avoid publicity over his cures and seeking to keep a secret concerning his person? If only one allows this, then the alleged inconsistencies (taken to be evidence of the imposition of a theological construction on the traditions) largely disappear. In the whole Gospel there is only one passage (8.30) where a strictly messianic secrecy is enjoined, and that need be only a temporary injunction, like that in 9.9 about the transfiguration. This would not be incompatible with the public messianic gesture (if such it was) of the 'triumphal entry', or the confession before the High Priest, when Jesus was a prisoner and there was no longer any danger of its leading to a political explosion. The handling in Mark of the secrecy-motifs, and the representation of Jesus as constantly interpreting 'Messiah' and 'Son of God' in terms of 'the Son of Man', contain nothing essentially incompatible with historical reporting, even if certain details are implausible, such as the injunction to Jairus and the others not to talk about his daughter's restoration to life (5.43), or to a former deaf mute and his friends to say not a word about his cure (7.36)!

In 1959 I published an essay looking in more or less the same direction as this one, although with a different 'slant' and with the use of other instances for support. It has been seldom referred to[10] and never, to my knowledge, expressly refuted. It is since then that I have noticed the phenomenon of the Lucan use of ὁ κύριος and become interested in the theory of a truncation of Mark at the beginning as well as at the end (see above). And now, Lemcio's essay (1986 and see, further, 1991) has taken up the cudgels for parts, at least, of this same thesis. It must be emphasized again that it is not my intention here, any more than it was formerly, to deny that post-resurrection attitudes have entered the Synoptic Gospels, or to argue for strict historical accuracy in them. My main intention is simply to question the assumption that the Synoptic Gospels were intended to present the full Christology and the full Christian theology of the Evangelists who wrote them or of any communities they may have represented.[11] I propose, instead, that it is more reasonable to assume that the Synoptic Gospels were intended to be ancillary to, and only a part of, the full

Christian kerygma. In the preaching of 'Jesus, crucified, raised, Messiah, Son of God, according to the Scriptures', questions were bound to arise: Who was this Jesus? What manner of man was he? Why did he come into collision with authority? Why do you say that a crucified man is Messiah? What makes you claim that it was all according to the Scriptures? It is precisely these questions that the Synoptic Gospels purport to answer, and it is *a priori* probable that, from the beginning, ancillary material of a historical kind such as this was therefore in demand. The hints and clues in the Gospels indicating that the Evangelists were deliberately refraining from stating their own full gospel support the *a priori* assumption of the need for such material; and, as has been shown, there is sufficient evidence to question the assumption that the early Christians had no concern for it. Such material is essential and integral to the kerygma, but is not the whole of it. Here, then, is a plea for a reconsideration of the whole situation. In my 1959 essay, I identified the Synoptic Gospels as 'kerygma'; but then I was using 'kerygma' to denote exclusively initial evangelism, that is, material for Christians to use in evangelizing non-Christians, as distinguished from material that those who were already Christians would need reiterated for themselves. The terms in that essay were slightly different, but the main contention was the same – that it is a false assumption that the Synoptics are preaching the full gospel; and I still stand by the thesis of that earlier essay:

> It would be ludicrous to deny that ecclesiastical interests and theological value-judgments ever overlaid the story. It has been as good as demonstrated that they do. But that is not the point. The point is that the Christians knew the difference between the two – between the pre-resurrection situation and the post-resurrection situation – and that their aim was to try to tell faithfully the story of how the former led to the latter. And in actual fact they succeeded better than is often allowed. (p. 173)

It may be added as a postscript that two early traditions about the purpose of Mark might be enlisted in at least partial support of this thesis, namely Papias', *apud* Eus. *HE* 3.39.15, and that of Morton Smith's Clement Fragment 1973 if it is genuine. These do not concur with the assumptions that have been criticized. Papias' description of Mark as preserving what Peter had said about Jesus is nearer to what is proposed in this essay; and Clement's (if his it is) shows the canonical Gospel as preliminary only, and propaedeutic. So far as Luke's Gospel is concerned, Luke's own prologue also supports it. It seems reasonable to see Mark, and, in their measure, Matthew and Luke, as meant for the instruction of catechumens about the circumstances of the life of Jesus rather than as a full statement of what it means to embrace the Christian faith. St John's Gospel is unlike the Synoptic Gospels precisely in that it does contain distinctively Christian answers to the question: 'What must I do to be saved?'

Notes

1. Kilpatrick 1946; Carrington 1952; etc.
2. In spite of the general attitude of St John's Gospel alluded to above, there is a point at which great care is taken to distinguish pre- and post-resurrection understanding: John 12.16.
3. Moule 1977[a], pp. 175f.
4. See note 1 above.
5. A more balanced presentation of this position is to be found in Boring 1982.
6. Discussion and bibliography in Moule 1970[b], pp. 15ff.
7. Lemcio 1986. See now 1991, and further bibliography there. He applies the principle to other items of belief as well as Christology.
8. See Moule 1981, p. 131 n. 1.
9. Wrede 1901; Moule 1975, with bibliography there; Tuckett 1984; Lemcio, as in note 7.
10. Though Lemcio 1986, p. 202 n. 10 refers to J. Roloff, *Das Kerygma und der irdische Jesus*, 1970, pp. 44f., and R. Pesch, *Das Markusevangelium*, I, 1976, p. 63.
11. Lemcio 1986, p. 205 n. 64, quotes an extreme example of the assumption from Marxsen 1968, pp. 132, 137: 'The Risen Lord (the glorified One, the Son of Man, the Son of God) goes to his Cross. This makes it quite clear that the story is not meant to be read as an account of an historical sequence of events.'

11

AN UNSOLVED PROBLEM
IN THE TEMPTATION-CLAUSE
IN THE LORD'S PRAYER

The Reformed Theological Review, vol. xxxiii, no. 3 (1974),
pp. 65–75.

The clause 'lead us not into temptation' in the Lord's Prayer
(Matt. 6.13; Luke 11.4) and the injunction in Mark 14.38
(Matt. 26.41; Luke 22.46) 'pray that you may not enter into
temptation', are notoriously problematic; but the heart of the
problem is not always defined with precision. It is the contention of this paper that nowhere else in the New Testament is
there quite so unqualified an injunction to pray for escape
from temptation; and that, since temptation is inevitable, the
prayer is usually turned by those who use it into a prayer,
rather, for escape from *succumbing* to temptation. The problem,
therefore, is why was this prayer ever recorded in this apparently illogical form? It is my main concern in the following
observations, not to solve the problem but simply to clarify it.
If this acts as an incentive to someone better qualified than the
writer to take the matter forward towards solution so much
the better.

It is none of my intention to go over the familiar ground once
more in detail. Presupposed here is an examination not only of
the occurrences of the πειράζειν-group of words and of the
standard works of the less recent past on the Lord's Prayer but
also, more recently, of the lucid article by C. W. F. Smith in
IDB ('Lord's Prayer'), the full and learned monograph by
the Abbé J. Carmignac (1969), the *TDNT* article on the
πειράζειν-group of words by H. Seesemann, and a weighty
paper by K. G. Kuhn (1952) on πειρασμός and other words.
These, between them, cover nearly all the relevant data, and
leave us free to take up certain matters that seem to remain
still to be reconsidered.

One stumbling-block to the understanding of the clause in the Lord's Prayer will not here be dwelt upon. From very early days (Tertullian's allusion to this is the stock example)[1] Christians have been puzzled by the logic of 'lead us not' – as though it were likely that God would deliberately lead anyone into temptation! But, although Carmignac is not altogether satisfied by the standard solution, I, for my part, am not concerned to dispute that, if the words be not too literalistically pressed, 'lead' (or, more accurately, 'bring')[2] 'us not into' need mean no more than 'do not let us be brought into', on the analogy of the 'deliver us from evil (or the evil one)' of the clause which, in the Matthean though not the Lucan version, is parallel to this clause.

A much more substantial problem, and one which this paper is concerned to define, though it is able to offer no solution, is the meaning of 'bringing into temptation'. It is intelligible enough to pray, 'Do not let us succumb to temptation when we are brought to the test', but 'Do not let us even be brought to testing' is harder to explain. By way of starting to think round this problem, the familiar question of the meaning of πειρασμός itself must be raised, although it is not this word so much as the phrase, 'into πειρασμός', that constitutes the problem. The Vulgate *temtatio* and the English 'temptation' suggest, to most modern readers, some kind of enticement to sin. But πειρασμός (like *tentamentum* in Latin) strictly means 'testing' rather than 'enticement'; and many scholars have urged that the word refers to external circumstances – testing times which need not, in themselves, be viewed as designed to entice – rather than to such inward, psychological allurement as is normally implied by 'temptation'. Further, there are those who relate the word to one notorious 'testing time' in particular, namely, the so-called 'messianic woes', the crisis that Jewish apocalyptic expected at the climax of history – the pains before the birth, the darkness before the dawn.[3] This is hinted at by the type of rendering that has become popular, and has been (for instance) accepted into the New English Bible both in the Lord's Prayer ('do not bring us to the test') and in Mark 14.38 and parallels ('that you may be spared the test'), and is proposed for an international version of the Lord's Prayer.

It is difficult to be satisfied with this last suggestion. In the first place, if the ultimate climax had been intended, one would have expected the definite article with πειρασμός.[4] Not that New Testament Greek is consistent or rigorous in its uses of the article; but it would be surprising to find it as lax as this. But, secondly and more weightily, Kuhn (1952) brings a great deal of evidence to bear in favour of interpreting πειρασμός here with reference to the constant, standing conflict between God and the devil, in which all are involved constantly and not only at the end. Besides, where is the evidence that πειρασμός was a recognized term for the climactic test? In Rev. 3.10 there is a promise: 'I will also keep you from the ordeal [literally, the hour of the ordeal, πειρασμός] that is to fall upon the whole world and test its inhabitants' (NEB). But that is no evidence that πειρασμός by itself was a recognizable technical term for the ultimate crisis of apocalyptic expectation. On the contrary, it only shows how carefully it is defined and given the definite article when it has to mean this.

But if one does not relate πειρασμός in the Lord's Prayer to the climactic test, a case certainly remains for interpreting it with reference to external circumstances – testing times – rather than to inward, psychological enticement: temptation in the commonly accepted sense of the word. Yet, that being said, the question arises how much difference ultimately exists between the one and the other. External testing circumstances, no less than inward lusting, may constitute an inducement to sin, even when not deliberately directed to that end. The way from the use of πειρασμός for 'testing' to its use for 'temptation', is, therefore, intelligible enough; and there is at least one passage in the New Testament where that way has clearly been traversed. In James 1.13f. the verb πειράζειν is explicitly enlarged upon in such a way that it means what we normally mean by 'tempting' as contrasted with 'testing'. Denying that God is the origin of πειράζειν, the writer says, instead, that a man πειράζεται 'when ... enticed and turned away by his own lust' (NEB). Thus, although the majority of scholars may still hold (against the view of Carmignac – who has Calvin as an ally)[5] that, in the Lord's Prayer, πειρασμός most probably refers to external, testing circumstances, the passage in James shows that the way from the one to the other need not be a long way; and perhaps it may similarly be said that *tentamenta* (or *temptamenta*) *fide* (=*fidei*) in Ovid, *M* 7.728, comes very near to making the transition from 'tests of faith' to 'temptations to break faith'. There is one other passage in the New Testament, 1 Tim. 6.9, where πειρασμός is close to a word of definitely sinister meaning, παγίς, 'a snare': to this we must return later.

But whatever the *results* of πειρασμός, and however much it keeps company with words meaning enticement to sin, it remains that the word itself does not normally mean enticement to sin or ruin; and that sharp distinctions can and should be drawn with regard to the *intention* with which the pressure of πειρασμός is applied. It may be that the result is much the same, whether one's loyalty is strained with intent to break it or not, and whether by outward circumstances or by inward lust; but this does not alter the fact that there is a clear distinction between the various ends to which a force that may be an inducement to sin may be applied. Without intent to harm, it may be applied as a purely experimental testing, like the assaying of a metal, to ascertain its quality – as when God 'tested' Abraham's loyalty[6] or allowed the Satan to test Job's (cf. Job 23.10). Or it may be applied as a refining process, which not only tests so as to show up what is genuine but positively frees the precious metal from the dross (cf. Zech. 13.9, Mal. 3.2). Admittedly, πειρασμός and πειράζειν are not used for this last; but the idea is not far away. δοκιμασία and δοκιμάζειν[7] are the natural words for 'assaying'; and from this word-group comes the word δοκίμιον, which is related, in the New Testament, to the metaphor of refining. It is true that δοκίμιον in James 1.3 appears, to judge by its context, to be only another word for 'test'; but the same word in 1 Pet. 1.7 appears to mean the tested and approved part of that which has been subjected to the refiner's fire; and this metaphor comes in the context of a reference to 'testing circumstances' (verse 6, ἐν ποικίλοις πειρασμοῖς). (There is a *v.l.* δόκιμον in both places, which, if correct, would still represent the same metaphor.) Further, 1 Pet. 4.12 applies the metaphor of the refiner's use of fire (πύρωσις) to persecution, and says that it takes place in order (or in such a way as) to test the sufferers – πρὸς πειρασμὸν ὑμῖν γινομένῃ. So, in *Didache* 16.5, the ultimate, eschatological test is called ἡ πύρωσις τῆς δοκιμασίας. From both of these at least neutral, if not good intentions, namely, testing and refining, it is necessary to distinguish the deliberate intention to cause ruin or moral downfall – 'temptation' in the ordinarily accepted sense; and it is only when πειράζειν is glossed in the manner of James 1.13f., with metaphors such as 'lure' and 'bait', that its meaning becomes unambiguously that of temptation (cf., perhaps, 1 Tim. 6.9 again, where Carmignac (1969, pp. 273f.), takes πειρασμὸς καὶ παγίς as a hendiadys). It is significant that, in the earlier verses of this very same chapter – James 1.2f. – πειρασμός means simply 'testing', which, successfully endured, turns out to be a benefit, because it leads to the refining and strengthening of character.

These attempts at definition have uncovered two sets of distinctions: (i) between πειρασμός as (a) external circumstances and (b) inward lust; and (ii) between πειρασμός as (a) experiment, (b) refining process, (c) attempt to pervert. (i) (b) is almost necessarily equal to (ii) (c) (unless one interprets lust in a neutral sense such as it does not normally bear); but (ii) (c) might also take an external form, (i) (a). Further, it is evident that (ii) (c) can act, even if not so intended by its author, in those other ways, as a test (ii) (a), or a refining (ii) (b). The devil may apply the pressure (external or inward) with intent to pervert; but God may use it as a test and a refinement, or may enable the sufferer so to use it. So, in the Matthean and Lucan narratives of the temptations of Jesus, although the language of enticement is not used, the fact that the devil is the one who applies the test means that enticement to evil is intended; but Jesus emerges like refined metal, authenticated and ready to exercise a ministry of power.

Interestingly enough, however, in spite of this affinity of meanings which is illustrated in the New Testament, the words for 'testing' do not seem often or commonly to be used in ancient literature for 'temptation' – possibly not at all until the New Testament. It is easy to think of countless temptation stories before the New Testament, such as (to take a few, at random) Odysseus and his men tempted by the Sirens (*Od.* 12.39ff. – θέλγειν); Hippolytus resisting the approaches of his step-mother Phaedra, and suffering for it; Joseph, comparably, resisting Potiphar's wife, and paying the price (Gen. 39); Regulus nobly resisting the temptation to escape torture at the expense of his nation's honour (Horace, *Odes* 3. 5. 45ff.). So, too, the moralists and philosophers know well enough what it is to resist temptation. Xenophon (*Mem.* 2. 5. 5) says that it is 'tempting' (ἐπαγωγόν) to sell a bad friend for gain; Plato (*Philebus* 44C) says that pleasure's lure (ἐπαγωγόν again) is enchantment (γοήτευμα) and not real pleasure. Seneca speaks of the true philosopher as having an unconquerable power of mind (*V.B.* 4.3, *animum ... extra cupiditatem positum*). But *tentare*, πειράζειν, are, in the main, not so used: they are neutral and fall more naturally into (ii) (a) or (b) of our categories than (ii) (c). The metaphors for tempting in literature before the New Testament tend to be such as those used in James 1.14 and 1 Tim. 6.9 – the unambiguously sinister metaphors of the bait and the lure and the trap. This applies not only to 'secular' literature, but also to the Old Testament, where מוֹקֵשׁ and מִכְשׁוֹל ('bait' and 'occasion for stumbling', 'cause of downfall') play a considerable part, and are both largely rendered in the LXX by those important words σκάνδαλον and σκανδαλίζειν (see *TDNT* s.v.) By contrast, the πειράζειν-group of words, like the *tentamentum*-group in Latin, seems to be kept for the neutral meaning of 'test' or 'testing'. Even in a passage like Deut. 13.1–3 (MT 2–4),[8] where the loyalty of the people is 'tested' by the evil proposal of a false prophet saying 'Let us go after other gods', so that testing and tempting are constituted by one and the same event, it is still God who is said to do the testing (מְנַסֶּה, πειράζει), and what the false prophet himself does – namely, what in English would be called tempting – is not so described. And this holds for the use of πειράζειν in the LXX generally. It describes God testing men and men testing God, but perhaps never explicitly actual enticement to sin.[9] The only clear exception in Hatch and Redpath is a variant reading confined to the first hand of Sinaiticus at 1 Macc. 1.15b, which read ἐπειράθησαν τοῦ ποιῆσαι τὸ πονηρόν, 'they were tempted to do evil'; but the corrector of Sinaiticus, and other mss, read ἐπράθησαν, 'they were sold ...'

Thus, the New Testament seems to stand alone, up to its date, in widening the use of the πειράζειν-group to embrace deliberate enticement to sin; and even in the New Testament, James 1.13f. is the only quite explicit passage, although 1 Tim. 6.9 has yet to be considered; and although whenever the devil or Satan is named as the tester it is clear that the intention is evil and that the word means 'temptation' (see Matt. 4.1, 3 with Mark 1.13, Luke 4.2, 13; 1 Cor. 7.5; 1 Thess. 3.5 (ὁ πειράζων), Rev. 2.10). Is it possible that πειράζειν takes on this special connotation in such passages of the New Testament chiefly because the pressures and strains of life ('tests') are there placed in the context of the unremitting warfare against evil ('temptation')? The 'psychological' temptation to which all are subject is recognized as part of the 'objective' warfare in which all are involved. With the paradigm of Jesus' temptations in their traditions (cf. also Luke 22.28), New Testament writers are able, even without resort to the usual metaphors of bait and enticement, to indicate that the struggle with temptation is part of the constant test of loyalty to which, as warriors of God, they are subjected. The Qumran sect, as Kuhn (1952) shows, were committed to just such a holy war; and, as Carmignac (1969, pp. 260f.), shows, the verb נסה is occasionally used in the Qumran literature. But the sectarians of the Dead Sea do not appear to have linked up this word so closely as the New Testament does with the battle against sin and its enticements. For this latter, like the Old Testament, they use words such as מוֹקֵשׁ ('bait') and מִכְשׁוֹל ('cause of stumbling').[10]

So tentative answers, at least, have been found to certain questions that need to be asked about the clause in the Lord's Prayer from which we set out: (i) What of the suggestion that 'lead us not into temptation' implies that God is likely to lead us into it? Answer: perhaps it is only a way of saying 'let us not be brought into temptation'. (ii) Is the temptation in question constituted by inward lusts and desires or by testing circumstances of persecution and distress, or, indeed, by the ultimate, climactic, messianic test? Answer: probably not the last; but, if one had to choose between the first and the second, perhaps more likely the second, namely, the constant, unremitting testing circumstances that beset any loyal believer. But (iii) can one, in fact, distinguish between, on the one hand, such circumstances in their pressure towards sin and, on the other hand, psychological, inward desires exercising a similar pressure? Answer: the line of demarcation is thin, so far as the results are concerned, as James 1.13f. shows; for there the verb πειράζει is associated with the language of bait and seduction, such as is usually used for what we call 'temptation' (cf. 1 Tim. 6.9). But the πειράζειν-group still properly belongs to the neutral meaning, 'test', and such 'testing' has to be shown to be with malign intent before it approximates to 'temptation'. (iv) What, if any, is the special feature of New Testament usage? Perhaps it is that it shows a special readiness in certain passages to attribute the testing to Satan and thus to define it as virtually temptation. It should be added here that, quite apart from the distinctive traditions of the New Testament, later Judaism in general showed an anxiety to exonerate God from testing with intent to cause sin (cf. James 1.13); and the logic of this would be to prepare the way for the New Testament's attribution of πειράζειν to Satan. Yet it remains true that the examples cited by Mayor (1897) on James 1.13 to illustrate this tendency in later Judaism show no instance outside Christian literature with the actual word πειράζειν or *tentare*.

But now we come back to the real problem: Why should anyone pray to escape testing – even if it is testing by the devil and constitutes temptation? If one knows that testing and temptation are inevitable; if one knows that, before the glorious climax of God's final triumph, there will be inescapable testing of an exceptionally severe kind; if, moreover, one knows that testing can be salutary[11] and that the Lord himself has pioneered the way through it to spiritual effectiveness – then what is the logic of praying for exemption? Would it not be about as logical as saying 'We know we are at war; but let there be no fighting!'? Certainly, one may dread being tested, and will pray for strength not to succumb when put to the test. In the remarkable passage, Luke 22.31f., Jesus is represented as knowing that the disciples are going to be 'sifted' by Satan. (The metaphor presumably relates to a hostile scrutiny[12] – the sifting of motives, and so forth, so as to expose the faults and failings: it is thus more or less equivalent to πειρασμός.) Jesus accepts that Satan has gained permission to do this; and his prayer for Peter is not that he may be spared it, but that his faith (or faithfulness?) may not give out (ἵνα μὴ ἐκλίπῃ ἡ πίστις σου). Again, certainly one will avoid gratuitously inducing temptation – as it were 'tempting Providence': one will not court temptation or walk deliberately into it. In 1 Cor. 7.5, Paul advises husbands and wives not to overstrain their self-control, 'that Satan may not tempt (πειράζῃ) you'. And there is 1 Cor. 10.13, about which something must be said later. So, too, in 1 Tim. 6.9, those who are over interested in money gratuitously incur 'testing', which, significantly, is associated with the metaphor of the snare, which, we have seen, is used for temptation: 'those who want to be rich fall into temptation (πειρασμός) and snares (παγίς) ...' (NEB).[13]

But it remains true that to pray to escape testing and temptation altogether seems useless and illogical. It is this that led the Abbé Carmignac to write his exhaustive book, in which he reaches a clear and logical conclusion, namely, that the verbs and the preposition used in the Lord's Prayer and in Mark 14.38, both in the Greek and in the original Hebrew (not Aramaic) that he conjectures for the Lord's Prayer, mean more than merely being brought, or coming, to the test: they mean actually yielding to the test so as to go 'inside' it – succumbing, in other words, to temptation. Dionysius of Alexandria, quoted by Carmignac (p. 274), as by J. B. Lightfoot before him,[14] expresses the same thought very clearly, though he merely asserts it, supporting it with scriptural quotations and a great deal of commonsense, but without syntactical arguments. Having first interpreted 'bring us not into' to mean 'let us not fall into', Dionysius goes on (I give my own paraphrastic rendering):

... and to show that this did not mean not being tested but being delivered from the evil one, he adds 'But deliver us from the evil one'. And what difference is there, perhaps you will say, between being tested and falling, or entering, into πειρασμός? [There is a difference,] because anyone who has been worsted by the evil one (and worsted he will be if he does not struggle and God does not shield him) has fallen and entered into πειρασμός, and is in it and has been brought like a prisoner under its power. But anyone who resists and endures has been tested, indeed, but has not entered or fallen into πειρασμός. Jesus, at any rate, was led out by the Spirit, not to enter into πειρασμός but to be tested by the devil; and Abraham did not enter into πειρασμός, and neither did God bring him into πειρασμός, but he tested him: he did not throw him into πειρασμός.

And, indeed, the Lord himself tested the disciples. For the evil one, in testing (πειράζων), drags into πειρασμοί, as a tempter to evil (πειραστὴς κακῶν); but God, in testing, causes the testings to pass (? τοὺς πειρασμοὺς παραφέρει – cf. Mark 14.36), since he is himself ἀπείραστος κακῶν: 'For God', it says (James 1.13) 'ἀπείραστός ἐστιν κακῶν'. 'For the devil drags men to destruction, and uses force (βιάζεται), but God trains (or exercises (γυμνάζων)) men and leads to salvation.'

Carmignac cites a long catena of other ancient writers in similar vein. J. B. Lightfoot[15] also quotes Hilary, who explains the clause by glossing πειρασμός so as to mean such πειρασμός as could not be sustained: '. . . "*Non derelinquas nos in tentatione*", *quam ferre non possimus* [This is reminiscent of 1 Cor. 10.13, which is discussed below.] . . . *Iob Deus tentationi permittens, a jure diaboli potestatem animae ejus excerpsit . . .*' Carmignac's own proposed rendering (1969, p. 396 (cf. p. 445)), is 'Et fais que nous n'entrions pas dans la tentation', and the Hebrew he postulates is וְאַל תְּבִיאֵנוּ בְמַסָּה. The Aramaic postulated by Jeremias (1971, pp. 196, 202) is very similar: *wᵉla ta'elinnan lᵉnisyon*, and he renders it boldly, 'Do not let us fall victim to temptation.' But whereas Carmignac is prepared to justify his rendering from the actual words, drawing a subtle distinction between coming to temptation and going inside it, Jeremias appeals, rather, to the parallel offered by the Jewish morning and evening prayer (b. Ber. 60b), 'Bring me not into the power of temptation.' But 'into the power of' (לִידֵי) is not the same as 'into', and it does not seem justifiable to render 'into' as though it were 'into the power of'.[16] On the other hand, Carmignac's exegesis seems to me far-fetched and unconvincing. If there is any distinction between coming *to* temptation and going *inside* it, it is 1 Tim. 6.9 with its ἐμπίπτειν that gets nearest to it: elsewhere in the New Testament this verb does seem to connote 'falling inside', 'coming into the power of' (Matt. 12.11; Luke 6.39, 10.36; 1 Tim. 3.6f.; Heb. 10.31). And it is significant that Dionysius of Alexandria, quoted above, uses precisely this verb throughout that passage when he wants to describe succumbing to temptation. He explicitly glosses εἰσελθεῖν, in our problematic clause, by ἐμπεσεῖν, and says that when God tested Abraham he did not 'throw him into' πειρασμός (οὐκ ἐνέβαλεν). Thus, Dionysius is interpreting the phrase in the Lord's Prayer exactly as Carmignac wishes to, but without any linguistic argument; and the fact remains that ἐμπίπτειν is not the verb used in the problematic phrase. So the problem remains. By all means, we must pray not to fall into the power of temptation but can we reasonably pray for exemption from testing or temptation itself? Will 'Do not bring us to the test' make sense?

There are three other passages in the New Testament concerning πειρασμός, which present a similar problem but in each of them there is some feature that makes this problem at least slightly easier.

(i) in 1 Cor. 10.13b, Paul says that God may be trusted not to allow the Corinthians to be tested beyond their endurance (ὑπὲρ ὃ δύνασθε), but that, together with the testing he will also provide the way out (ποιήσει ... τὴν ἔκβασιν), so that they may be able to endure it (ὑπενεγκεῖν). There are several matters here that call for comment. First, the logic of the verse in its context is elusive. 1 Cor. 10 opens with a warning against presumptuousness. Those whom Paul is addressing appear to have been wrongly confident that they were spiritually secure. He therefore appeals to the analogy of the Israelites' wanderings in the wilderness, when although duly 'initiated', as it were, into the community of God under Moses, they fell into sin and disaster. Accordingly, Paul sounds the warning (verse 12): 'Whoever thinks he stands firm must beware lest he fall.' And then comes verse 13a, which, in its context, must presumably be construed not as encouragement, but as a continuation of the warning: πειρασμὸς ὑμᾶς οὐκ εἴληφεν εἰ μὴ ἀνθρώπινος must, apparently, mean (as Barrett 1968, *in loc.*, puts it):

> *No testing has fallen upon you but what is the common lot of men.* They need not therefore claim that they themselves (or their prophylactics) have proved exceptionally resistant. It is implied by Paul's words that more severe trials are to be expected ...

If this is the correct interpretation, then we must assume a change in the direction of thought when, in the second part of the verse, with which we began, a note of reassurance is introduced. Barrett recognizes this when he continues his comment: '... he [Paul] himself seems to feel the implication that more severe trials are to be expected, and goes on to reassure his readers that though no human device can afford them security they may trust in God's faithfulness.'

If one accepts this interpretation of the sudden change between the mood of the two sections of the verse, one may go on to observe – and this is the main point, for the purpose of the present inquiry – that ἔκβασις admittedly sounds like exemption from the test rather than strength to endure it;[17] but that, if the first half of the verse is brought into the reckoning, it quite clearly implies, on the contrary, not escape from testing in general, but escape only from testing too severe for one's capacity to endure it. And the same thought, in a paradoxical form, returns at the end of the verse, where ἔκβασις is apparently equated, not with escape but with strength to endure. Accordingly, for all its difficulties and obscurities, 1 Cor. 10.13 does not present quite the unrelieved problem of the Lord's Prayer clause. It glosses the prospect of escape, illogically, perhaps, but significantly, by the prospect not, after all, of escape but of divinely given fortitude. Perhaps it is possible to explain the words even more logically. Dr J. A. T. Robinson suggested[18] that ἔκβασις might be taken to mean 'outcome' or 'result' (as it does in Wisd. 2.17, 11.14; Heb. 13.7). Then the translation might run: 'God ... will provide, together with the testing, the outcome that you are able to sustain it' (i.e. a result consisting in your being able to sustain it).

(ii) In 2 Pet. 2.9, the Lord knows how to rescue (ῥύεσθαι) the godly from (ἐκ) πειρασμός. Again, ῥύεσθαι, in itself, admittedly looks like escape; but this is illustrated by God's rescue of Lot from the destruction of Sodom, and suggests, therefore, that the rescue was not so much from the testing itself as from its ultimate sequel – the catastrophe at the end.

(iii) Rev. 3.10 (already quoted) promises 'I will also keep you from the ordeal (πειρασμός)' (NEB). But the fact that the verb is not strictly one of rescuing but of protecting (τηρεῖν) might, possibly, justify the conjecture that the phrase is a pregnant one, meaning 'Keep you safe in, and bring you out from...'.

Comparable is the thought in John 17.15 'I pray thee, not to take them out of the world, but to keep them from the evil one' (NEB). We could understand the Lord's Prayer clause if, correspondingly, it ran: 'When we are brought to testing, deliver us from the evil one.'

Thus, even if these three passages cannot fully be explained away, they are not quite so intransigent as the Lord's Prayer clause and the clause in Mark 14.38 (and parallels); and elsewhere in the New Testament (as a concordance shows) no such problem is presented by the πειράζειν-group. C. W. F. Smith (*IDB*) writes of the Lord's Prayer clause: 'Probably an eschatological reference is here modified for use in a prayer which seeks *deliverance from, but comes to imply deliverance within, testing*' (my italics). This is precisely what (with Carmignac) we desiderate. The question still remains, however: What, precisely, justifies the interpretation? Have we, perhaps, reached a position where we are confronted by a *logical* inconsequence, but one which expresses a *psychological* insight?

In this connection, two passages, in particular, are significant: Luke 21.36, and, still more, Mark 14.36. Luke 21.36 seems to be frankly 'escapist': ... praying that you may be strong enough to escape (ἵνα κατισχύσητε ἐκφυγεῖν) all these things that are going to happen ...' (though, all the same, 'to be strong enough' looks more like enduring than escaping). And the Lord's own prayer in Gethsemane is: 'take this cup away from me. Yet not what I will, but what thou wilt.' Admittedly, Jesus has not escaped testing: he is actually in it at the time. But it is, nevertheless, a prayer to escape at least one form of testing. Is it, then, true humility not to intellectualize, not to be over-logical, but, realizing one's weakness, to pray for escape even from what seems inevitable ('all these things that are going to happen'), while, at the same time, offering one's obedience: 'thy will be done'? The trouble is that practically all the rest of the traditions of Jesus' teaching emphasize the inevitability of suffering, and do not bid the disciples pray for escape. And it remains a fact that nearly all who pray the Lord's Prayer probably interpret it, often unconsciously, to mean 'Let us not succumb to temptation when we are tested'.[19] Indeed, it may be that the parallel clause in

St Matthew's version (Matt. 6.13), 'but deliver us from (the) evil (one)', represents one of the earliest interpretations in precisely this sense.[20]

Notes

1. *De Oratione* 8: ne nos inducas in temptationem, id est, ne nos patiaris induci, ab eo utique qui temptat, ceterum absit ut dominus temptare videatur, quasi aut ignoret fidem cuiusque aut deicere sit gestiens: diaboli est et infirmitas et malitia.
2. See J. B. Lightfoot, *On a Fresh Revision of the English New Testament*, London, Macmillan 1891, Appendix II, pp. 269ff. 'The Last Petition of the Lord's Prayer' (reprinted, in the 3rd edition only) from *Manchester Guardian*, 7, 14, 21 Sept. 1881 (p. 289). I owe the reference and the loan of the volume (the 3rd edition not being available in the Cambridge University Library or the Divinity School Library) to the Reverend Dr W. Horbury.
3. See, e.g., Jeremias 1971, p. 202.
4. See Marshall 1969, p. 50.
5. 1969, p. 267. It has to be admitted that the apparent dualism of Mark 14.38, 'the spirit is willing, but the flesh is weak', might lend weight to this view.
6. So Tertullian, *De Oratione* 8: nam et Abraham non temptandae fidei gratia sacrificare de filio iusserat, sed probandae ... And Augustine commonly distinguishes between the *tentatio* which is *probatio* and that which is *seductio*. I owe this observation to the late Professor J. Burnaby.
7. For this word-group, see Therrien 1973, especially pp. 9–26. The close connection between testing and refining is noted on p. 19. A full investigation of related words would involve also πειρᾶν, πεῖρα (see, e.g. Dan. 1:12); but this is not necessary for the present purpose.
8. To this the Reverend Dr W. Horbury has called my attention in this connection.
9. This conclusion is endorsed by Lyonnet 1958, pp. 27ff. Trench 1953 sums up the difference between this word-group and the πειράζειν-group: '... while *peirazein* may be used, but exceptionally of God, *dokimazein* could be used of Satan, seeing that he never proves that he may approve, or tests that he may accept.'
10. See, e.g., CD 14.2 (where the covenant is the defence against all the מוֹקְשֵׁי שַׁחַת), 1QS 2.17 (a curse on one who enters the covenant and then sets the מִכְשׁוֹל of his sin before him). But more often the Qumran literature uses even these words to

describe, rather, the attacks of human enemies. Incidentally, in CD 4.14, Isa. 24.17f., with its threefold, alliterative phrase, is quoted (פַחַד וָפַחַת וָפָח).

11. In Ps. 26.2 and elsewhere, the Psalmist actually invites God thus to test him.

12. Commentators point to Amos 9.9, but there it is doubtful whether the sifting is a threat (the wicked will be kept back for punishment, as pebbles stay in a sieve when the sand has gone through) or a promise (the faithful will be preserved like the good wheat in a grain-sieve – but can צְרוֹר mean 'wheat-grain', and was grain so sifted?). J. Schmid's 1955 Commentary *apud* Schürmann 1957, p. 105, is quoted as saying (of the Lucan passage): 'Dieses Bild besagt hier ..., dass er [Satan] sie gründlich "schütteln" wird, um sie zu erschüttern.'

13. For παγίς in this sense, see also 1 Tim. 3.7; 2 Tim. 2.26. Cf. the metaphors in Isa. 24.17f. (as in note 10, above), including, in the LXX, παγίς.

14. Loc. cit. in note 2 above, p. 308. The passage is in Migne, *P.G.* vol. 10, p. 1601. I have supplied in brackets what appears to be demanded by the argument.

15. Ibid. p. 314.

16. Meyer 1994, p. 10, however, regards this as a 'splendid parallel'.

17. Cf. Ps. 17.30 LXX (MT 18.30, *aliter*): ... ἐν σοὶ ῥυσθήσομαι ἀπὸ πειρατηρίου.

18. In a letter to me, 14 October 1973.

19. When I put the problem to a group of students at the Theological College of the Pacific at Suva in July 1974, several of them gave me the English equivalent of their own vernacular versions, and all of these represented some such sense.

20. For a careful essay on my investigation, leading to reflections on the devotional use of the Prayer, see now Demers 1993; and a detailed paper by Gibson (1998).

12

'THE SON OF MAN':
SOME OF THE FACTS

New Testament Studies, vol. 41 (1995), pp. 277–79.

Says the Psalmist, in Coverdale's (incorrect) version, 'while I was musing the fire kindled: and at last I spake ...' For many years I have been musing on why it is that otherwise excellent scholars seem to go blind to the facts when they discuss 'the Son of Man'. I exhibited most of the facts twenty years ago;[1] but here, at last, is a reminder.

(1) ὁ υἱὸς τοῦ ἀνθρώπου is not an exceptionally 'ponderous' phrase (to quote an epithet applied by a contemporary scholar) – no more ponderous, except by one syllable, than the common ὁ υἱὸς τοῦ θεοῦ. Neither is it linguistically odd, as has been asserted. It is an exact and idiomatic rendering of the sense '*the* Son of Man'. The definite article with the second noun represents a well-known Greek idiom.[2]

(2) In the New Testament, in the sayings traditions, including the saying of Stephen in Acts 7.56, this definite form is invariably used, with the solitary exception of John 5.27. The same definite form occurs again in the saying of James the Lord's brother related by Eusebius from Hegesippus (*HE* 2.23.13).

(3) In the New Testament outside the sayings, the anarthrous form correctly renders Psalm 8.5 (בֶּן־אָדָם parallel to אֱנוֹשׁ) at Heb. 2.6; and at Rev. 1.13, 14.14, a barbarously literal but nevertheless correctly anarthrous phrase, ὅμοιος υἱὸς ἀνθρώπου, renders the anarthrous Aramaic of Dan. 7.13, כְּבַר אֱנָשׁ.

(4) In Christian Greek literature after the New Testament, Justin correctly uses an anarthrous form when quoting Dan. 7, but uses the article when referring to a saying of Jesus (e.g. *Trypho* 100.8, illustrating both forms), thus adhering exactly to the New Testament usage.[3]

(5) In Hebrew literature prior to the New Testament, whereas various definite forms of a plural phrase, 'the sons of man', (בני האדם, LXX οἱ υἱοὶ [τῶν] ἀνθρώπων [τοῦ ἀνθρώπου] are common enough, especially in the Psalms, there is, to the best of my knowledge, only one solitary instance of the definite singular – 1QS 11.20 (בן האדם), but there the sign of the definite (the ה) is *over the line*, as though it were a correction or an afterthought.[4]

Thus if my facts are correctly stated, in the sayings traditions there is only one solitary instance of the anarthrous singular, but outside this only one solitary instance of the arthrous singular.

(6) In the *'Similitudes' of Enoch*, Dan. 7.13 is, if the English versions are correct, paraphrased with a correctly anarthrous phrase (46.1), which is subsequently referred to as 'this' or 'that Son of Man' (46.2, 4, 48.2); cf. John 12.34.

(7) Josephus (*Ant.* 10.267–8) provides evidence that Daniel was current and widely known in his time; and although Josephus' paraphrase does not seem to carry any reference to chapter 7, it does not follow that this was no part of the book at the time. Thus, it is not unreasonable to assume that Dan. 7 was widely known at this period.

(8) In the dialogue about the vision of Dan. 7 between Daniel and the interpreter, which occupies the latter part of the chapter, verse 22 says (probably) that judgement was given in favour of 'the saints of the Most High' (who are represented by the Son of Man, the human figure) – דינא יהב לקדישי עליונין. This could, however, without much difficulty be interpreted to mean also that the *right to judge* was given them. It is not difficult to believe that this thought underlies such Son of Man sayings as relate to judgement (e.g. Luke 21.36); and, conversely, that sayings about 'the saints' as judges stem from the Son of Man sayings (Matt. 19.28; Luke 22.30; 1 Cor. 6.2; Rev. 20.4; in this last there is clear allusion to Dan. 7).

Everyone knows that the elucidation of these facts is a matter not of fact but of speculation. But I still believe that the simplest explanation of the almost entire consistency with which the definite singular is confined to Christian sayings is to postulate that Jesus did refer to Dan. 7, speaking of '*the* Son of man [whom you know from that vision]', and that he used Daniel's human figure as not primarily a title so much as a symbol for the vocation to victory through obedience and martyrdom to which he was called and to which he summoned his followers (so that they would together constitute 'the people of the saints of the Most High'). It has been asserted (though the assertion has not gone unchallenged) that in Palestinian Aramaic of this period *bar naš* and *bar naš'* were indistinguishable in meaning, so that an unambiguous definite – 'the Son of Man' – could not have been expressed. But it is hard to conceive that it would have been beyond the capacity of the language to indicate an unambiguously definite or deictic sense by some means or other – perhaps by a periphrasis.[5]

To attribute the phrase to Jesus himself is not to deny that some of the Son of Man sayings in the Gospels may well be additions modelled on the original sayings; but I can think of no reason why there should not be a dominical origin for each of the main types of saying.

Such Son of Man sayings in John as do not conform to Synoptic types could well represent the Evangelist's adaptation of the tradition to express a pre-existence Christology. But all this I set out long ago, and need not repeat the details. The purpose of this note is only to reiterate the facts, which are frequently neglected.

Notes

1. 1974 (reprinted 1982). See also 1977[a], pp. 11ff.
2. See, e.g., Middleton 1841, p. 36, summarizing a ruling of Apollonius Dyscolus. *BDF* only grazes the matter (§252). But see now Wallace 1996, pp. 239f.
3. I owe this observation to Borsch 1970, p. 43. I have not investigated other patristic writers.
4. Facsimile in Burrows with Trever and Brownlee 1951, II, Plate 11.
5. See Moule 1982, p. 84 n. 27. Appeal is sometimes made also to targumic usages. I am not competent to judge of their date and degree of relevance.

Part Six

The Authority of Scripture

13

THE HOLY SPIRIT
AND SCRIPTURE

A lecture in a series 'Where is the Holy Spirit?' under the aegis of the Faculty of Divinity and the Department of Education in the University of Cambridge, published in *Epworth Review*, 8.2 (May 1981), pp. 66–74.

I invite you to examine with me two assumptions commonly made by Christians. One is that the Bible has a distinctive and indispensable function, at the very heart of the Church's life. The other is that this distinctiveness is imparted by the Holy Spirit – an assumption often summarized in the statement 'The Bible is inspired'.

The thesis that I offer for your critical consideration can be simply stated, although it concerns a problem that is anything but simple, and moves in a veritable minefield of prejudice and shibboleths.

My thesis has a negative and a positive side to it. The negative side is critical of the second of those two assumptions – 'the Bible is inspired'. If one is not merely discussing features which the Bible shares in common with other literatures and other modes of expression, but is inquiring what, if anything, constitutes that distinctiveness which is claimed for it, then I am going to question whether the statement, 'the Bible is inspired', affords any help towards defining it, because I wonder whether any distinctive meaning can be satisfactorily attached to such a statement.

But on the positive side, my thesis is twofold: that there is a clear distinctiveness about the Bible; and that, if one is asking, 'How are distinctively Christian decisions reached and implemented?', then it is impossible to give an adequate answer without reference both to Scripture (and its distinctiveness) and to the Spirit of God. In other words, I find that Scripture and a doctrine of the Spirit converge more evidently when one examines the nature of Christian decision-making than when one examines the nature of Scripture. In short, I find myself denying that any significant meaning can be attached to the phrase: 'The Bible is inspired', but affirming that both the Bible and inspiration-by-the-Spirit-of-God are indispensable in reaching Christian decisions.

On the negative side, then, one needs to reflect only for a moment on the meaning of inspiration and on the character of Scripture to realize how unhelpful the concept of inspiration is for distinguishing any special character in the Bible.

Do not misunderstand me. Do not mis-report me. Of course I am not denying that God's Holy Spirit speaks through Scripture. When, in the New Testament itself, the writer to the Hebrews prefaces a quotation from the Jewish Scriptures by the formula, 'as the Holy Spirit says', he is only giving particularly direct and striking expression to what any devout reader would wish to say. But does this help? No doubt the Holy Spirit speaks through Scripture; but not through Scripture alone. Who is going to deny that the Spirit speaks through many writers and artists and circumstances? I can see no particular gain, therefore, in calling the Bible inspired, when one is searching for what (if anything) is *distinctive* of it. For, ask yourself what you understand by the term 'inspired Scripture'. You do not, I'm sure, mean that the Spirit of the living God – God's presence – has somehow permeated the paper and ink. There is a sense, no doubt, in which all who believe that God is immanent within his creation as well as beyond it do believe that God is in the very texture of things. But in *that* sense there is no reason why the ink and paper of the Bible should more distinctively have the Spirit of God in them than the ink and paper of, let us say, the Communist Manifesto; nor, for that matter, why an atomic bomb or a lethal parasite should be less inspired than a rose. The conception simply of God's immanence reduces all matter to a common level. But if you are using Spirit in the usual sense – of God's personal presence – and mean that the *writers* of Scripture were inspired – as seems to be intended in the much-quoted phrase from 2 Peter 1.21, which says that impelled by the Holy Spirit the prophets spoke the words of God: then, so, surely, were Beethoven and T. S. Eliot impelled by the Spirit. At least at their height, what is it that impels poets, artists, and composers, if not the Spirit of God? Most of us believe that human beings are sometimes caught up by a mysterious power beyond them, so as to attain heights which normally they could not reach: 'an inspired performance', we say, 'an inspired game', 'an inspired insight'. A person's normal powers are sometimes divinely enhanced, and we recognize it. We have to recognize it, if only because the artist himself cannot command it: if it comes at all, it comes unbidden from above. But such inspiration is not confined to what we might call religious themes. In early Judaism, from the Book of Daniel onwards, the capacity to interpret dreams and foretell coming events – 'second sight', as we call it – is attributed to the Spirit of God or of the gods. Daniel says to King Nebuchadnezzar: 'No wise men, enchanters, magicians, or astrologers can show the king the mystery which the king has asked, but there is a God in heaven who reveals mysteries...' (2.27f.). And none of us, I imagine, would wish to limit this divinely enhanced capacity for vision exclusively to those writers who are represented in the Bible, any more than Jewish thinkers did. In the Dead Sea Scrolls, a worshipper – perhaps the great leader of the sect, the Teacher of Righteousness himself – explicitly claims it for himself, in one of the Psalms of Praise: 'by thy Holy Spirit I have faithfully harkened to thy marvellous counsel' (1QH 12.12, tr. G. Vermes). For my part, conversely, I find it hard to believe that the more pedestrian writers within the canonical Scriptures – in the Book of Ezra, for instance – were, in this sense, inspired at all, let alone more inspired than the great poets. No: inspiration, in this general sense of the heightening of human powers above the normal, gets you nowhere if you are looking for a definition of what is special about the Bible.

Is it, then, a special *kind* of inspiration that we must reckon with? Many, I think, will answer, 'Yes!' But what is this special kind of inspiration? Those who attribute special inspiration to the Bible are usually found to be talking not of inspiration at all, but of something else. They are using the word illegitimately to mean infallibility. They do not really want to say that God's presence took and endowed the writers merely with enhanced capacities, enabling them to write with a heightened sensitivity to reality. What they want to believe, rather, is that they were overpowered by God and made the mouthpiece for messages straight from him – that the fallible mind and imperfect character of the human agent were not allowed to hinder the authentic message from heaven. They were overridden by the divine.

But where is the evidence that this was the case with the biblical writers? I know of none. Why should 'impelling' by the Spirit be so interpreted? What is more, if one believes in God as personal it follows that he would not and could not treat a person like an instrument. There is no denying that writers, Jewish and Christian, have asserted that he does. Both Philo the Jew and the Christian apologist Athenagoras used without qualification the analogy of a flute-player: God used his prophets exactly as a performer manipulates his instrument. But is the analogy really tolerable? It seems to me totally out of character with the God whom a theist acknowledges. As a modern writer, John Ziesler, says (1980, pp. 127f.),

> God is he who enables everything to be what it is ... *This includes enabling my actions, thoughts, and choices to be genuinely my own* ... It is not (he continues) that God controls or supersedes my decisions and so on, so that I think they are mine though they are really being manipulated by God, but that my genuine freedom, my character, my personality, and all my decisions can be mine only because God enables them to be so ... God ... does not threaten man's humanness or freedom or integrity – he guarantees them!

And Christians can never forget their conviction that God's ultimate utterance to us is not a statement but a Man.

Thus, a conception of inspiration as the mechanical prevention of error is not only an illegitimate stretching of the meaning of the word; it is a sub-personal, sub-theistic conception of God: least of all is it compatible with a fully Christian understanding of God and of the Word made flesh.

Besides, even supposing that the writers of Scripture could have been divinely compelled to write without error, who is going to assure me that I am interpreting and understanding them without error? Infallible broadcasting is not much use without infallible radio sets.

... everybody knows [said Professor G. B. Caird (1980, p. 40)] how hard it is to be sure that what is received is exactly what is transmitted, without interference or distortion. That people habitually attach a meaning of their own to what they hear or read is beyond doubt, but it does not follow that this kind of hearer's meaning is in any sense a part of what is spoken or written.

So, what I am saying is that inspiration does not mean infallibility; and infallibility does not seem to be God's way; and even if it were, how could we profit from it?

But, in saying that inspiration is not a useful term to apply when one is trying to understand the distinctiveness of Scripture, am I not ignoring the famous phrase in 2 Tim. 3.16, which does seem to declare the Scriptures inspired? 'All Scripture' (does it not say?) 'is *theopneustos*', which is usually translated 'inspired'. Well, regarding this, I have three things to say.

First, it was one of the most consistent and learned fundamentalists of a past generation, B. B. Warfield, of Princeton, who himself questioned that translation of the phrase. He pointed out (see Kelsey 1975, p. 20) that *theopneustos* – literally, 'God-breathed' – more probably meant '*ex-spired*', 'breathed *out* by God'. The phrase means not that God's Spirit is in all Scripture so much as that all Scripture is God's utterance, his 'out-breathing'. In any case, we are no nearer to the sense 'infallible', which is what inspirationists want, nor – which I am searching for – to any distinctive description of Scripture not shared with other media, for they, too, undeniably can convey messages from God.

Secondly, remember that the term 'Scripture' in 2 Tim. 3.16 refers in any case to an undefined range of Jewish literature; for, by that time, although the Torah, the Books of Moses, were almost certainly a fixed entity, there was not a defined Jewish canon of Scripture as a whole. If the phrase in 2 Tim. 3.16 were accepted in a rigorous sense as a declaration of the infallibility of Scripture, it would refer to a range of Jewish writings of which we no longer know the contents, though we can be sure that it contains that terrible command to commit genocide, in 1 Sam. 15. And, unless 2 Tim. 3.16 is of a very late date, it would include no Christian scriptures in its reference.

Thirdly and finally, it is in any case poor logic to say that the accused is not guilty because he says so. At best, it would be questionable apologetics to defend the veracity of the Bible simply by a statement to this effect drawn from within it – even if that *were* the meaning of the statement. The same would apply if we appealed to the saying attributed to Jesus himself in the Fourth Gospel: 'the Scripture cannot be broken' (10.35). The argument would be perfectly circular.

Let me now reiterate that, in denying that 'inspired' is a term that has any legitimate or useful application to Scripture when we are trying to locate its distinctiveness, I am not for a moment (please do not misinterpret me) denying either that the Holy Spirit may speak through Scripture, or that Scripture is inspir*ing*. I am not denying any of the great things that God does for us in Scripture. He does speak to us through it. Scripture does 'find' us, as Coleridge said. It contains passages of stupendous grandeur, it probes the conscience, kindles the soul, exalts the spirit. The Bible knocks us down and lifts us up. It is, to a high degree, inspir*ing*. It is putting it mildly when that same 2 Tim. 3.16 says, rather prosaically, that Scripture is 'useful' for teaching, convicting, reforming, and educating. Most certainly it is all that. But that is not true exclusively of Scripture.

But if in describing Scripture itself there is nothing to warrant any distinctive or special use of the term inspiration, must it not at least be allowed that the canon was an inspired choice? The canon of Scripture – the list of the books comprising the Bible – is the list of those books which are deemed by the Church catholic to constitute the norm for faith and practice. This means, as the sixth of the Thirty-nine Articles puts it, that

> Holy Scripture containeth all things necessary to salvation: so that whatsoever is not read therein, nor may be proved thereby, is not to be required of any man, that it should be believed as an article of the faith, or be thought requisite or necessary to salvation.

This is not to say that everything outside Scripture is incorrect, nor everything in Scripture correct; but that the Church recognizes this body of writings as the norm and standard of the Faith, beyond which (in matters of controversy) nothing is to be deemed essential. Now, was it not the Holy Spirit that led the Fathers of the Church to this momentous decision about what constituted the entire Bible, and the Fathers of Judaism before them to the corresponding decision regarding the contents of that part of it that belongs to the Old Covenant? Surely we must say 'Yes!' But, once again, not in any recognizably distinctive sense. I can think of no evidence that the Church's choice was safeguarded in some special way, over and above ordinary human precautions, against a mistaken judgement. As everybody who has studied the matter knows, there was a great deal of doubt and a consider-able element of chance about certain fringe documents, and, in their case, the ultimate decision might easily have gone in another direction – not to mention that Church councils are not conspicuous for the purity and single-mindedness of their members. And as for the main nucleus of documents, both in the Old Testament and the New, they had come to stay in any case, without the decision of the councils: their intrinsic excel-lence and usefulness had established them before ever it came to a final choice. Was that the work of the Holy Spirit? Who can deny it? But I cannot see this as a special dispensation or as marking a unique act of divine overruling. The documents were established by their own antiquity and authenticity – and this, indeed, is endorsed by critical scholarship. Those bearing apostolic names may not all be by apostles; but it is im-possible to find an earlier or more authentic body of witness to the beginnings of Christianity. This is a striking process indeed, but nothing but a perfectly 'natural' process whereby excellence asserts itself. By all means call it a divine process if you like, as much as a human one. But I can detect no evidence of its being a special case.

I would, for my part, go on to say that, although the formation of a canon is an important datum for anyone who in-vestigates the truth-claims of Christianity, there is nothing to be gained by shutting one's eyes to what is pre-canonical or extra-canonical or post-canonical. The canon is the Church's norm: that is one of the facts which we have to recognize when examining the truth-claims of Christianity. We cannot alter it, even if we wanted to: it is an unalterable fact that by the fourth century these had been declared normative documents. People sometimes ask, 'Might we not revise and improve the canon? Ought not this and that to be included?' But that is to misunderstand what the canon is. It is not an anthology of the best devotional books. It is what the Church deemed their norm of doctrine: the canon is a historical fact. You may think its choice an error of judgement; but it remains a fact that these were the books chosen. And actually, as I have said, critical research has discovered nothing earlier or more directly relevant to the beginnings of Christianity than the books of the New Testament canon.

But that is not to say that those who chose and arranged the books were necessarily the best interpreters of them. Professor Brevard Childs of Yale has for some years espoused the view that Scripture – and as a Hebraist he is concerned chiefly with the Jewish Scriptures – may be properly interpreted only in such ways as are indicated or implied by their segregation into a closed canon and by the positions now occupied within that canon by each verse or section. (See 1972, 1979.) This seems to mean that some special inspiration was vouchsafed to the final editor or to the community he represented. We have to listen primarily not to what may have been the original meaning of a passage, but rather to the meaning with which it has been invested by its present position and the interpretation of it in the religious community for which the redactor acted. On this showing, scholarly research into earlier stages of the tradition becomes at best something ancillary, at worst something impertinent.

Now I am keen to listen, among other things, to what canonical arrangement and placing may tell me and to what an editor teaches me: but not to that alone, as though a special afflatus were attached to it: for this, again, there seems to me no warrant in the evidence. I want to examine, so far as is possible, aspects of what the Bible points to, at earlier stages of its composition as well as at a time when it had settled down into a recognized collection – and later still. I want to ask what kind of God this is, to whom men and women react thus and thus, at this period and that. The fact that a canon was eventually formed is itself part of the evidence to be examined; but this ought not to exclude scrutiny of its component parts or their pre-history, nor of the literature rejected by those who decided on the canon – for all these are significant in our quest for God, as well as in our quest for what, if anything, is distinctive of the canonical Scriptures. The selecting of books to form a canon, and the editing and interpreting that went into their final redaction are among the factors that need to be taken into account when one is asking about the nature and distinctiveness of Scripture.

Another factor to be reckoned with besides the canon – as another distinguished American scholar reminds us, John Reumann (e.g. 1977) – is the lectionary system. To read Scripture in association with assemblies for worship and in line with a religious calendar is itself to impose an interpretation on it; and this is one more of the phenomena to be examined when we ask ourselves how Scripture speaks and where the Holy Spirit of God is conspicuously at work. Are the compilers of lectionaries inspired? Sometimes, perhaps; sometimes, perhaps not. This is a question near to the bone for many of the Christian communions.

But my main point is that in none of the directions in which we have looked does there seem to be any clear reason for discerning a conspicuous or recognizably distinctive work of the Holy Spirit protecting selectors and interpreters from error or guaranteeing authentic transmission.

Wherein, then, lies any distinctiveness there may be in the canonical Bible? And what are we to say of the work of the Holy Spirit? If a doctrine of the Holy Spirit does not appear to offer a clue for this particular problem, is there some other way in which a distinctiveness may be defined, and is there some other aspect of authority to which a doctrine of Spirit *is* relevant? To both those questions I would answer 'yes'.

And here I must offer an analogy. In Arizona, near Winslow, there is a vast crater which is believed to have been formed by the impact of an enormous iron meteorite. By observing its shape and analysing the composition and formations of the rock and soil, it has been possible, I gather, to discover a good deal about the size and character of that meteorite. No doubt the investigations for this purpose would include distinguishing between what the original level of the ground was when the impact took place, and what has been deposited since then.

Altogether, the reconstruction of the original circumstances must involve an elaborate critical exercise by geologists, geophysicists, meteorologists and other specialists. Only so may the character and size of that meteorite be deduced.

Now, no analogy is perfect; but roughly you can see what I am getting at. The impact we are studying now is the impact of 'the Christ-event', as we have come (conveniently, though too loosely) to call the life, ministry, death, and resurrection of Jesus Christ, together with the emergence of the Christian movement. Our crater is the stamp of that impact in the earliest Christian literature and in any other literature or archaeological data that are relevant and that may throw light on the events. This includes the Jewish Scriptures, which were the matrix of the Christ-event. Part of the crater, also, is the very emergence of a canon of the Scriptures. Thus, Scripture's distinctive function is a historical one: it is the primary evidence for the Christ-event; it is the main part of our evidential crater. And the geologist's method of examining the successive layers and deposits is duly represented in the New Testament critic's procedures. Due account, too, is taken of the drawing of a line by the Christian community at a particular level, and the relevance of this for estimating the nature of the impact is weighed and assessed. Something comparable has to be taken account of for the Jewish canon in north Palestine at the end of the first century of the Christian era.

What is the result? What are we to say about the events and, above all, about the Person at their centre, that caused this impact? This is not a lecture on Christian beginnings, and I must not here and now go into details about an answer to that question. But in brief what I am now trying to say is that what the Scriptures point to is a self-authenticating reality which lends to the Scriptures the distinctiveness that we are seeking.

It always seems to me that the genesis of the Easter-belief – the reaching, that is, by certain of Jesus' followers of the conviction that Jesus was alive after the crucifixion (alive with permanent, irreversible, eternal life) – simply cannot be adequately described without using religious terms – terms of divine revelation. The secular historian cannot deny that the friends of Jesus did (rightly or wrongly) come to that preposterous conviction. If he is determined to acknowledge as real nothing outside the secular historian's field, he can suggest that this was due to hallucination or to deductions from already held religious beliefs or to superstitions and imaginative enthusiasm for a hero and a leader. But none of these suggestions (to my mind) is anything like adequate to account for the facts. It is positively more plausible and (I believe) more honest for the historian to admit that he can find, within his own terms of reference, no adequate explanation of how the friends of Jesus reached that conviction. If so, he must be ready to acknowledge that the evidence points beyond the frontiers of history to some religious conclusion, a conclusion in terms of revelation: Jesus, we have to say, showed himself alive; God raised him from among the dead. His supposed aliveness corresponds with reality. This is the distinctive statement. The historical evidence cumulatively, including both the Scriptures themselves and the fact that the Christian Church selected them, points, as it seems to me, to one who was not only a great, magnetic, supremely powerful man of superb integrity, but to this person's being, in an unparalleled way – in a distinctive way – one with God. Not, like our meteorite (for here the analogy completely fails), entering the earth's atmosphere from outside, colliding with the ground, and flying into a thousand fragments. No: Jesus clearly belonged to human kind and came from within. Yet, all the time, he belonged also, in an unparalleled way, to what I can only call 'the beyond'. And this mark has been left, embedded in the evidence, by the impact. This is a paradox; but it is one from which I see no way of escape.

Now, if so, then the whole of Scripture, not miraculously safeguarded against error but critically examined, points to the impact of One who is both within and beyond the world of human affairs. That is its distinctive character. Nothing can take its place for throwing a brilliant point of light on the mysterious appearing of God in Christ. Scripture performs its distinctive function when it brings us to God through Jesus Christ.

Finally, then, let us consider what happens when the Bible – Old Testament and New Testament, in its entirety – is allowed to perform this one proper and distinctive function (side by side with all the inspiring – yes, inspir*ing* – and uplifting and

soul-searching that it does, in common with some other literatures); the function, that is, of confronting the readers with a
portrait of Jesus Christ and with the events that show that he
lives and is with them. The Bible is then at the very heart of
the process by which Christians draw near to the living God,
and he to them. It is by constant study of the Bible that the
people of God are held to their historical roots, and held also
to faith in Christ, crucified, raised from among the dead, and
alive for evermore – the Christ through whom we draw near
to God and he draws near to us. In this steady holding of the
Church to the *fait accompli* under Pontius Pilate and to its
constant consequences, the Bible is distinctive, paramount,
and indispensable. Its character as the primary evidence
for the beginnings of Christianity and as a uniquely early
and authentic presentation of Christ is what lends it its distinctiveness.

But we cannot effectively use (or, rather, be used by) this
access to the living God through Jesus Christ to which the
Bible admits us, unless the Spirit of God is among us and
within us, making our minds alert and fortifying our resolve to
obey him in what we are shown. The ministers of the Christian
Church are ordained expressly as ministers of the Word and
the Sacraments; which means, I think, that all clergy are theologians: it is their professional duty and responsibility to communicate and interpret the knowledge of God. All are also
committed to leading their communities in Christian worship:
administering the Sacraments and the other means of grace.
And in both sides of their professional task, the Holy Spirit of
God is at work in them and in their communities: otherwise
they will toil in vain. God's presence as Spirit is the *sine qua non*.
As St Paul in effect says, it is the Spirit that utters in us the cry
'Abba! dear Father! Your will be done!' which was also on the
lips of Jesus. The Spirit reproduces in us his Sonship, and it is
the Scriptures that bring us and hold us to this knowledge of
the Son of God and this share in his Spirit.

So the Scriptures lead us to the Son – the living Son of God;
and in the presence of God, Father, Son, and Holy Spirit, we
are in a position to discern his will and find the moral strength
to follow it. It is no part of the function of Scripture to give us
moral direction. Scarcely any of the pressing moral problems

of the present day are so much as mentioned there. If, as does happen on occasion, some clear insight or compelling directive does come straight from what is written, that is a bonus. But it is not anything to be surprised or distressed at if the Bible does not guide us so. As I have ventured to say elsewhere (Moule 1977[b]), the Bible is not itself so much a compass or a chart, as directions for finding the Pilot; and he it is who will be to us both compass and chart and will steer us through the shoals. He is God's living Utterance. Putting it in terms of an elementary diagram, we are not to expect moral guidance normally to come straight along the base of the triangle, from the Bible to our predicament. Rather, we are to look to the Bible to help us to ascend the gradient up one side of the triangle to the living God through Jesus Christ; and it is from there, down the third side of the triangle that we may look for guidance to come, if we seek it seriously and realistically in obedience to the Holy Spirit and with the help of the experts in the relevant sciences and skills.

And in all this the Holy Spirit of God within us and among us will guide us, will purify our motives, and will strengthen us. St Paul gives a picture, in 1 Cor. 14, of a Christian assembly met for worship, for mutual edification, and for finding and following the will of God. The Scriptures of the Old Testament are represented there, in psalmody; the Scriptures of the New Testament are not yet in existence – they have not, for the most part, been written; but their substance is already there, in the traditions about Jesus and about his way and about his People; and the Spirit is there, uttering himself both through the inspired speakers, the Christian prophets, and through the Church's vital act of critically sifting and discerning what the prophets say. And thus it is that the will of God is felt after, found, and followed: we, incorporated in Christ Jesus; the Old Testament and the Christian Gospel behind us (that is, in effect, now, our Bible in our hands); the Holy Spirit in our midst; and the way of God ahead of us. By the Scriptures, through Christ, in the power of the Holy Spirit we make our pilgrimage in the whole company of the Church, to God. And here it is that the Scriptures and the Holy Spirit do converge.

Scripture is so precious to me that I have read it through from cover to cover scores of times, missing not a day in 50 years without steady reading. I hope that it is now clear why this is so. I do not believe that Scripture is infallible; I question the value of the language of inspiration for describing its distinctive qualities; I believe (as I have shown) that Scripture itself, and the fact that it is an accredited selection, need to be critically examined and sifted like any other matters of antiquity. But, precisely because it does constitute the body of documents most directly concerned with the impact of those events which culminated (so I read the evidence) in Jesus and the Christian movement, it constitutes (as a whole and taken in its entirety) a mirror held up to the face of God. And unless we gaze daily in that mirror we are deprived of the most vital agent in our access to God through Jesus Christ. That is why the Bible is indispensable and uniquely precious. But without the Spirit of God to nerve me to face, to respond to, and to obey that awesome presence, and to bind me to my fellow-seekers for our mutual help and encouragement in this activity, all the study and labour would be worse than useless. This is how I understand both the distinctiveness of Scripture and the relation to it of a doctrine of the Spirit.

ABBREVIATIONS

Ant.	Josephus, *Jewish Antiquities*
BAGD	Bauer, W., *A Greek-English Lexicon of the New Testament and Other Early Christian Literature*, tr., ed. and enlarged by Arndt, W. F., Gingrich, F. W. and Danker, F. W. University of Chicago, 1979
BDF	Blass, F., Debrumer, A., and Funk, R. W., *A Greek Grammar of the New Testament and Other Early Christian Literature* (tr., ed., enlarged). Cambridge University Press/University of Chicago Press, 1961
Bel.	Josephus, *The Jewish War*
BJRL	*Bulletin of the John Rylands Library*
CN	*Coniectanea Neotestamentica*
ET	*Expository Times*
FZPT	*Freiburger Zeitschrift für Philosophie und Theologie*
HE	Eusebius, *Historia Ecclesiastica*
HR	Hatch, E. and Redpath, H. A. *A Concordance to the Septuagint*. Oxford, Clarendon, 1897
HTR	*Harvard Theological Review*
IDB	*The Interpreter's Dictionary of the Bible*. Buttrick, G. A., *et al.* (eds), New York/Nashville, Abingdon, 1962
IKZ	*Internationale Katholische Zeitschrift*
JBL	*Journal of Biblical Literature*
JNTS	*Journal of New Testament Studies*: (subsequently *NTS*)
JSS	*Journal of Semitic Studies*
JTS	*Journal of Theological Studies*
M	Ovid, *Metamorphoses*
NovT	*Novum Testamentum*
NTS	*New Testament Studies*
PG	*Patrologica Graeca*, Paris, Garnier, 1857–91
RHPR	*Revue d'Histoire et de Philosophie Religieuses*
RSR	*Recherches des Sciences Religieuses*
RTP	*Revue de Théologie et Philosophie*
SB	Strack, H. L., und Billerbeck, P., *Kommentar zum Neuen Testament aus Talmud und Midrasch*. München, Beck, 1922–28
SBL	Society of Biblical Literature
SEÅ	*Svensk Exegetisk Årsbok*
SJT	*Scottish Journal of Theology*
TDNT	*Theological Dictionary of the New Testament* (tr. from Kittel, G., *et al.*, 1933–79), Grand Rapids, Eerdmans, 1964–76
TLZ	*Theologische Literaturzeitung*
ZNW	*Zeitschrift für die Neutestamentliche Wissenschaft*
ZTK	*Zeitschrift für Theologie und Kirche*
Zygon	*Zygon: Journal of Religion and Science*

REFERENCES AND
INDEX OF AUTHORS

Numbers shown in bold type indicate pages where references may be found to the titles listed below.

Aland, K., 'Bemerkungen zum Schluss des Markusevangeliums', Ellis, E. E. and Wilcox, M. (eds), *Neotestamentica et Semitica* (FS Matthew Black). Edinburgh, T. and T. Clark, 1969, pp. 157: **186**. (Cf. 'Der Schluss des Markusevangeliums', in K. Aland, *Neutestamentliche Entwürfe*. München, Kaiser, 1979, pp. 246ff.: **186**.)

Allison, S. F. *et al.* (eds) *The Fulness of Christ*. London, SPCK, 1950: **138**.

Bailie, G., *Violence Unveiled: Humanity at the Crossroads*. New York, Crossroad, 1995: **29**.

Baillie, D., *God was in Christ*. London, Faber, 1948: **158**.

Bammel, E., 'The Revolution Theory from Reimarus to Brandon', Bammel and Moule, 1984, pp. 11ff.: **113**.

Bammel, E., and Moule, C. F. D. (eds), *Jesus and the Politics of His Day*. Cambridge, Cambridge University Press, 1984: **113**.

Barrett, C. K., 'The Background of Mark 10:45', Higgins, A. J. B. (ed.), *New Testament Essays: studies in memory of T. W. Manson*. Manchester, Manchester University Press, 1959, pp. 1ff.: **79**.

Barrett, C. K., *A Commentary on the First Epistle to the Corinthians*. London, A. and C. Black, 1968: **200–1**.

Barrett, C. K., *A Commentary on the Second Epistle to the Corinthians*. London, A. and C. Black, 1973: **36, 39**.

Barrett, C. K., *Paul: an Introduction to His Thought*, London, Geoffrey Chapman, 1994: **114**.

Barrett, C. K., 'Stephen and the Son of Man', Eltester, W. (ed.), *Apophoreta: Festschrift für Ernest Haenchen*. Berlin, Töpelmann, 1964, pp. 32ff.: **78**.

Bauckham, R. J., 'Jesus' Demonstration in the Temple', Lindars, B. (ed.), *Law and Religion: essays on the place of the Law in Israel and Early Christianity*. Cambridge, James Clarke, 1988, pp.72ff.: **114**.

Best, E., *One Body in Christ*. London, SPCK, 1955: **175**.

Bittner, W., 'Gott-Menschensohn-Davidssohn', *FZPT* 32 (1985), pp. 343ff.: **115**.

Bockmuehl, M., *This Jesus: Martyr, Lord, Messiah*. Edinburgh, T. and T. Clark, 1994: **114**.

Boismard, M. E., ' "Constitué Fils de Dieu" (Rom. 1:4)', *RSR* 60 (1953), pp. 5ff.: **79**.

Borg, M. J., *Conflict, Holiness and Politics in the Teachings of Jesus*. New York/Toronto, Edwin Mellen, 1984: **101**.

Boring, M. E., *Sayings of the Risen Jesus: Christian Prophecy in the Synoptic Tradition*. Cambridge, Cambridge University Press, 1982: **189**.

Bornkamm, G., *Jesus of Nazareth*. London, Hodder and Stoughton, 1960: **108**.

Borsch, F. H., *The Christian and Gnostic Son of Man*. London, SCM Press, 1970: **207**.

Bouttier, M., *En Christ: Étude d'Exégèse et de Théologie Paulinienne*. Paris, Presses Universitaires de France, 1962: **94, 131**.

Bowers, W. P., 'Paul and Religious Propaganda in the First Century', *NovT* 22 (1980), pp. 316ff.: **114**.

Bowker, J. W., *The Religious Imagination and the Sense of God*. Oxford, Clarendon Press, 1978: **103, 109–10**.

Bowker, J. W., *The Targums and Rabbinic Literature*. Cambridge, Cambridge University Press, 1969: **130**.

Brandon, S. G. F., 'The Date of the Markan Gospel', *NTS* 7 (1960–61), pp. 126ff.: **113**.

Brandon, S. G. F., *The Fall of Jerusalem and the Christian Church. A Study of the Effects of the Jewish Overthrow of A.D. 70 on Christianity*. London, SPCK, 1957: **97, 113**.

Brandon, S. G. F., *Jesus and the Zealots*. Manchester, Manchester University Press, 1967: **113**.

Braun, H., 'Zur Terminologie der Acta von den Auferstehung Jesu', *TLZ* 77 (1952), pp. 533ff.: **78**.

Breech, J., *The Silence of Jesus: the Authentic Voice of the Historical Man*. Toronto, Doubleday, 1983: **182–3**.

Brown, R. E., *The Epistles of John*. New York, Garden City, Doubleday, 1982: **34**.

Bruce, F. F., 'The date and character of Mark', Bammel and Moule, 1984, pp. 69ff.: **113**.

Buchanan, G. W., 'Symbolic Money-Changers in the Temple', *NTS* 37 (1991), pp. 280ff.: **114**.

Burkitt, F. C., *Eucharist and Sacrifice*. Cambridge, Heffer and Son, 1927: **174**.

Burrows, M., with Trever, J. C. and Brownlee, W. H., *The Dead Sea Scrolls of St Mark's Monastery*. New Haven, The American School of Oriental Research, 1951: **207**.

Cadbury, H. J., 'The Titles of Jesus in Acts', Foakes Jackson, F. J. and Lake, K. (eds), *The Beginnings of Christianity*. London, Macmillan, vol. 5, 1933, pp. 354ff.: **53**.

Caird, G. B., *Jesus and the Jewish Nation*. London, Athlone Press, 1965: **114**.

Caird, G. B., *The Language and Imagery of the Bible*. Essex/London, Duckworth, 1980: **31, 215**.

Caird, G. B., *The Revelation of St John the Divine*. London, A. and C. Black, 1966: **33**.

Campbell, J. Y., 'ΚΟΙΝΩΝΙΑ and its Cognates in the New Testament', *JBL* 51 (1932), pp. 352ff.: **176**.

Carlston, C. E., 'The Christology of Acts', *Abstracts of Papers at the 99th meeting of the Society of Biblical Literature*, no. 31, Decatur, Georgia, Society of Biblical Literature, 1963: **78**.

Carmignac, J., *Recherche sur le 'Notre Père'*. Paris, Letouzey et Ané, 1969: **190, 191, 192, 194, 196, 198, 199, 200, 201**.

Carrington, P., *The Primitive Christian Catechism*. Cambridge, Cambridge University Press, 1952: **182, 189**.

Casey, R. P., 'The Earliest Christologies', *JTS* n.s. 9 (1958), pp. 253ff.: **78, 80**.

Catchpole, D. R., 'The Triumphal Entry', Bammel and Moule, 1984, pp. 319ff.: **101, 114**.

Catholicity, London, Dacre Press, 1947: **138**.

Catholicity of Protestantism, The. Eds R. N. Flew and R. E. Davies, London, Lutterworth Press, 1950: **138**.

Charlesworth, J. H., *The Old Testament Pseudepigrapha and the New Testament*. Cambridge, Cambridge University Press, 1985: **114**.

Childs, B. S., *Introduction to the Old Testament as Scripture*. London, SCM Press, 1979: **218**.

Childs, B. S., 'The Old Testament as Scripture of the Church', *Concordia Theological Monthly*, 43 (1972), pp. 709ff.: **218**.

Chilton, B. D., *God in Strength: Jesus' Announcement of the Kingdom*. Freistadt, Plöchl, 1979: **93**.

Chilton, B. D., 'Regnum Dei Deus Est', *SJT* 31 (1977–8), pp. 261ff.: **93**.

Conzelmann, H., *Die Apostelgeschichte*. Tübingen, Mohr, 1963: **53, 77, 78, 79, 80**; E.tr. *The Acts of the Apostles* (Hermeneia) Philadelphia, Fortress Press, 1987.

Conzelmann, H., *The Theology of St Luke*. London, Faber, 1961: **56, 77**.

Cullmann, O., *Baptism in the New Testament*. London, SCM Press, 1950: **175**.

Cullmann, O., *The Christology of the New Testament*. London, SCM Press, 1959: **54, 62, 77**.

Cullmann, O., *Peter: Disciple, Apostle, Martyr*. London, SCM Press, 1953: **62**.

Dahl, N. A., 'Die messianität Jesu bei Paulus', Sevenster, J. N., and van Unnik, W. C. (eds), *Studia Paulina* (FS J. de Zwaan). Haarlem, Bohr, 1953, pp. 83ff.: **80**.

Davies, W. D. and Sanders, E. P., 'Jesus: from the Semitic Point of View', Kevin Taylor (ed.), *The Cambridge History of Judaism III*. Cambridge, Cambridge University Press, forthcoming 1999: **114**.

Demers, M., 'The Temptation-Clause of the Lord's Prayer', unpub. dissertation for part of MA Degree, McMaster University, 1993: **204**.

Descamps, A., *Les Justes et la Justice dans les Évangiles et le Christianisme primitif hormis la Doctrine proprement paulinienne*. Louvain, Universitaires de Louvain, 1950: **72, 80**.

Dibelius, M., *Studies in the Acts of the Apostles*. London, SCM Press, 1956: **66**.

Dillistone, F. W., *The Structure of the Divine Society*. London, Lutterworth, 1951: **174**.

Dix, G., *The Shape of the Liturgy*. London, Dacre Press, 1945: **161–2, 167–9**.

Dodd, C. H., *The Founder of Christianity*. New York, Macmillan, 1970: **108**; London, Collins, 1971.

Dodd, C. H., *History and the Gospel*. London, Nisbet, 1938: **96**.

Doeve, J. W., *Jewish Hermeneutics in the Synoptic Gospels and Acts*. Assen, 1953: **80**.

Duling, A. C., 'The Promises to David and their Entrance into Christianity – Nailing Down a Likely Hypothesis', *NTS* 19 (1973–74), pp. 55–77: **79**.

Dunn, J. D. G., *Baptism in the Holy Spirit*. London, SCM Press, 1970: **94, 125, 128, 131**.

Dunn, J. D. G., *Christology in the Making*. London, SCM Press, 1980: **94**.

Dunn, J. D. G., '2 Corinthians III.17 – "the Lord is the Spirit"', *JTS* n.s. 21 (1970), pp. 309ff.: **94**.

Dunn, J. D. G., 'Paul's Understanding of the Death of Jesus', Banks, R. J. (ed.), *Reconciliation and Hope* (FS L. L. Morris), Exeter, Paternoster Press, 1974, pp. 125ff.: **18**.

Dunn, J. D. G., 'Spirit and Kingdom', *ET* 82 (1970), pp. 36ff.: **131**.

Dupont, J., 'Filius meus es Tu. L'Interprétation de Ps. II.7 dans le nouveau Testament', RSR 35 (1948), pp. 541ff.: **79**.

Dupont, J., *The Sources of Acts*. London, Darton, Longman & Todd, 1964: **79**.

Foakes Jackson, F. J., and Lake, K., 'Christology', Foakes Jackson, F. J. and Lake, K., (eds), *The Beginnings of Christianity*. London, Macmillan I (1920), pp. 345ff.: **80**.

Fox, D., *The Vagrant Lotus: an Introduction to Buddhist Philosophy*. Philadelphia, Westminster Press, 1973: **18**.

Frei, H., *The Identity of Jesus Christ*. Philadelphia, Fortress Press, 1975: **93**.

Fuchs, E., *Gesammelte Aufsätze*, Vol. II, Tübingen, Mohr, 1960: **108**.

Fulness of Christ: see Allison.

Gärtner, B., *Die rätselhaften Termini Nazoräer und Iskariot*, Uppsala, 1957: **59**.

Galling, K., 'Der Charakter der Chaosschilderung bei Gen. 1.2', *ZTK* 47 (1950), pp. 145ff.: **130**.

George, A. R., *Communion with God in the New Testament*. London, Epworth Press, 1953: **156**.

Gibson, J. 'Testing Temptation: The Meaning of Matt. 6:13ᵃ//Lk. 11:4ᵇ', a paper for Society of Biblical Literature, Annual Meeting, 1998: **204**.

Gore, C., *The Body of Christ*. London, John Murray, 1901: **140, 144, 170**.

Grässer, E., and Merk, O. (eds), *Glaube und Eschatologie: Festschrift für Werner Georg Kümmel zum 80. Geburtstag*. Tübingen, J. C. B. Mohr (1985), pp. 199–208: **179–89**.

Gundry, R. H., *Soma in Biblical Theology, with Emphasis on Pauline Anthropology*. Cambridge, Cambridge University Press, 1976: **18**.

Haenchen, E., *Die Apostlegeschichte*. Göttingen, Vandenhoeck & Ruprecht, 1961: **53, 80**; E. tr. *The Acts of the Apostles*, Oxford, Blackwell, 1971.

Hahn, F., *Christologische Hoheitstitel*. Göttingen, Vandenhoeck & Ruprecht, 1963: **17, 77, 78, 79**; *The Titles of Jesus in Christology* (abridged E. tr.). London, Lutterworth, 1969: **18**.

Hamerton-Kelly, R. G., *Sacred Violence: Paul's Hermeneutic of the Cross*. Minneapolis, Augsburg-Fortress, 1992: **29**.

Harvey, A. E., *Jesus and the Constraints of History: the Bampton Lectures, 1980*. London, Duckworth/Philadelphia, Fortress Press, 1982.

Hebert, G., *Ways of Worship*, London, SCM Press, 1951.

Hellwig, M., *Jesus the Compassion of God*. Dublin, Dominican Publications/Wilmington DE, Glazier, 1983: **99**.

Hengel, M., *The Charismatic Leader and His Followers*. Edinburgh, T. and T. Clark, 1981: **102, 109**.

Hengel, M., Review of Brandon 1967, *JSS* 14 (1969), pp. 231ff.: **113**.

Hengel, M., *Was Jesus a Revolutionist?* (E. tr. with Introduction by Reumann, J.). Philadelphia, Fortress Press, 1971: **113**.

Higgins, A. J. B., *Jesus and the Son of Man*. London, Lutterworth, 1964: **77**.

Hooker, M. D., *From Adam to Christ: Essays on Paul*. Cambridge, Cambridge University Press, 1990: **15**.

Hooker, M. D., *Jesus and the Servant*. London, SPCK, 1959: **79**.

Hooker, M. D., 'Traditions about the Temple in the Sayings of Jesus', *BJRL* 70 (1988) pp. 7ff.: **114**.

Hoover, R. W., 'The Harpagmos Enigma: a Philological Solution', *HTR* 64 (1971), pp. 95ff.: **36**

Horbury, W., 'The Messianic Association of "the Son of Man"', *JTS* n.s. 36 (1985), pp. 34ff.: **115**.

Housman, A. E., *More Poems*. London, Jonathan Cape, 1936: **18**.

Hunter, L. S., *John Hunter, D.D. A Life*. London, 1921: **94**.

Jeremias, J., *The Eucharistic Words of Jesus*. Oxford, Blackwell, 1955: **18**, **176**.

Jeremias, J., 'The Key to Pauline Theology', *ET* 76 (1964[a]), pp. 27ff.: **80**.

Jeremias, J., *New Testament Theology*, I. London, SCM Press, 1971: **38**, **93**, **199**, **203**.

Johnston, G., *The Spirit Paraclete in the Gospel of John*. Cambridge, Cambridge University Press, 1970: **127**.

Jones, D. R., 'ἀνάμνησις in the LXX and the Interpretation of 1 Cor. X1.25', *JTS* n.s. 6 (1955), pp. 183ff.: **176**.

Jones, L. G., *Embodying Forgiveness: A Theological Analysis*. Grand Rapids, Eerdmans, 1995: **29**.

Käsemann, E., 'The Problem of the Historical Jesus', *Essays on New Testament Themes* (E. tr.). London, SCM Press, 1964: **179–80**.

Kelsey, D. H., *The Uses of Scripture in Recent Theology*. Philadelphia, Fortress Press/London, SCM Press, 1975: **215**.

Kilpatrick, G. D., 'Acts VII: 52 ΕΛΕΥΣΙΣ', *JTS* n.s. 46 (1945), pp. 136ff.: **80**.

Kilpatrick, G. D., *The Origins of the Gospel according to St Matthew*. Oxford, Clarendon Press, 1946: **182**, **189**.

Kingsbury, J. D., *Jesus Christ in Matthew, Mark, and Luke*. Philadelphia, Fortress Press, 1981: **179**.

Kirk, K. E., 'The Evolution of the Doctrine of the Trinity', Rawlinson, A. E. J., (ed.), *Essays on the Trinity and the Incarnation*. London, Longmans, 1928, pp. 157ff.: **131**.

Klausner, J., *Jesus of Nazareth: His Times, His Life, and His Teaching*. London, Allen & Unwin, 1925: **113**.

Koch, K., 'Offenbaren wird sich das Reich Gottes', *NTS* 25 (1978–9), pp. 158ff.: **93**.

Kramer, W., *Christos, Kyrios, Gottessohn*. Zürich, Zwingli-Verlag, 1963: **80**; E. tr. *Christ, Lord, Son of God*, London, SCM Press, 1966.

Kühn, K. G., 'Peirasmos-hamartia-sarx im Neuen Testament und die damit zusammenhängenden Vorstellungen', *ZTK* 49 (1952), pp. 200ff.: **190**, **192**, **196**.

Lampe, G. W. H., *God as Spirit* (Bampton Lectures 1976). Oxford, Clarendon Press, 1977: **93**.

Lampe, G. W. H., 'The Holy Spirit and the Person of Christ', Sykes, S. W. and Clayton, J. P. (eds), *Christ, Faith and History*. Cambridge, Cambridge University Press, 1972, pp. 111ff.: **93**, **94**.

Lampe, G. W. H., *The Seal of the Spirit*. London, Longmans, 1951: **131**; London, SPCK, 1969.

Lapide, P., *The Resurrection of Jesus: A Jewish Perspective*. Augsburg/ London, SPCK, 1983: **109**.

Lemcio, E. E., 'The Intention of the Evangelist Mark', *NTS* 32, 1986, pp. 187ff.: **187, 189**.

Lemcio, E. E., *The Past of Jesus in the Gospels*. Cambridge, Cambridge University Press, 1991: **187, 189**.

Lightfoot, J. B., *On a Fresh Revision of the English New Testament*. London, Macmillan (1891), Appendix II, pp. 269ff.: **198, 199, 203**.

Lindars, B., *Jesus, Son of Man*. London, SPCK, 1983: **37**.

Lindars, B. and Smalley, S. S. (eds), *Christ and Spirit in the New Testament* (FS C. F. D. Moule). Cambridge, Cambridge University Press, 1973.

Lohse, E., *Märtyrer und Gottesknecht*. Göttingen, Vandenhoeck und Ruprecht, 1955: **17**.

Lövestam, F., *Son and Saviour, A Study of Acts 13, 32–37*. Lund, CWK Gleerup, 1961: **79**.

Lyonnet, S., 'Le sens de peirazein en Sap. 2.24 et la doctrine du péché originel', *Biblica* 39 (1958), pp. 27ff.: **203**.

Mackintosh, H. R., *The Christian Apprehension of God*. London, SCM Press, 1929: **94**.

McLean, B. H., 'The Absence of Atoning Sacrifice in Paul's Soteriology', *NTS* 38 (1992), pp. 531ff.: **29**.

Marrow, S. B., 'Principles for Interpreting the New Testament Soteriological Terms', *NTS* 36 (1990), pp. 268ff.: **29**.

Marshall, I. H., *Kept by the Power of God: a Study of Perseverance and Falling Away*. London, Epworth Press, 1969: **203**.

Martin, R. A., 'Evidence of Aramaic Sources in Acts I-XV', *NTS* 11 (1964), pp. 38ff.: **79**.

Martin, R. P., *A Hymn of Christ: Philippians 2:5–11 in Recent Interpretation and in the Setting of Early Christian Worship*. Downers Grove, IL, Inter-Varsity Press, 1997: **40**.

Marxsen, W., *Introduction to the New Testament* (E. tr.). Oxford, Blackwell, 1968: **189**.

Mascall, E. L., *Corpus Christi*. London, Longmans, 1953: **140, 162**; ²1965.

Masson, C., *L'Épitre de Saint Paul aux Éphesiens* (in one volume with P. Bonnard, *aux Galates*). Neuchâtel/Paris. Delachaux et Niestlé, 1952: **175**.

Mayor, J. B., *The Epistle of St James*. London, Macmillan, 1897: **197**.

Merkel, H., 'Jesus im Widerstreit', in *Glaube und Gesellschaft* (FS W. F. Kasch), Bayreuth, 1981, pp. 207ff.: **179**.

Merkel, H., 'The Opposition between Jesus and Judaism', Bammel and Moule 1984, pp. 129ff.: **179**.

Merritt, R. L., 'Jesus Barabbas and the Paschal Pardon', *JBL* 104 (1985), pp. 57ff.: **113**.

Metzger, B. M., *A Textual Commentary on the Greek New Testament*. London/New York, United Bible Societies, 1971: **10**.

Meyer, B. F., *The Aims of Jesus*. London, SCM Press, 1979: **38**, **99**, **112**.

Meyer, B. F., *Reality and Illusion in New Testament Scholarship*. Collegeville, MN, Glazier, 1994: **204**.

Michel, O., and Betz, O., 'Von Gott gezeugt', in *Judentum, Urchristentum, Kirche*, (FS J. Jeremias) (BZNW 26) Berlin, Töpelmann, 1960, pp. 3ff.: **79**.

Middleton, T. F., *The Doctrine of the Greek Article*. London, 1841: **207**.

Moberly, E., *Suffering, Innocent and Guilty*. London, SPCK, 1978: **42**.

Moberly, W., *The Ethics of Punishment*. London, Faber and Faber, 1968: **42**.

Moody, C. N., *The Mind of the Early Converts*. London, Hodder and Stoughton, n.d. (Preface dated 1920): **76**.

Morgan, R. C., *The Nature of New Testament Theology*. London, SCM Press, 1973: **ix**.

Moule, C. F. D., *The Birth of the New Testament*. London, A. and C. Black, ³1981: **79**, **80**, **189**.

Moule, C. F. D., 'The Christ of Experience and the Christ of History', *Theology* 81 (1978ᵇ), pp. 164ff.: **93**.

Moule, C. F. D., '2 Cor. 3:18ᵇ, καθάπερ ἀπὸ κυρίου πνευματος', Baltensweiler, H., and Reicke, B. (eds), *Neues Testament und Geschichte* (FS Oscar Cullmann), Zürich, Theologischer Verlag/Tübingen, Mohr, 1972, pp. 231ff.: **94**, **129**; Repr. in Moule 1982, pp. 227ff.

Moule, C. F. D., *Essays in New Testament Interpretation*. Cambridge, Cambridge University Press, 1982: **207**.

Moule, C. F. D., 'From Defendant to Judge – and Deliverer', *SNTS Bulletin* 3, Cambridge University Press, 1952, pp. 40ff.: **77**, **79**; reprinted, *The Phenomenon of the New Testament*, London, SCM Press, 1967, pp. 82ff.: **77**.

Moule, C. F. D., 'Further Reflexions on Philippians 2:5–11', Gasque, W. W., and Martin, R. P. (eds), *Apostolic History and the Gospel: Biblical and Historical Essays* (FS F. F. Bruce). Exeter, Paternoster Press, 1970ᵃ, pp. 264ff.: **36**.

Moule, C. F. D., *The Holy Spirit*. London and Oxford, Mowbray, 1978ᵃ: **xi**.

Moule, C. F. D., 'The Individualism of the Fourth Gospel', *NovT* 5 (1962), pp. 171f.: **79**, **80**, **128**, **235**; repr. *Essays in New Testament Interpretation*. Cambridge, Cambridge University Press, 1982, pp. 91ff.

Moule, C. F. D., 'The Influence of Circumstances on the Use of Christological Terms', *JTS* n.s. 10 (1959ᵃ), pp. 247ff.: **79**, **80**, **187–8**; repr. *Essays in New Testament Interpretation*. Cambridge, Cambridge University Press, 1982, pp. 165ff.

Moule, C. F. D., 'The Intention of the Evangelists', Higgins, A. J. B. (ed.), *New Testament Essays: Studies in Memory of Thomas Walter*

Manson (1893–1958), Manchester, Manchester University Press, 1959[b], pp. 165ff.: **187, 188**.

Moule, C. F. D., 'Jesus in New Testament Kerygma', Böcher, O., and Haacker, K. (eds), *Verborum Veritas* (FS Gustav Stählin). Wuppertal, Brockhaus, 1970[b], pp. 15ff.: **189**.

Moule, C. F. D., 'Jesus, Judaism, and Paul', Hawthorne, G. F., with Betz, O. (ed.), *Tradition and Interpretation in the New Testament* (FS E. E. Ellis), Grand Rapids, Eerdmans/Tübingen, Mohr, 1987, pp. 43ff.: **113**.

Moule, C. F. D., 'On Defining the Messianic Secret in Mark', Ellis, E. E., and Grässer, E. (eds), *Jesus und Paulus*: (FS Werner Georg Kümmel), Göttingen, Vandenhoeck und Ruprecht, 1975, pp. 239ff.: **189**.

Moule, C. F. D., *The Origin of Christology*. Cambridge, Cambridge University Press, 1977[a]: **xi, 3–18, 94, 113, 189, 207**.

Moule, C. F. D., 'A Neglected Factor in the Interpretation of Johannine Eschatology', *Studies in John* (FS J. N. Sevenster). Leiden, Brill 1970[c], pp. 155ff.: **128**.

Moule, C. F. D., 'Neglected Features in the Problem of "the Son of Man"', Gnilka, J. (ed.), *Neues Testament und Kirche* (FS Rudolf Schnackenburg), Freiburg/Basel/Wien, Herder 1974, pp. 413ff.; repr. in Moule 1982, pp. 75ff.: **115, 207**.

Moule, C. F. D., 'The New Testament and the Doctrine of the Trinity', *ET* 78 (1976), pp. 16ff.: **94**

Moule, C. F. D., ' "Through Jesus Christ our Lord": Some Questions about the Use of Scripture', *Theology* 80 (1977[b]), pp. 30ff.: **93, 223**.

Neill, S. C., *Christian Holiness*. London, Lutterworth, 1960: **131**.

Neugebauer, F., *In Christus, Untersuchung zum Paulinischen Glaubensverständnis*. Göttingen, Vandenhoeck und Ruprecht, 1961: **131**.

Neusner, J., 'Money-Changers in the Temple: the Mishnah's Explanation', *NTS* 35 (1989), pp. 287: **114**.

Newbigin, L., *The Finality of Christ*. London, SCM Press, 1969: **38**.

Newbigin, L., *The Reunion of the Church*. London, SCM Press, 1948: **176**.

O'Collins, G., *The Easter Jesus*. London, Darton, Longman & Todd, 1973: **15**.

O'Neill, J. C., *The Theology of Acts in its Historical Setting*. London, SPCK, 1961: **60, 80**; revised and rewritten, 1970.

Owen, H. P., 'Stephen's Vision in Acts vii. 55–56', *JNTS* 1 (1954), pp. 224ff.: **78**.

Palgrave, F. T. (selected by), *The Golden Treasury of the Best Songs and Lyrical Poems in the English Language*. Oxford, Oxford University Press, 1920.

Peacocke, A. R., 'The Nature and Purpose of Man in Science and Christian Theology', *Zygon* 8 (1973), pp. 373ff.: **18**.

Peacocke, A. R., *Science and the Christian Experiment*. Oxford, Oxford University Press, 1971: **18**.

Reicke, B., *Glaube und Leben der Urgemeinde*. Zürich. Zwingli-Verlag, 1957: **80**.

Reumann, J., 'A History of Lectionaries: From the Synagogue at Nazareth to Post-Vatican II', *Interpretation* 31 (1977), pp. 116ff.: **219**.

Richardson, A., review of *The Fulness of Christ* in *The Churchman*, June 1951: **138–9**.

Robinson, J. A. T., *Jesus and His Coming*. London, SCM Press, 1957: **78**.

Robinson, J. A. T., 'The Most Primitive Christology of All?', *JTS* n.s. 7 (1956), pp. 177ff.: **60**, repr. *Twelve New Testament Studies*, London, SCM Press, 1962ᵃ, pp. 139ff.: **78, 175**. (Cf. *Jesus and His Coming*, London, SCM Press, 1957, pp. 143ff.)

Robinson, J. A. T., *The Priority of John* (ed. J. Coakley), London, SCM Press, 1985: **113, 185**.

Roloff, J., 'Anfänge der Soteriologischen Deutung des Todes Jesu (Mk. x.45 und Lk. xxii.27)', *NTS* 19 (1972), pp. 38ff.: **18**.

Ross, J., 'ΑΡΠΑΓΜΟΣ (Phil. ii.6)', *JTS* 10 (1909), pp. 573f.: **36**.

Rowland, C. C., *Christian Origins: an Account of the Setting and Character of the Most Important Sect of Judaism*. London, SPCK, 1985: **102, 103, 106, 109**.

Samartha, S. J., *The Hindu Response to the Unbound Christ*. Madras, Christian Literature Society, 1974: **18**.

Sanders, E. P., *Jesus and Judaism*. London, SCM Press, 1985ᵃ: **96, 98, 100–1, 102–4, 110, 111, 112, 113, 114, 115**.

Sanders, E. P., 'Judaism and the Grand "Christian" Abstractions: Love, Mercy and Grace', *Interpretation* 39 (1985ᵇ), pp. 357ff.: **100**.

Sanders, E. P., *Paul and Palestinian Judaism*. London, SCM Press, 1977: **100**.

Sanders, E. P., *Paul, the Law, and the Jewish People*. Philadelphia, Fortress Press, 1983: **114**.

Schürmann, H., *Quellenkritische Untersuchungen des Lukanischen Abendmahlsberichtes Lk 22, 7–38. III Teil: Jesu Abschiedsrede, LK 22, 21–38*. Münster, Aschendorff, 1957: **204**.

Schweizer, E., 'The Concept of the Church in the Gospel and Epistles of St John', Higgins, A. J. B. (ed.), *New Testament Essays: studies in memory of T. W. Manson*. Manchester, Manchester University Press, 1959ᵃ, pp. 230ff.: **94**.

Schweizer, E., '"Er wird Nazoräer heissen" (zu Mc 1 24; Mt 2 23)', *Judentum, Urchristentum, Kirche* (FS J. Jeremias). ed. W. Eltester, BZNW 26, Töpelmann, Berlin, 1960: **59**.

Schweizer, E., *Gemeinde und Gemeindeordnung im Neuen Testament*. Zürich, 1959ᵇ, 11 a ff.: **94**; E. tr. *Church Order in the New Testament*. London, SCM Press, 1961: **94**.

Scroggs, R., 'Paul: Σοφός and Πνευματικός', *NTS* 14 (1967), pp. 33ff.: **131**.

Seesemann, H., 'πεῖρα, etc.' *TDNT* VI, pp. 23ff.: **190**.

Smalley, S. S., 'The Christology of Acts', *ET* 73 (1962), p. 362: **79**, **80**.

Smith, M., *Clement of Alexandria and a Secret Gospel of Mark*. Cambridge, MA, Harvard University Press, 1973: **188**.

Snodgrass, K. R., 'Justification by Grace – to Doers: an Analysis of the Place of Romans 2 in the Theology of Paul', *NTS* 32 (1986), pp. 72ff., n. 48.: **113**, **114**.

Styler, G. M., 'The Basis of Obligation in Paul's Christology and Ethics', Lindars and Smalley 1973, pp. 175ff.: **16**.

Sweet, J. P. M., *Revelation*. London, SCM Press, 1979: **33**.

Sykes, S., *The Story of Atonement*, London, Darton, Longman & Todd, 1997: **29**.

Taille, Maurice de la, *The Mystery of Faith and Human Opinion: Contrasted and Defined*. London, Sheed and Ward, 1930: **162**.

Temple, W., *Christus Veritas*. London, Macmillan, 1924: **172–3**.

Therrien, G., *Le Discernement dans les Écrits Paulinniens*. Paris, Gabalda, 1973: **203**.

Traina, R. *The Atonement, History, and Kerygma: a Study in Protestant Theology* (University Microfilms, Drew University). Ann Arbor, MI, 1966: **18**.

Travis, S. H., *Christ and the Judgement of God: Divine Retribution in the New Testament*. Basingstoke, Marshall Pickering, 1986: **47**.

Trench, R. C., *Synonyms of the New Testament* (repr. from 1880). Grand Rapids, Eerdmans, 1953: **203**.

Trocmé, E., *The Passion as Liturgy. A Study in the Origins of the Passion Narratives in the Four Gospels*. London, SCM Press, 1983: **180**.

Tuckett, C. (ed.), *The Messianic Secret*. London, SPCK, 1984: **189**.

Turner, M. M. B., *The Holy Spirit and Spiritual Gifts, Then and Now*. Carlisle, Paternoster, 1996[b]: **131**.

Turner, M. M. B., *Power from on High: the Spirit in Israel's Restoration and Witness in Luke-Acts*. Sheffield, Sheffield Academic Press, 1996[a]: **57**, **131**.

Turner, M. M. B., 'The Spirit of Christ and Christology', H. H. Rowdon (ed.), *Christ the Lord: Studies in Christology Presented to Donald Guthrie*. Leicester, Inter-Varsity Press, 1982, pp. 168ff.: **57**.

van Iersel, B. M. F., *'Der Sohn' in den synoptischen Jesusworten*, (*NovT* Supplements, 3). Leiden, Brill, 1961: **78**, **79**.

van Unnik, W. C., 'Jesus: Anathema or Kyrios (1 Cor. 12:2)', in Lindars and Smalley 1973, pp. 113ff.: **18**.

Vanstone, W. H., *Love's Endeavour, Love's Expense*. London, Darton, Longman & Todd, 1977: **31**.

Vanstone, W. H., *The Stature of Waiting*. London, Darton, Longman & Todd, [2]1982: **31**.

Vermes, G., *The Dead Sea Scrolls in English*. Harmondsworth, Penguin Books, 1962 (and subsequent edns): **131, 213**.

Vermes, G., *Jesus the Jew: a Historian's Reading of the Gospels*. London, Collins, 1973: **108–9**.

Vielhauer, P., 'On the "Paulinism" of Acts', Keck, L. E., and Martyn, J. L. (eds), *Studies in Luke-Acts* (FS Paul Schubert), Nashville/New York, Abingdon, 1966, pp. 33ff.: **79**.

Vonier, Dom Anscar, *A Key to the Doctrine of the Eucharist*. London, Burns and Oates, 1925: **162**.

Waddell, H., *Peter Abelard*. London, Constable, 1933: **156–8**.

Wallace, D. B., *Greek Grammar Beyond the Basics*. Grand Rapids, Zondervan, 1996: **207**.

Walls, R. C., review of J. A. T. Robinson's *Communion Manual*. Cambridge, Cambridge University Press (repr. in Robinson, J. A. T., *Liturgy Coming to Life*, London, Mowbray, 1960), in *The Cambridge Review*, 76 (Oct. 1954–June 1955): **140**.

Watson, F. B., 'Why was Jesus Crucified?', *Theology* 88 (1984–5), pp. 105ff.: **113**.

Weiss, J., *Paul and Jesus*. London, Harper & Brothers, 1909: **180**.

Westcott, B. F., *The Epistle to the Hebrews*. London, Macmillan, 1889: **145, 165, 169**.

Williams, Rowan, *Resurrection*. London, Darton, Longman & Todd, 1982: **24**.

Williams, Rowan, *The Truce of God*. London, Collins, 1983: **38**.

Wrede, W., *Das Messiasgeheimnis in den Evangelien*, 1901, 3rd edn, Göttingen, Vandenhoeck & Ruprecht, 1963: **189**; E. tr. *The Messianic Secret*. Cambridge, Jas Clarke, 1971.

Wright, N. T., '*Harpagmos* and the Meaning of Phil. 2:5–11', *JTS* n.s. 37 (1986), pp. 321ff.: **37**.

Wright, N. T., *Jesus and the Victory of God*. London, SPCK, 1996: **115**.

Wright, N. T., 'Jesus, Israel and the Cross', Richards, K. H. (ed.), Society of Biblical Literature Seminar Papers 1985, Chico, California, Scholars Press, 1985, pp. 75ff.: **101**.

Young, F., 'New Wine in Old Wineskins: XIV Sacrifice', *ET* 86 (1975[a]), pp. 305ff.: **18**.

Young, F., *Sacrifice and the Death of Christ*. London, SPCK, 1975[b]: **18**.

Zehr, H., *Changing Lenses: a New Focus for Crime and Justice*. Scottdale, PA/Waterloo, Ontario, Herald Press, 1990: **43, 45–6**.

Ziesler, J., *The Jesus Question*. Guildford/London, Lutterworth, 1980: **214**.

INDEX OF ANCIENT SOURCES

The Society for Promoting Christian Knowledge (SPCK) was founded in 1698. It has as its purpose three main tasks:

- **Communicating the Christian faith in its rich diversity**
- **Helping people to understand the Christian faith and to develop their personal faith**
- **Equipping Christians for mission and ministry**

SPCK Worldwide serves the Church through Christian literature and communication projects in over 100 countries. Special schemes also provide books for those training for ministry in many parts of the developing world. SPCK Worldwide's ministry involves Churches of many traditions. This worldwide service depends upon the generosity of others and all gifts are spent wholly on ministry programmes, without deductions.

SPCK Bookshops support the life of the Christian community by making available a full range of Christian literature and other resources, and by providing support to bookstalls and book agents throughout the UK. SPCK Bookshops' mail order department meets the needs of overseas customers and those unable to have access to local bookshops.

SPCK Publishing produces Christian books and resources, covering a wide range of inspirational, pastoral, practical and academic subjects. Authors are drawn from many different Christian traditions, and publications aim to meet the needs of a wide variety of readers in the UK and throughout the world.

The Society does not necessarily endorse the individual views contained in its publications, but hopes they stimulate readers to think about and further develop their Christian faith.

For further information about the Society, please write to:
SPCK, Holy Trinity Church, Marylebone Road,
London NW1 4DU, United Kingdom.
Telephone: 0171 387 5282